GIFT THIS BOOK

When we really like something, w̲ ̲.̲.̲ ̲.̲.̲ others, like books, films and restaurants.

The impact of this book has the power to change people's lives. We all can resonate with stories, and the women in this book have bared their souls so they can connect with you. We all have endured adversity, challenges and life-changing experiences. The real power is in sharing this with others, so that they can see once you find your courage to voice your truth, it can have a transformational impact on others.

For these reasons and more, the intention is to share these stories with thousands of others around the globe. We have stories in Voices of Hope by women from six continents that exemplifies the reach of this wonderful, inspirational and powerful book.

When you purchase two copies you will receive one half price. In addition, 10 % of all profits will go to Healing Houses of Hope in Africa. This is to help create a safe space where young people can go to set them on the road to a brighter future.

Let's pay the gift of story forward so you too can transform other people's lives.

Brenda Dempsey
Creator and Editor

This book is for you if...

- You like reading real-life inspirational stories
- You are looking for inspiration about your current situation or a challenge
- You like short stories that you can dip in and out of as you choose
- You are looking to connect with other like-minded women who have experienced what you are experiencing in your life
- You may be considering writing about your own inspirational story
- You want to speak to inspire others
- You want to shape and grow your business using your story
- You are searching for the hope to find your own voice

Brenda Dempsey

Love for Voices of Hope

Years ago, stories about overcoming challenges against nature such as climbing Mount Everest and rowing across the Atlantic Ocean, were used to inspire us to be the best. 'Voices Of Hope' brings together true inspirational stories about overcoming a new kind of mountain ... the mountain of overcoming grief, illness and the ups and downs of life. These ladies have all found an inner strength and found their passion and purpose. With hope you can do anything and with a voice, you can share the hope with others. These ladies inspire you to be you, in all your frickin' awesomeness.

DR. CHERYL CHAPMAN
BEST-SELLING AUTHOR, "FIND YOUR WHY" www.cheryl-chapman.com

The conditioning that we've endured through the ages is now finding its Voice to no longer be bound by prejudice, victimhood or any boundaries that don't give us the space to choose for ourselves.
Voices of Hope is inspiration for women by women, who are breaking the barriers of fear. They give a voice to guilt and shame that hold back beautiful visions and missions that are needed to impact parts of the world for growth and expansion. A must read.

SASHKA HANNA-RAPPL
LEADING BUSINESS AND BRAND STRATEGIST FOR CREATIVE VISIONARIES
www.brandsashka.com

Brenda Dempsey's new anthology, Voices of Hope, is a collection of global testimonies of women who have risen above what life has thrown at them and have come through the other side.

Their stories have an urgency and vigour that will make you sit up and take notice - they are highly personal statements which will resonate with women and men all over the world. These true-life accounts are astonishing, raw, brutal, incredible and powerful but above all, HONEST. With great care and consideration, Brenda Dempsey has shaped and guided the authors into offering us moving and compelling narratives which shine with wisdom and compassion. Their stories will haunt you long after you have finished reading.

This timely book is a testament to the power of the human spirit and gives a voice to those women who have often been silenced.

OLIVIA EISINGER
FREELANCE EDITOR

These stories are tender, real, raw and beyond inspiring. They are weaved with the energy of these beautiful souls to not only inspire you but ignite your truth to come to life now. I felt my power growing as I connected with each of these stories. Phenomenal. Warning - be ready to change your life as you read about what's possible and know it's possible for you.

ANITA GOSHAL
INTERNATIONAL COACH AND SPEAKER
www.anitaghosal.com

Voices of Hope is a reflection on women of great courage and determination who've honoured their authentic nature despite their challenges, and found their 'song line.' Being in alignment with their true nature has taken spirit to overcome adversities and their stories are inspiring and unique to remind us of our own. Each one of us has the ability to find our 'own story' and Brenda's book reminds us of this beautifully.

AMANDA HART
INTUITIVE CONSULTANT, SPEAKER & AUTHOR   www.amanda-hart.co.uk

Voices of Hope is filled with inspirational stories of ordinary women overcoming incredible struggles and doubt, creating extraordinary things as a result. As a man, I am inspired by the honesty with which these woman were able to voice their truth and would love to see such a book created and compiled filled with similar stories from a male perspective. Hearing real life stories, connects us and helps us to remember this when we often feel alone when we are faced with challenges. Thank you.

DAVID LAKEY
SPONSOR & MD OF D & G COMPUTER SERVICES LIMITED

About the Creator

Brenda Dempsey (Domestic Abuse Survivor, Catalyst and Problem Solver), is a Master Coach, Teacher, Mentor, Speaker and #1 International Best-selling Author. She is already published in the anthology *Book of Inspiration for Women by Women* created by Australian Ruth Stuettgen and *Conceived to Lead, Dismantling the Glass Ceiling Mindset* created by American author Carla Wynn Hall. She has found a love of writing and speaking and uses this to assist other women in raising their voices with their own stories. She is the creator of *Voices of Courage* – a trilogy of anthologies full of transformational stories of Strength, Courage and Change, inspiring hope in others written by women from around the globe.

Brenda believes that women can find their voice through writing and speaking about their stories. This sets off a catalytic reaction, increasing their confidence, belief and courage to step into the spotlight and share their stories with other women, illustrating their conviction to make a difference in the world today.

As a Transformational Success Coach, Brenda successfully empowers, inspires and enables women to create, shape and grow their business so they too can be free to live their life on their terms and achieve their dreams. Her vision is to create more leaders through the education and Diamond ripple effect of Holistic Leadership.

Brenda has founded a charity for homeless women, focusing on their sanitary and hygiene, called Helping Handbags Worldwide featured on BBC. She is a mother of four smart kids and grandmother to seven beautiful grandchildren. Brenda loves to travel around the world with David, her guardian angel, leaving her mark on the lives of those she touches. She is a Scot who now lives in Surrey, UK.

Connect with Brenda

Facebook	Brendadempsey/diamondsuccesscoaching
Website	www.brendadempsey.co.uk
Instagram	@brendadempsey
Twitter	@1diamondsuccess
Email	hello@brendadempsey.co.uk

Dedication

To the women who have yet
to find their voice.

Rising from the Ashes
when all seemed lost

Voices of HOPE

True Stories - Changed Lives

Brenda Dempsey

The Life Changer

HOPE

Be the Light

Published by
Filament Publishing Ltd
16 Croydon Road, Beddington, Croydon,
Surrey, CR0 4PA, United Kingdom.
www.filamentpublishing.com
email: info@filamentpublishing.com
Telephone: +44(0)20 8688 2598

Voices of Hope by Brenda Dempsey
© 2019 Brenda Dempsey

ISBN 978-1-913192-68-6

Printed in the UK by 4edge Ltd.

Table of Contents

FOREWORD

PENNY POWER OBE

All generations can talk of the adversity and challenges they have faced, and all those people who have faced them have chosen their own way to manage these set-backs and traumas.

There has never been a time in history when women have been as creative, bold and determined to independently stride out into business and make their mark. I strongly believe that those who have the wisdom of pain and adversity and the pride when they found their way through it and experienced the strength and power of their recovery, can be the ones who will have the greatest impact.

There is a certain character that emerges when life has broken you and you have found a way to become whole again, perhaps whole for the first time in your life.

The humility of these people, the empathy and the gratitude of the smallest of things, turn the potential of being a victim into a survivor that will enable their impact on the world. It is through adversity that we discover why we were born.

In 'Voices of Hope', you will read about these women, you will want to stand beside them, you will thank them, and you will grow. Through their words, your fear may turn to love, and this could be the greatest turning point in your life.

Penny Power OBE
Director Social Power (Surrey) Ltd
Founder of The Business Cafe
Author of "Business is Personal"
Believe that "Business is Personal, and you should lead the life and business you want"

HOPE

Be the Light

Introduction

The first book, *"Voices of Courage"* illustrated the depths of adversity that many women face on a day to day basis. It was not written to evoke pity for the women but to realise that anything can happen to anyone at any time. It's not so much about what you face but how you rise. Yes, there is the time when the anguish you may face is all consuming but when this begins to fade because 'enough is enough is enough', then you discover a new you. Like a phoenix rising from the ashes, you emerge with a determination never before experienced.

I am a lover of Dr. David Hawkins' work on Levels of Consciousness. This is not the time to go into detail about his work but suffice to say that it is an awakening of living life consciously as contrastingly allowing life to happen to you and being another cog of drudgery that many face each day.

He talks about two ideas: emotions that suppress life like jealousy, judgement and bitterness as opposed to emotions that support life like Courage, Hope and Love and all the shades in between in both camps. I was shocked to learn that only 15%

of people in the world live in the Supporting Life while 85% of people live in the Suppressing Life. I believe that it is a duty to share your story. Stories Heal, Inspire and Transform both the lives of the author and the reader. By encouraging others to tell their personal stories, it gives others permission to share their stories too.

When I started on this writing journey and decided to call Book 1 *Voices of Courage,* it was in response to my personal story and discovery of courage that I chose that particular word. For me, it's associated with being a Braveheart – someone who finds courage to take action and see it through.

I had not joined the dots of Dr. David Hawkins' Level of Consciousness work. It came to mind recently, when talking about my work with a fellow author, that I was awakening something powerful within me in relation to the Voices Series of books. I found myself reaching for his Map of Consciousness which lists all the emotions and traits of humans. That was my 'aha' moment!

The first step to sustaining life is **Courage,** at a light frequency measurement of 200. This book *'Voices of Hope'* is the third step in the sequence. WOW, it hit me that I was guided to this work because I enable others to transform their lives and that each subsequent book in the Series of four journeys towards total sustenance of life, is gathering strength and power to change lives.

When I was thinking about '*Voices of Hope*' and how could I make it different yet familiar, once again I looked inward and at my own life. Today, after being in education for twenty five years, I am a woman in business. This was who my co-authors were going to be - Women in Business. Why? I knew they would be like-minded and that they too were on a mission to make a difference in the world. They were on their path of transformation and I knew that they would have used their personal story, perhaps not in a conscious way for some, but consequently, they are determined to create that ripple effect of change.

Furthermore, being a woman in business opens doors of opportunity to spread your message as your values underpin your very vision and mission. In the online world of today you can reach people on a global scale. We have witnessed many videos and posts go viral when they capture the hearts and imaginations of others.

I too know a little about this phenomenon myself through my social enterprise Helping Handbags Worldwide. Within six weeks of reposting a meme on Facebook, we collected, donated and distributed over ten thousand handbags UK wide and have now pushed into America. With everything that is happening in my life, it's becoming more apparent why I left education to do the work I do today.

I can make a positive impact for change by influencing and working with other women in business to create a ripple effect of change worldwide.

It is without a doubt, to me, that adversity and challenge, birth Hope. Hardship, emotional tornadoes and familiar situations are just some of the key ingredients that bind us together. More importantly though, I am interested in what turns women from victim to victor as they battle and triumph in their situations and life.

These were the traits that I wanted to explore and highlight in the stories. People want to know detail and how you managed to break free, take a different path and find happiness, hope and a passion for life again.

These experiences mark a PIVOTAL MOMENT.

A Pivotal Moment is a 'turning point in time'. A turning point, when you make a decision like no other decision ever made. Why? It comes from the depth of your soul. It's a decision that spurs you on, no matter what.

It's a decision that has you looking at your challenge in a different and transformational way. It's a decision that will change you and your life forever. Pivotal moments bring hope, clarity and light. They unlock your paralysis, unveil your voice and unleash a latent power within. I like to call this your Inner Diamond Power. You see, you have been in the dark, yes. You have endured incredible pressure, yes. You awaken the indestructible rough diamond that has potential to be brilliant, strong and unique.

'Voices of Hope' reveals resilience, strength and courage. You have a vision that you keep in your mind's eye, no matter what. You have unleashed your incredible WHY and nothing will stop you from achieving your goal.

I have learned this from the many pivotal moments in my life, and there's more…

When you spark hope and re-ignite your passion you experience an acceptance of your Pivotal Moment which gives you courage, strength and a common bond in which to connect with other women. When you experience a sisterhood, there is an unspoken knowing that you can achieve more in unison than alone. Understanding, knowing and soul connections bind us together as one. That is why Anthologies are powerful. They unite and attract like-minded souls.

My mission is to assist women in being the best version of them, living in super consciousness and manifesting their dreams whatever they may be, with an I CAN Mindset, Soul Purpose and a Passion fuelling unstoppable Success, whatever that is for them.

One approach I have learned is through unlocking women's courage, belief and confidence to raise their voices so they can share their stories; in writing and speaking, as well as through their business. You see we have always had these qualities within us.

You all know the power of stories. Since time began, stories have been a vehicle for connecting us at a deeper level than mere words. A neuro-scientific study explained why telling stories builds empathy, brain synchronicity with people acting as if they're watching it unfold before them. We love human stories.

It is my vision to connect women from around the world. In finding a common bond, more than simply being a woman, yet as women, know the real power of our feminine essence and energy. Embracing this Divine Feminine Energy uplifts us and the world in which we live.

Joining in its harmony generates a powerful energy that creates change for the better with us and others.

For these reasons and more, I have been the vessel of the creation of this book, 'Voices of Hope'. By creating a platform for Real Women, their Real Stories and revealing their Real Lives, it has produced a place of healing, empowerment and realisation that they have everything they need to create the life and business of their dreams so they can make a difference and live fulfilled happy and prosperous lives.

I am humbled and privileged by all the brave, bold and beautiful women who said, "YES" to being part of *'Voices of Hope'* and joined the sisterhood of Voices of Change with their fellow authors in *'Voices of Courage'*. They are re-energised, excited and hopeful for their futures. They illustrate strength, courage and transformation through their experiences and I know that when you read them, you too will feel the power of their unique stories bringing renewed hope to you.

Be BRAVE - Be BOLD - Be BEAUTIFUL
Brenda Dempsey

HOPE

Voices of Hope can be found in Nietszche,
in the all-too-human wards of bureaucracy,
where the nurses are not authorised to diagnose
anything except whether you will be famous
and which medicine to take when you are.
I must warn you now, there is a cure,
but involves a lot of waiting around,
and then daily meditation.

Commissioned
Lewis (Poet)
Morbid Books

VOICES OF HOPE

Selina Boshorin, London, UK.

Finding My Purpose

Selina's story of Strength, Hope and Pivotal Moments is one that shares the process catapulting her to finally take the plunge and start her own business, five years ago. It was March 2014 and has certainly been a journey strewn with decisions, faith and trust since then. Setting out on her journey is undoubtedly one of the best and most significant decisions she says she has made and truly right for her at that point in her life.

Brenda Dempsey
Creator & Editor

Transformation #1

Finding My Purpose

Selina Boshorin

Business Systems Strategist

"There is no greater agony than bearing an untold story inside you."

Maya Angelou

I know my story and the events that led me to start my business are not uncommon, and there are many of us who, even though we hold a particular dream or really want to take the first step, something keeps us back from taking it even though we know we need to. Usually we wait until the time comes or something happens when we know we have no choice but to make that move or make the decision to move.

What I want to show by sharing my story is that life is too short to put up with indecision, and that we do have a choice. It is down to us to decide and take the actions, create the plans and re-frame the boundaries that are much needed. I am thankful for this experience for the learning I have gained and for the events that led up to this and that have occurred on my journey in life, my Career and Business since that point.

The event I am going to share occurred over the course of a few weeks to a month, was really part of a much longer process and culmination of maybe one year plus and long overdue in many ways; but as timing would have it, was 'perfect timing.'

I was working as a Careers Advisor - Freelancing, it was one of the many moments I realised it was time to take my power back and regain control over my destiny.

I had been working in the industry for almost five years and had moved from a smaller organisation to a main organisation within the Industry. About a year ago, I had started dabbling in my own Business ventures, but somehow not yet felt confident to take the plunge. I had launched my Events Business about three years prior and was also doing a lot of my Careers/Training and Private Coaching/ Consultancy Work on the side in addition to my Community Projects.

For the last few years I had been doing a lot of media /PR work for the organisation and the cause, and was being invited to participate in radio interviews, live events and even print media, including the Huffington Post. What a major honour! I was taking part in additional projects, and the centres I was working in and new business I was developing for the organisation were going really well.

I somehow had this feeling that something wasn't right, that there was more to what I had to give than what I was doing. There was the back drop of experiencing that myself and my colleagues were being undervalued, lacking resources, with extreme stress and burn out. There was much negativity, hopelessness and no action behind the scenes, but always putting on our show/performance face in public. It all felt false, glamorous and full of great opportunities on the outside, which I'm grateful for, however I knew something needed to be done.

The other major truth that I kept being reminded of was that whilst I continued to work here, it was taking away my physical time for anything else. My work/life balance was non-existent, as even when I left the venues, I was expected to go home and work late hours completing admin and working on tasks. For many colleagues it was normal to be working 7 days a week or having to continue working late after putting children to bed, after they had already completed a long full day. I knew that working in a way where I had freedom and flexibility during my business hours was a key factor in my decision making. It would allow me the space to live a life of my choosing as well as create the time to do what I desired and be with the people who were important to me, to travel and much more.

Ironically, my career focus was all about supporting and assisting others in their Career Development, Career Satisfaction, Confidence, thinking about Skills, Growth, Training and Education yet here I was feeling stagnant, burnt out, undervalued, frustrated and exasperated. I loved helping people, but also saw there was so much more that needed to be done to help people as well as considering my own growth, satisfaction, and development.

The crunch point came one day when I was asked to participate in a morning of creating/shooting Promotional Careers Advice YouTube videos. I was told that I had been specially requested along with a few other advisors across the country to front this special campaign – how exciting was this opportunity? But the double blow came when I spoke to my manager who told me, that as I was a Freelance Consultant, although I had been selected and specially asked for, I would not be able to be paid anything! It would require a whole morning of my time and travelling to the office, but not being a permanent member of staff, meant that was just how it had to be. Of course I thought whilst it was a great opportunity; significantly what hit me was how undervalued I really was and that principally I needed to decline. I did just that. I thanked my manager and advised her that, although it was a great opportunity, out of principle, I had to decline.

My response must have really surprised my manager and it put her into a total spin, particularly the talk of principles; usually people were made to feel that they had no choice and just had to be grateful for anything put in front of them. For me it wasn't about the money, but it was the idea that my talent, skill and expertise had been recognised, and I had been asked for, however my time was being undervalued and dismissed, which seemed to be an ongoing cycle for me in this current phase. I was giving more, doing more, and trying to please more, however somehow nothing was coming back in return. The irony also was that in the midst of this, I was seemingly not getting paid properly, and there were constant demands being placed on myself and my colleagues.

There was a real air of oppression, my confidence and the confidence of others were being attacked.

One of the things that really stood out for me, as I reflect, was the power of resilience, I knew there had to be another way and that this situation could not destroy me, and that I would need to take action and get out soon.

Interestingly, my manager did go to negotiate with her manager quite quickly, requesting payment to cover my time. Although I accepted, I knew that this had to be it. I had to make the decision in order for my business to succeed.

One of the amazing things that did happen to me during the month I was working my notice, was in being commissioned to undertake a major piece of Coaching/Training/Consultancy work which came via a contact. This situation was a huge pivotal and key moment in the launch of the start of my business and its next phase. This gave me the confidence and confirmation that no matter what, I had to take the plunge and step out.

During this time, I had been a School Governor in a local Primary School for around three to four years, and by that point was Vice-Chair. My Chair at the time was involved in several other things in the Community, including a Chair of Trustees for a cluster of Children's Centres. I had mentioned briefly about my Training, Coaching and

Consultancy Services at the time and fortunately they were looking for some support.

I was invited to present to the Board of Trustees and they advised me that they had a Centre requiring team work training. They were experiencing challenges with cohesion. Another Centre needed support and services to develop key members of staff, particularly around their confidence and assertiveness and lastly, another Centre where leadership coaching, succession planning and productivity training and mentoring was needed with Business Development support across the board.

After attending the meeting I was able to put together a comprehensive proposal for the Organisation. After researching and ruminating I put together the pricing and packages before submitting them to the Trustees for approval. Subsequently, I nervously awaited a response. It was accepted and the dates booked in to start and support a run for three months and would start immediately after I left. This decision was just the encouragement I needed to get me through that final month. Knowing that I would be able to make a difference, increasing my confidence in my abilities, and being well-rewarded financially too for my services, left me feeling fantastic! I was exactly where I wanted to be.

One of the things that I will never forget was the reaction of some of my friends and family.

When I expressed that I was finally leaving, it was a universal "about time too" as they could see the negative effects on me, particularly the last month of working. I discovered, as much as we may try to continue as normal, some things can't be hidden. I even had a friend whom I texted a few days after leaving, who said that I sounded happier. I could not believe it! Looking back I can see that my energy was being attacked and the subconscious stress that was there prior to leaving, was the push I needed to finally go.

Over the last few years I have been running my business; it has certainly been a journey, but I am really pleased that I made the decision and took the step. There have been many pivotal moments and experiences that have definitely contributed to my growth, not to mention helped to inform and under pin the services I offer. Even now I experience transitions, so there is always ongoing growth.

Today I support Business Owners, Leaders and CEOs who are experiencing overwhelm or feeling overloaded in their personal or professional life. In fact they are simply looking to find a different way of working, leading and being. Through the journey and processes, I support them with achieving more clarity, greater focus and helping to create the right strategies and ways of making things more simplified, and streamlined. In particular connecting them with their priorities, vision, values, legacy and reducing the 'to do' list.

From my journey and from working with my clients over the years I have seen that the more space we have to think, and connect to our priorities, the more we become more intentional, think bigger and support our leadership. I still run my Events Business and am involved in various Community projects too.

You have the capacity to do whatever you choose when you are in alignment with your purpose.

Dedication: *This is dedicated to my family and friends who have encouraged and supported me through this time, and have been there throughout my business journey.*

∞

Selina's story illustrates that you have to listen to your soul calling and make changes so you can live in purpose with passion and peace. Important human needs are to be heard, understood and appreciated. Selina's determination to begin her own business began with courage. She is giving hope to other women out there who feel trapped and undervalued in their current status. Selina's desire to inspire women who have a bigger mission and don't know where to start is to begin by listening; take action and never stop until you are aligned with your purpose.

Thank you Selina for your vulnerability and honesty shared in your story.

Brenda Dempsey
Creator & Editor

VOICES OF HOPE

Hannah Ingram, Leicestershire, UK

Unleashing the Warrior Queen

Many of us look for role models. Hannah Ingram's story is one of great adventure, self-realisation and being free-spirited. Despite much trauma in her life, she listened to a burning desire for a better more abundant life.

Throwing caution to the wind, she showed great entrepreneurial spirit when she found the courage to travel the world not alone but with a 3-year-old in tow; her son Morgan.

This was a journey of self-discovery and joy. A journey back to her African roots. A journey that would unleash the Warrior Queen that is ready to take on the world has she consciously chosen and created a life on her terms.

Hannah has bared her soul in her moving story of Hope for you. Be Inspired.

Brenda Dempsey
Creator and Editor

Transformation #2

Unleashing the Warrior Queen

Hannah Ingram

Events Organiser

"Think like a queen. A queen is not afraid to fail. Failure is another stepping stone to greatness."

Oprah Winfrey

This is the story of how I became a Warrior Queen. Looking back, I lived the first 30 years of my life feeling insecure, seeking approval, lacking love and fearing that I didn't deserve it.

From the beginning, my birth father left before I was born, and my step-dad took over when I was one year old, however, I have had, and continue to have, a challenging relationship with them both. Throughout the years I lived a roller coaster of rejection, disapproval, and control which had repeatedly deflated my confidence and manifested in a string of dysfunctional relationships, both romantic and platonic. These experiences have seen me flip-flopping between being abandoned or controlled. I link this to a double dose of 'daddy issues'; subconscious feelings of abandonment rooted in my father leaving before I was born and then dipping in and out of my life on a whim, promising me he had changed and then disappearing again with no explanation.

On the other hand, I had a very dominant figure telling me how to think and feel. He was always there for me and loved me (maybe too much), but my step-dad was very overpowering and controlling.

Looking back, my self-worth and confidence were through the floor. Although it wasn't visible from the outside, on the inside I was a victim and my energy attracted more of the same from almost every man I met. Desperate to be loved for being me, I have repeatedly given 'too much' to people who are emotionally unavailable, often to be taken advantage of. In my relationships, it manifested as mental, emotional and physical abuse, even rape.

Thankfully these were relatively short-lived experiences and often took me to a breaking point where I was able to escape the situation. But I also manifested my fear of abandonment in my relationships; with an extremely short-lived marriage to which I gave everything and he still walked away, the crux point coming when my ex-partner abandoned me whilst I was 6 months pregnant.

Each time this happened my heart broke a little more and I was forced to permanently wear a mask. Behind the mask was a wounded little girl, who spoke to herself in the most despicable manner, and physically abused herself. There is nowhere to hide when your worst enemy is living inside your head and it saddens me when I think about the pain I experienced and inflicted on myself every single day. From bulimia to medication overdoses, to cutting, to suicide attempts, it's a miracle that I am still here and healthy today.

But there was always a little fire burning inside of me, I wanted to do and be more. Throughout these dark days, I always managed to reach out for help and I have met some incredible spiritual teachers along the way who kept me growing; I made slow, steady progress.

At the end of 2013, I decided to give up my successful Personal Training business in Leicestershire because it just didn't feel fulfilling anymore. I'm so grateful for this period of my life because fitness and sport was a huge passion and entering this industry may well have saved my life.

Through my training, I learnt about and earned respect for my body and managed to end my ten-year battle with bulimia. From here I decided to follow a dream and move to London, and within a few months I met a guy who seemed different to anyone I had dated before. We had a lot of fun but unfortunately, it was short lived when I realised that I was pregnant. Suddenly life became serious and it was too much for him so I walked this journey alone and I struggled not to fall into being the victim of abandonment once again.

For me, becoming a single Mum really was rock bottom, I was solely responsible for a fragile little life, learning the ropes of motherhood and trying to find a way to continue working. Morgan's Dad wouldn't commit to physical or financial support, so I was exhausted, scared and barely making ends meet. At my lowest point, I considered having Morgan adopted as I really felt I couldn't give him what he needed. But this story was starting to sound way too similar to my early childhood so I promised myself and my son that we would write a different story for him.

One small decision can lead to a totally different life…so after months of struggling, one day I woke up and realised enough was enough. I had spent too long being angry at my son's Dad for 'leaving me in this situation' and I finally took control of the situation by accepting my current circumstances as they were, realising that I couldn't change anyone but myself and the only way I could do that was by changing the way I responded to the situation.

I stopped 'fighting' with my son's Dad and our parenting relationship improved remarkably, almost overnight. I stopped living as a victim and finally asked for and accepted help. I reluctantly started claiming benefits and it was just what I needed to get back on my feet.

I have always believed that children are a blessing and I can honestly say that Morgan is the best thing that could have happened to me. He joined me on this journey in 2014 and this bundle of joy immediately became the best teacher and healer I could ever have. He introduced me to unconditional love, the first time I had experienced it and probably the first time I had given it. He was my inspiration to stop being a 'victim' and find the best version of myself.

From a positive perspective, the only way was up and deep down I was still full of hopes, dreams and ideas, so I rekindled my self-development fire and started working on my self-worth and confidence again.

Knowing the difference it would make, I began investing the little money I had on myself because I realised I owed it to my son to live my best version. I joined an amazing online self-development group, which connected me with women all over the world who were on a similar journey. It led me to life-changing books, transformational daily practices and encouraged me to do things simply for fun.

I instructed the services of a coach and mentor to keep me focused and accountable and as a consequence, my life saw some incredible shifts.

Despite my increase in spending, money actually started flowing to me to support my desires, I managed to evict the negative chatter from my head and I felt more peaceful, happy and inspired each day. It was a challenging journey to self-love, but Morgan was my motivation all the way. He gave me a reason to step up and to focus on my healing. Arriving two weeks before my 30th birthday, he marked the beginning of a new chapter in my life.

"It is our wounds that create in us a desire to reach for miracles. The fulfilment of such miracles depends on whether we let our wounds pull us down or lift us up towards our dreams."- Jocelyn Soriano

One of the most exciting and pivotal moments of this chapter was when I made the decision that I would finally fulfil a long-standing experience on my bucket list, to have a gap year and travel the world. I had been doing some inner child work and had rediscovered an inner longing for an adventure, so as 2017 drew to a close I pledged to live 2018 entirely through joy. Not only had I managed to get back on my feet financially and regained my independence, but I somehow managed to save £15k as well. I have no idea where it really came from; I can only put it down to the law of attraction and my internal transformation.

It was time to give up our life in London, to travel and become the citizens of the world that we were called to be. We were stepping into the unknown with no idea where it would lead us, what would happen next, or where we would be at the end of the year. We were so excited to find out, but the only commitment I vowed to myself was to let our experiences and my intuition decide everything and so Morgan and I sold all our belongings, packed our bags and started booking tickets to travel the world.

We did four car boot sales, mainly with Morgan's toys and gave a huge amount to charity. We were left with two small boxes of items of sentimental value which a friend put in storage for me; everything else was either gone or was coming with us. This was the most cleansing, transformative processes I have ever experienced. Over the course of the weeks leading up to our departure, I spent my time organising, laughing, crying, reminiscing and releasing so many items and with it my emotions. I realised I had been holding on to so much physical and emotional baggage and through this process I let so much go, my load was lightened and I think it was the best preparation for the freedom of travelling.

Our first stop was Ghana, West Africa, the homeland of my estranged father, a country I had longed to visit, but never had the opportunity. I wanted to discover my roots and experience Ghana first-hand. Since I don't have a close relationship with my birth father and his family, we decided to explore Ghana by joining a volunteer organisation. So Morgan, my then 3-year-old son and I, spent a month in rural Ghana, teaching in the schools and doing outreach programmes to struggling rural communities. What an incredible experience it was for both of us, we were humbled by the happiness and positivity of people despite the poverty we saw. Ghana burst open my heart, this was well and truly my homecoming.

During my time in Ghana, I found myself, as a lady of dual heritage who knew nothing about her Ghanaian inheritance; I realised I had been living like half a person and I finally began to feel whole. Before we even left Ghana, I wanted to go back, my heart had a calling which I was compelled to answer. If we hadn't planned the next stage of our journey we would have stayed but equally, I knew this was the beginning of many visits to Ghana.

From Ghana, we continued our adventure, with eight weeks touring around New Zealand in a camper-van; four weeks in Sydney; six weeks on the West Coast of America and finally two months in Croatia and Italy. These were some of the most empowering, interesting and memorable weeks of my life. Morgan shared my wonder at the beautiful sights and exciting experiences that filled our journey. At times it was hard work travelling alone with a 3-year-old but he was also my motivation. However, the true beauty of this time was that each day was lived entirely through joy and spontaneity, and as a consequence, we were literally manifesting experiences as we went along. It really was a magical experience.

A pivotal moment came during my time in the USA which birthed a relationship with God and this has turned out to be a key feature of our gap year.

Having grown up with many negative connotations of church and God, I had no interest in Christianity and would avoid it at all costs. I was very spiritual and believed in a higher being, which I referred to as the universe. I expressed gratitude and my intentions but, couldn't bear to say the word 'God' or to pray. However, whilst staying with our friends in Denver, Colorado, they invited us to join them at a service. I reluctantly agreed to tag along, in a bid to be polite, but little did I know that this would ignite and then lead to a blossoming relationship with God.

Whilst singing along to the upbeat, pop Christian songs and then listening to a shaven, casually dressed man who was delivering the message that God is a friend, and father-figure who unconditionally loves and supports me, something shifted. This was reinforced when I was reunited with Morgan who had learnt in Sunday school that God made everything. He was full of wonder and intrigue which fuelled me to feel the same.

After six months of exploring the globe, I decided to return to Ghana and investigate the possibility of setting up a business and living there. We lived in Ghana for four months and experienced a real taste of what our lifestyle would be. The pace of life, the community and the food were wonderful, however, life was laborious and making money was a battle. It also gifted me time for reflection, soul searching, finding myself and continuing to live a joyful life.

We worshipped in church every Sunday and our relationship with God continued to develop. We were ready to create a life here, I was ready to take on the challenge, even willing to live a simpler life and to give up my dream of financial freedom to enjoy the daily freedom. But then I received a phone call from my best friend and in that second everything changed.

Earlier in my trip, she had let me know she was fighting cancer but as a 33-year-old super-fit woman we believed she would beat it, so I carried on with my journey and supported her from a distance. But she had just been told by her consultant that she had three months to live. We were life-long friends so within a week I was by her bedside and we spent one and a half months of relatively quality time together. In that time she taught me that I really had to make the most of every second I have on this planet and make the most of the benefits that I have been graced with. So I decided that I would come back to the UK and work towards the 'boss babe' status I had always dreamt of. I said goodbye to her, not knowing if I would see her again and left to organise my affairs in Ghana in order to return to the UK.

In the three weeks I was gone she passed away and I realised how priceless that time with her really had been. My new relationship with God and my new partner Alex really gave me strength at this painful time.

Back in the UK, in January 2019 I decided to dive into the challenge of joining the family business; a business I know well but have to learn thoroughly over the next two years as my step-dad prepares to retire.

Despite being in the industry for decades, I never felt able to commit to it due to the difficult relationship with my step-dad.

I grew up working in the family business. From the age of fifteen, I had worked with him. He is a creative, business-minded and successful guy who has high aspirations for me. I enjoyed working with him; it also gave me a taste of freedom and therefore I never wanted to work for anyone else. Despite his desire for me to work with him, taking over his business just wasn't an option either as we had a love/hate relationship with one another. He has always been a huge inspiration and role model to me, but he is also my biggest critic and at times I have felt like he smothered me.

Following my year of healing, I finally felt ready to show up and deal with my step-dad and the business on my own terms. For the first time in my life, I am mentally and emotionally free and I am consciously choosing rather than being coerced into following a path. My gap year was the catalyst for me to claim my power and commit to living and creating a joyful, abundant life. During this year I have found and unleashed the Warrior Queen within me who is capable of making her dreams a reality and I am finally well on my way to being the 'boss babe' I have always longed to be.

Today life looks completely different, I have travelled the dream far enough to find a home. Morgan and I are creating a life back in Leicestershire and despite the fact he is physically in Ghana, I have a great man by my side who respects, values and adores me and my son.

I met Alex the first time I travelled to Ghana and during our time there and our time apart he has been and continues to be a rock to me, he supports my wild and free mind and lifestyle but helps me to keep focused on being the best version of myself. It's a great comfort to know that I manifested the life I am living right now and this gives me more hope than ever; it has shown me that anything is possible.

When I look back I realise that 'suffering' had become my norm, I didn't realise that there was any other way to live and I am so grateful that I have reached a space of being so happy and peaceful. It's not that I never experience anything negative anymore, but I can now be confident that it's temporary, I can embrace these feelings and ride the wave of the emotion so that I am able to gain answers from their message. I continue to work on my emotional intelligence, and I am freed by the fact that my thoughts and feelings no longer control me.

"True freedom and the end of suffering is living in such a way as if you had completely chosen whatever you feel or experience at this moment."
Eckhart Tolle

My story is here to show you that there is always hope, no matter how low you go, no matter how dark the days look, things can change in an instant. You have the power to reinvent yourself, on your terms. Personally, I needed to travel the world to find myself and therefore find a home, but you may never have to venture this far as what you are looking for is inside of you. However, I do encourage you to listen to the whispers of your heart and to respond, to step out of your comfort zone, to do what everyone around you thinks is crazy, to do what you need to do to find yourself.

Before I discovered my whole and full self, I was broken, I was alone, I was scared, I was humiliated and lost and that's just what I needed to experience in order to ultimately recreate myself. I am grateful for those lessons and those who broke me because as a result, I am stronger.

"You might never fail on the scale I did, but some failure in life is inevitable. It is impossible to live without failing at something unless you live so cautiously that you might as well not have lived at all - in which case you fail by default." J. K. Rowling

I am full of hope, faith and I intend to quantum leap towards my dreams. This Warrior Queen is ready, she has the audacity to go after and take what she desires and deserves.

She has choices, so she chooses to be her own champion - a noble, fearless, compassionate Warrior Queen.

Dedication:

To my son Morgan, my inspiration, my life.

∞

Hannah's story can only leave you feeling inspired and full of hope. A courageous young woman and mother whose life has been filled with much trauma, illustrates that with a positive mindset, determination and a warrior queen-like spirit you can achieve the impossible.

Coming full circle after a great world adventure, Hannah has a burning ambition to become the 'boss babe' she dreamed of as a young woman full of dreams and ambition.

Armed with the tools and knowledge she has learned along her journey so far, I believe that Hannah will achieve whatever she sets her mind to. Morgan is one blessed young boy to have such a courageous, strong and fearless mother.

I wish Hannah, Alex and Morgan every happiness as they embark on their new chapter in life.

Brenda Dempsey
Creator & Editor

The Art of Feminine Beauty

Another Mountain To Climb

One sunny April day, breast cancer announced itself in my life,
Unleashing on my family and I, an unprecedented era of strife.

"But this was going to be my year!", I protested.
"Did you think you were in charge?", God contested.

And so it began, months of pricks and prods,
As I decided to beat cancer, whatever my odds.

First came the chemo, with its unwelcome hair loss,
Sprinkled with muscle pains, and a river of emotions to cross.

"I can't take any more!", on days I'd cry,
Only to pick myself up, and give it another try.

Spring turns into summer, and that also fades,
And all too soon, autumn's displayed its many shades.

Surgery now looms, to complete the clearing,
And in my heart, emotions are searing.

Another mountain, still left to climb,
Best to take it, one day at a time.

It hasn't been easy, the road to beat cancer,
But I know my prayers, God will answer!

Caroline Emile

VOICES OF HOPE

Johanna Burkhardt (USA)

You Have to Feel It to Heal It

Many of us can relate to being an ostrich. We often bury our heads in the sand rather than face challenges or even feel pain.

Johanna's story shines a light for many of us who do this throughout our lives. From trauma experienced in childhood, to painful relationships to total breakdowns.

The Truth Johanna reveals in her story is remarkable and gives us permission to do the same so we too can find ourselves once more.

It's time to take your head out of the sand, drop the mask and honour yourself.

Johanna has revealed many of the painful experiences in her moving, insightful and inspiring story of Hope for you.

Brenda Dempsey
Creator & Editor

Transformation #3

You Have To Feel It To Heal It

Johanna Burkhardt

Soul Shaman, Medium, Quantum Energy Facilitator,
Certified DNA Restructuror, Author and Creator of The
Purification Process and Healing Method.

"Be yourself; everyone else is already taken."

Oscar Wilde

I have spent most of my life wearing a mask of bravery. My childhood was filled with moments of excitement, love, and joy, but it was outweighed by the moments of abuse, pain, and shame.

As an adult, I never wanted to talk about my past, I didn't want to think about it, and I surely didn't want people to know about it. I just wanted to be "normal". I tried to move on with my life, and create the life I actually wanted to have. I wanted my children to never have to know the pain I experienced.

What happened was precisely the opposite. I did not see it this way though because I was in such denial of the life I had grown up in, I had buried it so deep that, it was as if it had never happened. In fact, I couldn't even remember most of my childhood, I had huge blocks of time that were just completely black, and I was okay with that.

In 2011, things began to shift for me. After coming out of severe depression, walking away from my second marriage, feeling like a complete failure, and living back at home with my father, I began to have these shifts within me that were unexplainable.

Other than I didn't want to be where I was anymore, I didn't know who I was anymore, what I wanted or where I was going.

On top of that, I was being faced with some uncomfortable emotions, and I was ready to run, and just start afresh like I was in a witness protection program.

In 2013, I packed up my car with what I could fit in it, with my son and a good friend and we drove cross country from California to North Carolina, where my son and I would start our "new life" with my now husband. Filled with expectations of my son having lots of friends, running in the countryside, me making new friends, having barbecues and just loving life, I was filled to the brim with expectations of how I wanted my life to look. I was sadly disappointed and feeling very alone, out of place and rejected. Two months in I get the first phone call that would forever change my life,;my grandma was dying. I didn't even know she was sick. How could she be dying? This woman was like a mom to me, and she didn't tell me she was dying?

I was the executor of her will so of course, had to fly back to California to be with her during her final weeks. While I cried a little bit, not what you would expect from someone who had just lost one of the closest people to her, on top of that my dad wasn't dealing well with this, and my now husband didn't know how to help me, so I did what I did best. I buried it.

In 2014, about seven months after my grandma had passed, she came to me in the middle of the night. So vivid, standing there looking young and healthy, I sat straight up, and was in awe that this was happening. She wasn't speaking, and her mouth was not moving, but I still knew everything she was telling me. My dad was now sick, and he wasn't telling me. This was her trying to say to me so that I could help him. I never told my dad that story, I was too afraid he would think I was crazy.

However, soon after that, he would no longer Skype with me, only call on the phone once a week or so. My dad, the engineer, said his computer was broken, and he didn't know what was wrong with it. That year he was in and out of the hospital about five times, and all he would tell me was that he was fine, not to worry about him. I knew deep down he was lying to me, and not telling me the truth, because he was afraid to admit what was happening himself.

In 2015, I receive the second call that would forever change my life, that my dad was dying, and I needed to fly back to California because he would no longer be able to take care of himself. This call I was actually prepared for, I had seen him just days prior on a trip to watch my daughter graduate. I knew he was really sick, but he would not talk about it. What I was not prepared for was the downward spiral that was about to happen.

He was given four months to live. I had weeks to sell the childhood home I had grown up in, retire him from his job of thirty-plus years and move him across the country. I had just taken a massive promotion at work, I was in the middle of planning my wedding, and we were in the middle of a home loan to build a new home on our existing property. We hadn't even secured a house to stay in temporarily while the building was happening. I could not have had more balls in the air at one of the worst moments in my life. And they all came crashing down. I lost my job, we almost lost our home loan, and we almost lost me. Three days after our wedding, I was misdiagnosed with a stroke when half of my body shut down from all the pain I was repressing. I sank into a profound depression after this event.

I was angry that this was happening, that my dad was dying, that he wasn't fighting, that this was my life. I was so mad I finally told my dad, he was given a death sentence, I told him what I swore I never would, that they had given him four months to live and he was on month four. I told him this in the hope he would fight harder; instead, he gave up, and he died weeks later, three days before Thanksgiving.

Once again, I didn't grieve as someone who had just lost the most important person in her life. I buried it, and I felt deep shame for telling him. I blamed myself for this death. Each day after his death I had to be "seen", to be doing things, I wore the mask of having it together and doing okay. I was really good at that, I had done it my whole life.

Most people thought I was happy and would tell me how strong I was for all that had happened and how I handled it.

This time it was different though, it got harder and harder to wear the mask, to keep up with the lies I was telling people and the lies I was telling myself. I was downing two wine bottles a night, shopping, eating, and doing everything I could to avoid the pain that was coming up from the depths of the well inside of me. Memories from childhood that were once black were flooding back. The pain I had never wanted to feel was creeping in, most days, it was a battle to get out of bed. I was snappy, judgemental and my poor husband took the brunt of it.

After months and months of this, my husband looked at me one day and said, 'please go back to the doctor and get a new medicine'. I looked at him, and with tears welling up in my eyes, I said 'I can't'. When he asked why I told him they would put me in a straightjacket because I want to die. 'I just can't take being here anymore. Inside, I really felt this way. I would rather die than feel the pain.' I said.

Something happened at that moment. When I was speaking those words out loud to someone who loved me more than anything, I knew it wasn't right. I was hearing myself and watching myself as if I was out of my body. My husband immediately wrapped his arms around me, and I let go.

At that moment a light came on, and I knew, I really didn't want to die, I just didn't want to be in pain anymore. I was tired of running from the pain that was coming. I surrendered.

That was the day I got my life back. That was the day, I realized all the masks I had been wearing to make people happy, not to appear weak, to be the big girl and take care of things had to be put down and burned. I wish I could say life was rainbows and roses from here on out, but it wasn't.

I found this quote by Elizabeth Taylor that helped me get up each day and begin to heal the pain; it read:

"You just do it. You force yourself to get up. You force yourself to put one foot in front of the other, and God Damn it, you refuse to let it get to you. You fight, You cry. You curse. Then you go about the business of living. That's how I've done it. There's no other way."

That was what I needed to see every day. I printed an 8 x10 size picture of this quote and taped it to the wall on the side of my bed. Every morning when I laid there not wanting to get up and face the pain, I would read it, and I would get up and put two feet on the ground to brave the world and the pain that was inside of me.

After about seven months of reading all the self-help and spiritual books I could get my hands on, getting mediumship readings and spending thousands and thousands of dollars on courses, I did the thing that shifted my entire journey. I detoxed my life. For 40 days I vowed to eat no refined carbs, no sugar, no alcohol (this was a big one for me), to journal and meditate. This was my first time journaling and meditating. I didn't know why I had to do this, I just knew I did. Looking outside me for the answer was not working. All the courses, all the training, all the readings were not making me better. It was time just to shut it all off and go within.

After 40 days, my life was completely different. I began feeling the spirit, seeing the spirit, and knowing information, I had no idea how I knew it. My intuitive gifts had burst wide open, and I knew I was here for way more; I had a purpose. There was just one thing I had to do first - HEAL. I had to do the work. I had to lead by example, something I had never done before. I had to help people see the answers they were seeking were inside of them, they just had to be brave enough to enter into the dark and turn the light on to receive them.

After two years of deep healing, and teaching what I learned to anyone who paid attention to me, one thing was more apparent than ever. We don't actually fear failure, rejection, an accident, heartbreak or death. We fear what it will feel like at that moment. No matter how many times I thought I healed it with mindset work or energy work, it always returned with a new mask on to play a new way again. This can get quite exhausting after enough times around the same rabbit hole.

You see, I had most of the pieces. I was already teaching others in my courses, readings, and coaching sessions that there was a purpose behind the pain, that it didn't all happen for nothing. I was already teaching them how to clear the "clutter" in their mind, body and home to reveal the pain they were avoiding. What I wasn't teaching them was to feel it. It was during another detox, I had this revelation that to create neutrality and peace in the body, we had to stop trying to "fix" the pain, the problem, the fear. We had to accept it. Not just take it, but we had to embody the pain completely. It is like eating poison so that the poison can never hurt you again.

When we face the feeling we fear and enter into a state of neutrality with it, we can live life from a more courageous and confident place. We can be free of the masks, the blame, the shame, the pain. We step out of the cage we placed ourselves in.

Today, I am a practising Shaman, a medium, a quantum energy facilitator and author, who helps people every day find the God within them. A Shaman is "the wounded healer", the bridge between the dark and light. We help bring you into balance by integrating the two worlds into one. To become one with the pain, and the joy and know that it isn't about one, or the other but that they are one and the same. Today, while I still have triggers, healing, and obstacles to overcome, I am not afraid. When the fear comes, it only occurs for a moment because I know, I am the creator of my reality and to help humanity, I must take the next step courageously and with all of me.

The flames we walk through today create a beautiful new pathway for those walking behind us. When you heal yourself, you improve the world. It's not a roadblock, it's a step up.

Feel it. Heal it. Then Lead with it. Do you see? We came here to find the shadow and envelope it. What you have experienced becomes what you are here to teach. Do it courageously.

Dedication:

I dedicate this to my Husband for loving me where I was and all the way through.

∞

It takes courage to face your demons, the dark side and the lies before you can find your Truth. Johanna's incredible story of one challenge after another illustrates the strength of the human spirit. It is often during our darkest times that we are reborn. We discover our purpose which fuels our passion and drive to create a new way of being, a new way of living. Johanna certainly has done that and today helps many other lost souls to find their path home.

Brenda Dempsey
Creator and Editor

VOICES OF HOPE

Phyllis Marlene-Benstein, Colorado, USA

My Detoxing Journey

Phyllis has a zest for life that has been ignited by a passion to improve not only her life but that of the women and men she inspires.

Suppressing her dream of a life on the stage, Phyllis chose to please her father's wish for her to become an engineer.

A rocky road lay ahead but her grit and determination to change her life and the opportunity to embrace entrepreneurship has enabled her to create a global business.

Phyllis' story allows the reader to see hope in the darkest of places and times.

Brenda Dempsey
Creator & Editor

Transformation #4

My Detoxing Journey

Ind. Market Partner with Manat

Phyllis Marlene-Benstein

"Surround yourself with people who reflect who you want to be, and how you want to feel. Energies are contagious."

Rachel Wolchin

I emerge from very humble beginnings.

My mom, Rhoda, was my hero and my biggest influence. She was a registered nurse who worked the night shift so she could send me off to school, sleep while I was at school, have a normal afternoon and evening, then go to work as I slept. My mom was confident, educated, and funny. She loved the finer things in life even though we were a bit mediocre as a family. She taught me to be the best me that I could be and not be like everyone else. She said that everyone can be ordinary and like everyone else but the beauty comes from being different and standing out.

Some of the other things she taught me were, being unique is special, to be myself, to be genuine, and see the good in everyone.

My dad, Jack, was a mathematician and computer programmer who taught me to find my passion, no matter what I decided to do in life. He encouraged me to be the best at whatever I choose and to be at the top of my game. I was always a math whiz with great training from my dad. Since he wouldn't pay for me to go to Carnegie Mellon or NYU Greenwich Village to pursue my dream of being an actress, I went to engineering school instead. My dad was the first dream-buster I had met. I graduated and was hired by a major defence contractor. I loved my J.O.B. for many years. If you haven't heard, J.O.B stands for "journey of the broke."

Some years later, I thought I had it all, four beautiful kids, a husband, a luxury home and a six-figure corporate job as an electrical engineer.

What transpired was a nasty divorce and becoming a single mom. I turned to network marketing as an outlet to be around other successful women and a change from the male dominated environment I endured at work daily. I surprisingly found a community, and sisterhood as well as a support network that taught me compassion, and how to compartmentalize and put my best face forward, even if I was hurting on the inside, so I could serve others. Not to mention the possibilities... I went on to pay off $40,000 in divorce debt and felt grateful for second chances. I was passionate about serving others so it was easy to show others how to empower themselves and live their dreams.

I'm passionate and dedicated to helping others discover their true potential and gifts outside the four walls of corporate. You see I was overworked and under-appreciated, overstressed and underpaid. Does this describe you?

Not long after starting work, I soon discovered years ago, my life was defined by corporate America. Although my heart was in the fashion and beauty industry, I graduated from college with a Bachelor of Science in Electrical Engineering and began a 25-year career in a male-dominated, fast-paced and demanding environment. I was a high frequency (rF) Design engineer. I loved my job and the intellectual stimulation, but needed some new creative and positively inspiring challenges.

I went to work in the dark; I came home in the dark, travelled a lot, and sacrificed time with my precious children to climb the corporate ladder.

I had little work-life balance. I had irritable bowel syndrome, frequent migraines, heart palpitations and sometimes an irritated bladder. I grew more and more unhappy. I decided it was time for a self-assessment and reality check about halfway through my career, only to determine that I was no longer doing something that was in alignment with my core values, and beliefs. I knew in my gut, my core that I was meant for something more, and that I could serve and make an impact on far more people outside the walls of corporate America.

One afternoon I asked a female co-worker if she wanted to go to a local networking business mixer to meet some other women. We went and it was there that I met someone who introduced me to the world of direct sales. Several months later I started my first business alongside my tech career. It was all about make-up and image. I quickly noticed that the women around me in my tech job, didn't care about their looks, not even to enhance their natural beauty and features, and this deeply saddened me.

There were beautiful women walking around in baggy t-shirts, casual unflattering jeans, and not a bit of lip gloss or mascara to be seen. I always found it disturbing that these same women would "glam" it up though if they got divorced or widowed.

For many years I worked my beauty business alongside my tech career. I continued to fall in love with the environment, freedom, flexibility, extreme positivity and the opportunity to work with other men and women who genuinely wanted to empower themselves and each other to be all they could be and in the process, reach mind-blowing levels of success.

Direct Sales is also a huge course in personal development, professional development, and leadership. I was taking in as much as possible! I began to seriously evaluate the possibilities of transitioning from Engineer to Entrepreneur completely.

A few months into that business I decided to file for divorce to end my very unhappy marriage and my relationship with an emotionally abusive man. My waning self-worth was beginning to grow again.

It gave me great joy, and a pay check of the heart to make other women look good, feel good, and radiate their inner beauty on the outside with confidence.

I became hungry to serve other women, and inspire them to wake their own sleeping giants and live life on their terms.

I eventually stopped the make-up business and joined a start-up handbag business. Again I grew personally, professionally, and stepped into leadership. I filled in working on my business in all the cracks of my life. I did work on my business before work hours, during my lunch time, and many evening hours. I went on amazing trips including conventions, conferences, award nights, and incentive trips. My confidence in being able to sustain myself with this type of business was growing.

I've always been very in tune with my body. One day I felt a moving lump in my left abdomen. It ended up being a growing fluid filled ovarian cyst that grew to the size of an orange. My gynaecologist did some testing, and there was a grainy portion that was possibly cancer, so I was scheduled for a full hysterectomy, with a vertical incision that ran between my bellybutton and my pelvic bone. By the grace of God, there was no cancer.

My recuperation meant six weeks off work, and as I was so exhausted it turned into eight weeks. During those eight weeks, I worked my business from a recliner chair or a lawn chair for a few hours a day in the beginning, and more near the end of the eight weeks.

My downtime gave me so much time to reflect, and re-evaluate my career, my vision, my time with my family, and the lifestyle that I wanted for myself and my family.

At the end of those eight weeks I now had a burning desire to get out of Corporate America.

My dad way back had suppressed my soul's desires so much that I couldn't give birth to my dreams! The hysterectomy was closure and I was ready to give birth to my wildest dreams. It was during my healing months, that it had felt so good spending a few hours, even with low energy, sitting outside in the warmth of the sun, listening to the birds, and smelling the beautiful flowers all around me. I realized at this point how fragile life is and that it could turn sour any minute. It was time to start following my heart.

Despite the misery I endured, I did re-marry the most incredible man, Harry Benstein, whom I met thirty one years ago at work. We had become good friends. Over the next decades we each were divorced. Harry was a gentleman, pure class, always polite and positive. He stood out as the crown jewel in that environment and was so much more outside of work. He was the knight in shining armour that saved me from my negative life and choices. He embraced my four children Mac, now 24, Mike 25, Shannon 28, and Rachel 29 that were only 7, 8, 11, and 12 when we got together. My kids have a bonus father that they love and respect. Harry is my life partner, my business partner, my soul mate and my best friend. I am more in love with him every day and so grateful to have him in my life.

I stayed in corporate America for another year. Right after my 25th anniversary, I walked into my boss's office for a review, when he explained that I would get a zero raise, for my zero contribution to the organization for the previous year. But actually I had bought many hundred thousands of dollars of work into the department. I was well-known and respected by industry leaders and those in niche technical groups in which I participated.

A few weeks later my company offered a voluntary layoff, and after consulting with my husband, I applied and was accepted. No one deserves the type of negativity and disrespect that I endured. During some of the discussions before I left, I was horrified to find out that in the year 2011, I still wasn't paid the same as my male counterparts.

I was elated to finally be able to stay at home with my now high-schooler boys, as well as my daughters who were already in college.

I stayed with that handbag company for two years out of corporate, building a 2 million-dollar organization, and growing more personally and professionally. That company folded in the summer of 2013 due to the inexperience of the two founders.

One and a half years later I reconnected with my business partner from that handbag company, who had found a new network marketing company that was a start-up for anti-ageing, non-toxic hair care. This was ideal for I'm definitely hair challenged. Image though is very important to me. At the time we reconnected, I was still experiencing hair dryness, breakage and loss, due to the early onset of the menopause caused by my hysterectomy. That combined with the extreme cold weather and climate in Chicago, and the toxic based normal professional salon products, it left my hair thin and my scalp and follicles clogged as a result. I couldn't imagine myself selling shampoo, although I was intrigued with being part of another start up, a 'founder' opportunity with a profit sharing option, and the desire to get my beautiful hair back. Also for the past 5 years I was "clean "with all my cleaning products, self-care products, and relationships to literally detox my life.

On January 23, 2015 I joined Monat Global and started the most incredible journey of a lifetime.

I'm passionate and dedicated to helping others discover their true potential and gifts outside the four walls of corporate. I currently lead, train, and inspire a team of 3,400 with 100+ hair professionals. I help men and women run successful businesses, get paid what they are worth and design the life of their dreams on their terms by selling shampoo or helping people start a lucrative business. I seriously help women wake their sleeping giant, discover what they truly worth and start a new path irrespective of how old they are.

I finally know my purpose. It's to help people reconnect with their core values, transition out of Corporate, and detox as well as design and live their dream life with a vision that pulls them toward their greatness, with confidence on the inside and being stylish on the outside. Your hair is the crown you never take off. I love the metaphor; get your head in the game.

I've learned that your skin is your biggest organ. Whatever product you use on your hair or your skin - for example, whatever shampoo you use - it's documented that it goes into your bloodstream in about 26 seconds, so increasing that toxic load was only making me sicker. I had migraines, heart palpitations, and back aches so I started that cleaner lifestyle and really looked at the products that I was using. Monat Global is premium hair care brand specialising in naturally botanically based products.

My tag-line is 'conscious beauty - why wait?' and I'm just really passionate about helping women be more conscious about what they put in and on their body so they do not increase their toxic load.
When women feel good, they look great.

Monat has also provided me with the opportunity to educate hair and health professionals, and the public about being conscious about the toxins in their every day products. I'm on a mission to help hair professionals choose safe products that they will touch and breathe as well as use with their client base.

Toxins lead to illness, cancers, stress, and it is never too soon to reduce our toxic loads.

I hope you too will discover yourself and embrace and love your God-given gifts as well as your precious bodies. Choose healthy non-toxic products and have a lifestyle at home and at work in sync with your personality and core values. Then you can truly live your life on path and purpose.

And lastly, as women please stand in your power and let your inner beauty radiate out so you can enlighten and inspire others with your gifts, talents and messages.

I'm now ready for the next chapter which will allow me to grow my brand and business to live a life of ease.

Dedication:

This chapter is dedicated to my mom Rhoda, who was my number one cheerleader, who loved me unconditionally and was the driving force behind me stepping out of my corporate comfort zone and into entrepreneurship.

HOPE

Be the Light

Once you awaken your awareness like Phyllis, you can begin to re-frame the way you think and change your life. In this process you can release old limiting beliefs that do not serve you and find a new path to follow. Phyllis' courage to totally transform her life from one that focused on a masculine energy to a more feminine way of being, illustrates how you can reveal you inner beauty. Now working in the well-being industry, Phyllis uses her transformation to help others change their lives to be more financially independent and free. She has accepted the beacon of light in which she now lives her life, lighting the way for others to see and follow.

Brenda Dempsey
Creator & Editor

The Art of Feminine Beauty

GODDESS

Dovile Strazdiene

Dovile Strazdiene is an abstract artist, wife, mother, cancer survivor and optimistic soul who featured in 'Voices of Courage'.

VOICES OF HOPE

Cathlene Miner - Florida, USA

I was Put in a Position Where I Had to be Quiet and Listen

This is a story of Karma. Cathlene found her courage and voice to sit up and take notice of the truth that was ringing in her ears. Like many people, we often know we are making wrong choices, yet we somehow cannot control ourselves. We believe that we are invincible, especially when we are young. It often takes something serious and even life-threatening before we acknowledge that it's time to make new choices. You could say that Cathlene's story is a coming of age tale. The life lessons she learnt have transformed her life and now she sees the power in adopting her new way of being.

Brenda Dempsey
Creator & Editor

Transformation #5

I Was Put In a Position Where I Had To Be Quiet And Listen

Cathlene Miner

Manifesting Expert, Radio Host,
Founder of Hopeful Handbags

*"Hope is what get us over the Hump.
Never Underestimate the Power of Hope."*

Cathlene Miner

When the universe is trying to reconnect and you will not slow down enough to listen, it will eventually put you in a position where you have no choice but to listen.

There I was lying in a hospital bed. I made some promises to God, the universe, angels, and anybody that would listen at the time. I knew that I had not taken very good care of myself for the past few years and now I found myself lying in this bed...

Let me rewind to my early life and high school before I found myself in the hospital bed. In addition to anxiety, depression, and always feeling like I had to have a boyfriend or some other outside "thing" to attempt to fill the empty gaps inside, I had an eating disorder. It consisted of flip-flopping between binge eating, bulimia and anorexia - eventually adding excessive exercising to this exhausting regime.

My eating disorder started when I was in high school. Looking back, I can admit I had a very poor self-image. I was always being told from people around me that I have no reason to be self-conscious. Instead, I should be very confident. "You are a pretty girl with an amazing family and a bright future ahead." I heard this way too often.

There was no huge outside influence that was making me feel this way. I was like any typical girl always looking at the happy skinny girls and models in the magazines. There were girls in my school that by definition were bullies to others and even their own friends; however for some reason I thought that because they were thin, they were the happy ones. I thought that they probably did not have any empty spaces inside like I did. They were happy with themselves. I would sometimes fall victim to the bullying, but for the most part I was always the girl that had a big friendship group, however, very few close friends. I was never the popular girl, the smart girl, or even the nerdy girl. I was just a girl who everybody knew and had a reputation of just sort of keeping quiet and being nice. I made decent grades, not an honor student but overall an average student.

I entered into the work program during my senior year of high school so I could make money. I was always, and still am to this day, very independent. I prided myself on being able to pay my own car payment and help out with whatever I possibly could for myself. The job was great, I thought it would fill the void in me but it never did.

I had absolutely amazing parents and still do to this day. My mom was 15 when I was born, my dad was 17 and I just have to say as a little side note, that they are still together and absolutely amazing. We did not have a lot, but we had just what we needed to be a very happy family. I tried to always hide my struggle with food from my parents. Coming home conveniently after dinner, pretending my stomach was too upset to eat, turning on the shower while being sick... I thought I was doing a good job of being "normal."

I guess I did not hide it as well as I thought I did - considering I do not know how I thought I could hide my increasingly emaciated body from my mom. She caught onto my eating disorder and of course she tried to make it better for me. She took me to doctors, counsellors, all of the things that you would do for your child. But still, the eating disorder never released me from its grasp. Now I look back and I know why I was not getting any relief from its strong grip on me. It was something I needed to work on from the inside, no outside influence was going to help me. I tried again to not let my parents see my struggle. I tried to make them believe that the help was truly working.

I would still go awhile without eating and somehow that made me feel better inside, hungry but yet full in a sense. It made me feel very in control. Plus, I loved the feeling of my clothes being loose on me and the comments I would get about how skinny I was. The times when I would eat, it was usually something sweet. I always seem to crave sweet things - candy corn especially. But then I would immediately go and throw what I ate up. The boyfriend that I had at the time knew what I was struggling with. Every time I would excuse myself after eating, he would come to find me, trying to help me as best he knew how. He truly did help too, until I found myself alone again and the disordered voice in my head was too loud to shut out. Even though I had so many caring people by my side, I still felt so lost. I felt like something was missing. I did not feel complete by any means. I graduated from high school, worked and supported myself. I always felt that I needed to have a boyfriend at all times. Somehow I thought that a boyfriend would make me feel complete and fill the gaps and voids that I was feeling. I was always looking for an outside thing to make me feel better.

As I said before, I have an amazing family, amazing parents and an amazing sister, but I was not full on the inside. As soon as I graduated from high school, I craved to be on my own. I did not have to move out of my parents' house but I wanted to be more independent.

I was not going away to college, but I craved that independence. I was still working and keeping busy with developing my independence.

We only lived about a half a mile from the ocean, so a simple bike ride would bring me to my happy place. However, I wanted to be even closer to the ocean. That, combined with the craving of being on my own, finally pushed me hard enough to move out. I thought that being on my own and living only one block away from my happy place would surely fill the empty void in me. The only thing I brought with me was my bed. I had a roommate and we had nothing. When I say nothing, I mean there was nothing in that apartment except for a cardboard box that we ate our dinner on. We each had only a bed in our bedrooms but I felt accomplished because I was doing it on my own.

Every day I would get up early, go to work, go take a nap on the beach when I finished work, and found that the empty void was still there. Additionally, I was continually being haunted by the eating disorder and I was starting to exercise excessively. I walked everywhere. So not only was I doing my regular hard-core workout, but I was walking between five and ten miles a day down the beach.

I pushed the thought out of my head on how my body would function with the minimal amount of food. I knew deep down that this was not healthy for me and long-term I was going to be doing a lot of damage to my body and mind. My mom would try to talk to me about this a lot, but I did not want to hear anything about it. I would tell her how I had everything under control and everything was fine. I was fine.

Fast forward a year and a half later to where I had just started dating a guy that I had been friends with in school. It was not too serious of a relationship yet. We had talked about getting married at some point, but I had talked to other boyfriends about that too like most girls do. I still was being imprisoned by the eating disorders, but I was going through life as normally as I could.

I went for a routine Pap smear that came back abnormal and was told I needed to have the LEEP procedure (Loop Electrosurgical Excision) on my cervix. They said they had found precancerous cells and just to be cautious the procedure would be the best choice. The doctor said my cervix will eventually grow back. I was just turning 19 when I had the procedure done. The doctors informed me that I would not be able to carry a pregnancy any time soon because my cervix needed time to grow back. I was fine with this fact because I was not planning on getting pregnant anytime soon.

After the procedure I went back for my six week check up. They had me do the usual urine analysis and sent me to the room to wait for the doctor. The nurse came in and asked how I have been feeling lately, I replied that I was feeling okay. What the nurse said next flooded me with so many emotions. "Well, you are pregnant." Unexpectedly, a true feeling of excitement came over me. So many overwhelming thoughts at once. I was extremely excited, yet I was scared. Some anxiety started taking over my thoughts. In that doctors' office I pledged to never make myself throw up again and to start eating right for my baby. "Oh my gosh, maybe this is what I needed? How did this happen? Will I be able to maintain this pregnancy?" It is amazing how many thoughts and feelings can come rushing into your head in a matter of seconds.

The doctor came in and answered the dreaded last question on my mind. I may not be able to maintain this pregnancy. "Oh my gosh," I thought. The feeling of fear was still lingering and the excitement was replaced with disappointment. I knew I had to go home to tell my parents this news. So many thoughts at one time. So I walked out to the lobby and to my boyfriend that had driven me to my appointment. We were walking down the hall and talking. I remember saying, "I'm pregnant" and I just kept walking. I turned around and he was still standing at the other end of the hall, in shock.

After the shock wore off enough, to where he could move, we went to my mother's work. I told her the news and she was extremely excited and positive as she always is, so there was some relief in her response. Next, I had to go and tell my father. I knew I would be able to find him in his usual place, which was working on his car in the driveway of the house. The first two questions he had for me were, "Do you have health insurance?" and "When are you getting married?" It was a nice slap of reality for me that I was left to ponder and deal with.

A few days later, I started throwing up. I thought this was ironic, I was not making myself sick. I spent a lot of time in the bathroom though. My mom would take me to the doctors, and they always found that I was dehydrated. They would read me a slew of questions. They would send doctors and nurses into the room one by one and asked me if I was making myself throw up. One particular doctor would say to me every time I saw her that I was too young to have a baby anyway.

I was shocked when they asked me if I was being abused. None of this was true. It was as if they thought that by asking me enough times, I would eventually say 'yes' to at least one of these things. Consequently, they would put me on an IV drip to get me hydrated before sending me home. The very next day, I would be back in the doctor's office, back in the hospital and back on IV. It got to the point where they put me on IV at my parents' house. I would still throw up and get more dehydrated and be back in the hospital again.

Fast forward a couple of days to me lying in the hospital bed. This was the universe trying to teach me a huge, huge lesson…

I was diagnosed with hyperemesis gravidarum (a condition characterized by severe nausea, vomiting, weight loss, and electrolyte disturbance during pregnancy). Imagine waking up everyday, feeling like you had the worse hangover… but I did not even drink in general, let alone of course not touch alcohol when I was pregnant. Every hour of the day I was either being sick, or feeling like I was on the verge of being sick to where there was nothing left to come up but bile. The whole pregnancy was spent bent over, over the toilet or bent over, crawling place to place due to my lack of energy.

Occasionally I would find relief curled up in a ball, but it never lasted long.

I had lost a lot of weight, but my baby was growing and healthy because he was getting everything he needed through IVs.

I promised the universe that I would never ever make myself throw up again. How can somebody that suffered from bulimia and anorexia now have hyperemesis, where they cannot control the amount they are throwing up? I thought this was a lovely joke that the universe was playing on me. I started thinking back to when I was little, about seven or eight years old and I was very connected to my spiritual self and I would sometimes hear things.

I would have severe anxiety and panic attacks trying to stop the thoughts I was having. I guess being in such a weak state most of the time during my pregnancy caused me to have a lot of quiet time.

No more running around for a while. I would lay there and just think. Those panic attacks and anxiousness I used to experience as a child started creeping back into my life. I felt like I was being told something. I would hear all the things I tried to ignore when I was a little girl. The constant voice in my head was telling me that it had always been with me, trying to give me guidance. "There is nothing to be afraid of," the voice assured me. Those familiar visions, voices and knowing were coming back to me. It began to dawn on me that I was trying to block out all of that because it was not "normal" - right?

I knew the universe was trying to get my attention and to help this baby; I was ready to listen.

As I lay there thinking about these things, the doctors would have counsellors come in and talk to me, wanting to know why I was making myself throw up. Asking me again if I was being abused. Then the doctors told me that if I did not stop making myself throw up, there was a chance it would not end well for myself or for my baby. They would have to put a feeding tube in and I would have to keep it in for the rest of the pregnancy. I did a whole lot of crying, especially as I had not purposely "made" myself throw up since I had found out I was pregnant.

I started to reconnect to those old familiar feelings from when I was younger, but this time without FEAR. I began to connect to my inner guidance again and talk to the visions I was seeing and hearing. I started asking them to PLEASE help my little boy and help me make it through this pregnancy. And they did. That was when I knew that this void inside of me was my spirit, which I had disconnected from. By listening and being quiet, really quiet, I could reconnect. After reconnecting with my spirit and feeling stronger, I was able to fight off the eating disorder that had a firm grip on me.

Thank you Universe! The universe taught me that no one around me was able to fix this for me. It was something that I had to do myself by looking deep within and finding my true strength.

Although the bulimia and anorexia were over, I had done such damage to my body that I had many other hurdles to overcome. And YES, the UNIVERSE got me through those too. Now I have four children and am happily married, living just a quick bike ride away from the beach.

Dedictation:
To my mom and dad;
Thanks to your unconditional love and support over the years, I have learned to believe in my internal strength and intuition. You have taught me the importance of slowing down and listening to my internal guidance and having the confidence to follow it. Thank you also for showing my children and grandchildren the same unconditional love. I love you.

Cathlene's story described a soulful journey that is filled with many challenges that she has overcome. These experiences have been crafted into her work which she carries out with great empathy, compassion and love. Her positivity, determination and passion to help others on their journey, is a testament to everything she endured to become the remarkable vibrant women she is today.

Brenda Dempsey
Creator & Editor

VOICES OF HOPE

Willow Sterrick - Buckinghamshire, UK

Ditch Shame and Guilt, Find Authenticity, Discover Your Truth!

Willow is one of the most courageous women I have met. She has totally surrendered to who she is; learning to let go of her past and move on. Her experiences have led her to create a new life and business where she can help other women, like her, find the light within themselves.

She is using the journey of her own mental health to help others recognise that they DO have options and that one of the best ways to make different choices is to reach out to others and ask for help.

This takes great courage and Willow has learned many practices through becoming a Shaman to help her sisters in need. She is totally empathetic to their situations. Be marvelled at her story.

Brenda Dempsey
Creator & Editor

Transformation #6

Ditch Shame and Guilt, Find Authenticity, Discover Your Truth!

Willow Sterrick

Shaman

"If you want to find the secrets of the universe, think in terms of energy, frequency and vibration."

Nikola Tesla

D o you long to be heard, in a world that desperately needs your authenticity, love, nurturing, care, compassion and Truth?

Do Shame and Guilt hold you back?

What if I revealed to you that this is the perfect place to start? The 'How' will come when the passion is fired by your Truth! The Shame and Guilt will disperse as you find love, nurturing, care and compassion for yourself making you authentic and ready to face your Truth!

In my first Transformation story in *Voices of Courage,* I was afraid to openly share my soul and kept the 'thing' that was a pivotal moment for me quite cryptic. In some ways now, when I read it over, it's like a huge part of me that held me back. Now the guilt and shame has gone, vanished, dispersed within me. Since writing about it, I can easily see how much I have grown, so it now feels ancient history!

I am now ready to share what lies deeper and deeper down that rabbit hole of darkness; like going off into the night to find respite from the mundanity of my life. The lack of connection with friends and family, having no real ambitions and waiting for life to happen for me, is a consequence of not facing my Truth. In *Voices of Courage*, when I said that 'Escorting' restored my faith in humanity, it is indeed what it felt like at the time.

95

Not being able to see myself in a better light and blaming the area I lived in, as well as the people I hung around with, was easier to face than the absence of seeing the bigger picture of the world or myself. It was just another consequence of shame and guilt.

For sure, meeting such a diverse range of folk in different counties, towns and villages really opened my eyes once more. As a child and a young adult into my twenties, I held a more diverse perspective of the world but allowed this to be closed down by people-pleasing and fitting in to the local status quo. Feeling dismayed, this was not the person I envisaged, yet something inside me stirred.

Through the unique and diverse clientele I met, I began to enjoy the conversation and connections being made. It felt more like companionship, counselling and listening time after time especially as I am a natural when it comes to folk opening up and feeling safe to do so with me. This ironic situation became quite common place and often the focus was on this experience rather than the actual service first sought.

I interestingly dodged the intimacy with more than one of my clients on more than one occasion as they preferred the talking, listening and non-judgemental environment I created. Ironically, the job was making me feel completely detached, unemotional and defensive, so this listening had indeed began as a way of taking my nurturing femininity back. However, at the time I had no idea of this lesson it was showing me. It ended up as self-loathing, resulting in self-harm and depression which further induced detachment from others. I allowed Shame and Guilt to creep in; my mind was consumed by the feelings of being outcast from society.

Over time, the intense destructive feelings created a catalyst for change. It was time to value myself once more, to see things in me that no one else was seeing. It was evident that my family and friends didn't appear to value me either. I hadn't realised it all started with me. I had been provided for all my life and now I had to take full responsibility which was not easy for me. It took me longer to realise that I had to truly 100% value 'me' first. I was still going through life's motions, waiting to be saved, rescued or for a miracle to happen without even asking!

I knew I had gifts but it appeared the world was not ready for the Depth of me, the Authenticity of me - I had to find my Truth, but how?

I attempted to give up drugs mainly as I had a puppy to take care of so my focus was on her.

A few months later, I ended being an Escort, when I met a new partner who was actually an old friend. Having experienced a taste of self-employment, we decided to start a business writing and co-producing a magazine on mental clarity, emotional well-being and spirituality. However, we weren't ready due to our underlying emotional issues. Moreover, the coping strategies we both had in place were not healthy but we clearly yearned for this change. I knew I never wanted to be anything else but self-employed from now on!

These Dreams and Visions of a better life never left me. As a sensitive being, I had found a relationship which ended suddenly with every bit of hope resulting in a mini emotional breakdown.

I discovered that some of my most enlightening moments and conversation have been while in chemical romance. We all take different paths to enlightenment.

So drugs in essence helped me find my Truth. My inner deeper nature was experienced through meeting new folk who thought more like me. These meetings helped me see the never ending potential within the fractals of my mind -,but how to harness it I had no idea!

Drugs have a dark side and they can consume some people completely. I know, it happened to me for a short while. I also feel strongly that it is often our thoughts that are the things that consume us to the point of full detachment from reality and that, yes the drugs can be the catalyst that pushes us over the edge of our own mind, into the abyss.

The Shame and Guilt associated with drugs is what caused me to have a Psychotic Episode. The medical professionals blamed the drugs, as I had been trying out magic mushrooms in the summer of 2013. There was a catalogue of events that impacted on me, my thoughts, decisions and behaviour.

During this time I was shown things by higher level spiritual beings and lower level feral beings described as delusions of the mind, yet these things were scary as my understanding at the time was limited to what I was truly experiencing. From the Shamanic path I have chosen to follow, I now know that I was experiencing the other world we cannot see.

I believe what made my experience more frightening was the anti-psychotic medication I was given. This made me more open to what was going on and was in no way keeping me safer; it felt like it was hindering the entire experience. This was a Spiritual Awakening of a massive kind and all I needed was a Shamanic Healer to help me navigate all the healers and teachers coming into my energetic body.

They would show me the paths and how to navigate my chakras back into my body and be in peace to journey these parts of me safely. It's now my mission to help the medical profession see this side of insanity as often it can be an awakening for many folk.

This has been my experience of drugs and sometimes they have been the healer.

I see a world uneducated to the true teachings of what is readily available to us. We have varying perspectives of life, looking at situations in shallow ways. We rush through life without giving a thought to why so many people turn to drink and drugs; instead, we judge and label them alcoholics or addicts - yet many of these tormented souls are super talented!

I knew I had gifts but it appeared the world was not ready for the Depth of me, the Authenticity of me. I was laughed at, mocked and shut down by others when showing my emotions deeply so I had to find my truth, but how?

I found my Inner Voice was louder on drugs and consequently my Higher Self rose up! What if my experiences of drugs have helped me to access parts of my brain that were previously unlocked?

To discover more and to continue to use my past Shame and Guilt for good I am planning to complete a Neuro-Science Degree to find out just what was going on in my brain during these moments of clarity and self-realisation.

Perhaps this resonates for your Chemical Romance which you feel is holding you back in life when it could be propelling you forward. If this is the case,

I would love to hear from you! My details are in the back of the book.

Are you a functioning drug user that wants to be more in control or stop ?

What if through self-love, care and understanding you find your path out of the situations that you no longer wish to control you? Would you reach out and be guided to do so? I see the Light in you before you do, so it's always been there waiting for you to call it home.

My journey led me to feel deeply compassionate for others, especially the misunderstood folk of the world. These people often feel they don't deserve to take up space, especially those who never felt they fitted into the mainstream. Perhaps this is you?

I can help you find your Truth in a six month Journey that leaves you with life-long tools of inner discovery and helps you to propel yourself forward in ways that are beautifully grounding and deeply personal to you. A journey that is life-affirming and transformational, returning you to the Soul purpose you came to create.

With you in mind I have created Energetic Healing packages in my business Willow's Wisdom, from my story and journey, to work from the inside out!

Dedication:

To my dad - Dad I miss you every day – I know I am like you because I feel the love and gifts you gave me.

Willow's story is raw and real. Unapologetically she bares her soul and stands in a power that many people never experience. Her candid account of living with a drug problem provides a deeper insight to help the reader understand the turmoil and longing for something different. Through Personal Development and training, in rising up from her situation, Willow is determined to help other people who are experiencing mental health issues because of their choices.

Brenda Dempsey
Creator & Editor

VOICES OF HOPE

Lou Matson - Sheffield, UK

The Road Back to ALL that I AM – The Journey from Disempowerment to Empowerment.

Without a doubt, life is difficult and challenging when we ignore the little voice inside. We are so misinformed that we spend our lives pleasing others before ourselves.

Louise Matson finally woke up and listened to her truth. From a very young age she knew she was different. She knew she was born to stand out and not fit in.

Her struggles impacted the way she thought and behaved until one day. ... A very powerful day that is usually disguised in trauma.

Like Louise, you will have 'aha' moments when you read her tale...

Brenda Dempsey
Creator & Editor

Transformation #7

The Road Back to ALL that I AM – The Journey from Disempowerment to Empowerment.

Louise Matson
Postive Energy Healer

"I always wondered why somebody doesn't do something about that. Then I realised I am somebody."

Lily Tomlin

My earliest childhood memories are of being 'wrong', 'bad', 'mad', 'unwanted' and 'unloved'. The way I was made to feel like a child, especially during my teenage years, you would've thought I was a juvenile delinquent. But I wasn't, I was just an average child who happened to have been born knowing that we are all spiritual beings having a physical experience! I was born with the gifts of claircognisense (clear knowing, a sense of 'knowing'), clairsentience (precise sensing, the ability to feel energy), clairvoyance (clear seeing, the ability to see with the 3rd eye), the ability to heal and to channel messages. I was also born with a strong 'knowing' that I was here to serve others.

I could 'feel' people's pain, and feeling an intense urge to help people, would lay my hands on them to take the pain away. I would absorb the shock into my energy field, storing it within my body until it became too much for me to handle. At the point where it became too dense for me to carry, I would feel drawn to finding a tree happy to take the energy from me, place my hands on the tree and release the pain into the Earth for transmutation into love and light. As a young child, I assumed everyone was the same as me and would happily talk about my gifts; however, I learnt early on that this was not the case. My 'gifts' did not go down well in the very conservative upbringing my soul chose for me in this lifetime. Neither of my parents was strongly religious; however, both were very conservative regarding their views on life. My father worked within the armed forces, and life was very rigid and full of rules about how one should behave and BE.

My need and desire to be loved and fit in with my family and immediate society won out over my desire to be authentic and real to my Self. So, my life from the age of six onwards was one of doing whatever it took to fit in, I just wanted to be loved, accepted and have a comfortable life. I consciously chose to lock away my gifts, my 'knowing' of who we are and everything spiritual, firmly in a box. This led to me developing shape-shifting, chameleon-like behaviour; using my intuitive gifts to work out what people wanted of me and doing everything possible to give it to them. I became a people-pleaser extraordinaire!

It only struck me how far I had gone with this behaviour when someone asked me my name in secondary school, and I answered, "What do you want it to be?" But by that point, it was too late as the behaviour pattern was so deeply embedded in my programming, into my identity, that I felt incapable of doing anything different. I no longer had any sense of who I was or what I wanted in life, the only aspect I had held onto was my 'knowing' that I was here to serve others and this became my main focus to the detriment of my personal needs.

I focused my energy on making others feel happy. I gave of myself and my energy always and acquiesced to the wishes and desires of friends and family often going way beyond my personal boundaries to the point where I felt utterly miserable. The ironic thing, I was completely unaware of my misery as I was in complete denial. Like most people, I built walls around my heart and any pain within me so that I wouldn't feel it. The constant energetic alterations I made to my physical appearance, posture, accent, and personality just to fit in were draining to the extreme and left no energy for me to consider what MY wants and desires were even if I had wanted to.

There were moments during my teenage years and early adulthood where the Universe would 'nudge' me with regards my true identity, my gifts and my soul mission, attempting to steer me back in alignment with my truth. But these 'nudges' were often subtle and easily ignored due to fear of losing what I had and the unknown. Those instances when I did follow the Universe's guidance and 'lift the lid' on my spiritual box, opening myself up to spiritual experiences, the overwhelm I felt from the messages, experiences and sensations that flooded in, was such that I 'freaked out' and immediately locked that part of myself back in the box.

One thing I do know is that the 'nudges' may start off small and subtle but if ignored, become louder and bigger until eventually you can no longer ignore them and have to take action in alignment with your truth. I was so deeply entrenched on the path of disempowerment, consciously disempowering myself, that I chose to ignore the very many red flags the Universe, my higher Self, whatever you want to call it used to 'wake me up' that it took an almighty 'shove' from the Universe to alter my course and redirect me on the path to Empowerment.

This 'shove' by the Universe was the first significant pivotal moment in my life, and it happened in September 1996. I was living a desolate existence so far removed from my truth, it was scary. I was living in Sheffield with my partner and our child. My partner was deeply into the club scene using drugs and regularly having affairs with women he met on the dance floor. Our relationship pushed my boundaries so far beyond what was acceptable for me that it brought me the closest I have ever been to ending my existence on this planet. The years of mental and emotional abuse I suffered during that relationship made me feel completely worthless, unlovable and insignificant.

To bring money in, I was working as an administrative assistant at the University, for a manager who amplified my feelings of worthlessness and insignificance by making me feel useless and invisible. I hated my life but was resigned to my pain, unable to see any way out. Then one morning, as I was walking down the stairs to go to work, the Universe gave me a mighty shove!

My foot slipped on the carpet at the top of the stairs, and I remember my head going back and thinking 'that went back too far!'. The next thing

I remember was finding myself at the bottom of the stairs! The result of this innocuous accident was me being hospitalised with no feeling from the neck down. I was paralysed, tetraplegic. Now thankfully, this experience only lasted a week, but it was one of the scariest episodes of my life and a resounding 'wake up' call.

I look back on moments like this in my life with absolute gratitude. I find these moments to be the best and most decisive moments of my life.

The accident and subsequent panic attacks and anxiety gave me many things; they showed me my courage, inner strength, resilience, compassion and immense capacity to love. The accident, the time spent in the hospital and recovering at home afterwards also gave me time and space to reflect. Time to review my life, my relationships, my behaviour, my wants, needs and desires, something I had never done. This period of reflection enabled me to take stock of my life, my journey thus far. I looked at my life with radical honesty, owning and accepting my part in my misery, taking progressive responsibility for my choices and actions and eventually starting the process of forgiveness. This, in turn, resulted in significant changes to my relationship with my parents and my career. I could see with real clarity, the patterns in my behaviour, and were not being true to myself had led me. It also made me realise that life is too short to waste and is there to be enjoyed! We have no idea what's around the corner, and all those little things that we worry about really are NOT that important! I subsequently left the job I hated; I completed a counselling course and retrained to become an Occupational Therapist. It took a little longer and another 'nudge' from the spirit to leave my partner but hey ho, one thing at a time!

I started to 'lift the lid' on my spiritual aspects training as a Reiki Master, Reflexologist and Crystal Healer and started to take on healing clients while still working full time for the NHS. I again didn't feel fully able to embrace ALL my gifts or spirituality (such as the channelling, clairvoyance), just the parts my parents found acceptable, but I felt better for starting to allow parts of myself out of 'the box'.

The next significant pivotal moment happened in January 2016 when my father died. My mother had been diagnosed with Alzheimer's 13 years earlier and stopped knowing who I was many years before my father's death. His death finally set me free from my self-imposed prison. I finally felt free to be me!

This realisation was, that on the one hand, I felt released from the bounds I had placed on myself to fit into my family and society, and on the other hand, I had the sudden realisation that I had no clue who I was. I was instantly plunged into depression as I wrestled with my feelings of grief for my loss, my sense of guilt for the pain I had caused myself and the confusion of not knowing who I was. I realised that my people-pleasing program was still powerful and that I had no idea what I truly wanted in life! I knew I had a soul mission, a soul purpose but felt wholly disconnected from it and had no clue how to reconnect.

At the time of my father's death I was a senior manager in the NHS. The realisation that although the role was fulfilling concerning the fact that I felt I could help people, I realised that this had been my father's dream and not my own. As I struggled with the internal turmoil of realising that I was not living my truth and in fact, didn't know what my reality was, I became increasingly stressed and depressed. I eventually went on sick leave from work as the stress resulted in physical and emotional symptoms, which made it impossible for me to 'carry on' with my job. Unhappy to take sick pay but 'knowing' that I needed to take time to really find myself, I chose to have a career break for 12 months to give myself the time I felt I needed to explore who I was and to reconnect with ALL that I am.

During those twelve months, I was on a fast track of spiritual development, finally allowing myself to reconnect with my truth, my higher Self and allow my gifts to resurface. I started to embrace my gifts of claircognizance and clairsentience fully, I reconnected with my guides, the angels and other higher energy beings, studied additional healing modalities that I felt divinely directed to learn and

I changed my lifestyle. As I reconnected to my truth, I started to follow my inner guidance with more confidence and conviction, practising daily meditation, connecting with nature and making energetic hygiene an essential aspect of my daily routine, basically following my direction to open up my energy channels and enable the flow of energy freely throughout my system. I undertook a period of 'healer heal thyself' and now feel ready to serve as I was meant to – a place of self - full, a replenished cup and not by giving entirely of myself selflessly.

The final pivotal moment came in January 2018. Two years after my father's death, my mother died. This experience taught me so much about soul contracts, love and forgiveness. The 'shackles' were finally wholly removed. I say that with the utmost appreciation for my mother but the experience of her passing and the sense of freedom I felt for us both was powerful and beautiful all at the same time. I knew in the moment of her passing that we were both freed from our karmic contracts and as her soul released from this world to the next I realised I had no more excuses for hiding my light.

I realised and accepted that I had lived my whole life on the sidelines, hiding, fearful of allowing the light of my truth, my power to radiate from within, afraid of shining too brightly and attracting attention! That was the moment I began to walk the path of Sovereignty.

I am not fully there yet, I still have some aspects of the fear and disempowerment program to release, but I am working on them as and when they 'trigger' with love and excitement. As each 'trigger' appears, I now surrender rather than deny, avoid or 'run away'. Understanding that my experiences from childhood were explicitly designed and beautifully, to give me the perfect life lessons my soul desired, enabling me to serve best those people I am here on this planet to assist.

I started a self-employed business as an intuitive energy healer, channel, way-shower and spiritual guide with an emphasis on assisting others in walking their own path from disempowerment to Empowerment so that we can all stand in our Sovereignty and live our truth, and I have started taking on clients. I now live my life fully in-line with spirit, listening to and following the guidance I receive. I openly share my gifts on Facebook and am allowing all opportunities to come to me.

I now feel as though I am moving towards the lifestyle I am here to live, and I think this is the tip of the iceberg and as I allow more and relax further into my gifts, I shall receive so much more. I feel more at peace within myself than I ever have, especially with the realisation that I chose the life that I have lived. I decided to experience all the lessons I've had to bring me here to the point where I am so that I can serve and assist others all the better for them.

While reintegrating my spiritual truths I had the realisation that I (like many people on the planet at this time) am a 'star seed', someone whose initial incarnation and the majority of previous lifetimes has been on other planets and unlike Earth, seeds do not naturally feel at home on Earth. This realisation has led to more of an understanding of why I felt so 'alien' as a child, why I felt so different to those around me. Why I thought I didn't belong with my family or here on Earth at all, struggling with the density of the energy on this planet. It also explained a lot about why I often wanted to leave this physical life on Earth, not necessarily to want to kill myself but just finding it unbearably heavy on my heart to be here. This more profound understanding of who I am, who we all are as multi-dimensional beings has meant that I can connect more fully to my soul purpose and channel messages from a more extensive source. I aim to assist others who are on similar journeys to my own.

Walking the path from Disempowerment to Empowerment has often felt really hard, and the desire to give up and turn back to what was known and felt safe has been immense. But I can honestly say that I feel so much happier where I am now, standing in and living my truth openly in the world and can't wait for what the future holds, 'knowing' that we are all divinely guided and protected.

Never give up hope, allow your hearts to open and reconnect with your light within.

Dedication:

For my mother and father, who taught me so much about myself. I am now able to fully appreciate what it is to be ALL that I am.

For my son Sol, my blessing and at times, my rock and my reason for being.

To all the souls that entered my life to teach me and help me grow and to my partner Duncan, thank you for your love, acceptance and support.

Facing her Truth, Lou found the courage to live her life as she was born to live it, fearless, limitless and of service to others. She is able to Face and Voice her Truth as she sees it. Her message of connection within is one we hear time and time again until one day we hear it with our heart and soul. That is the time when we are awakened to a new way of living, a new way of BEing. Louise has found her path to Sovereignty and invites you to join her. Louise, thank you for the invitation. Be moved...

Brenda Dempsey
Creator & Editor

VOICES OF HOPE

Paula Jarek - Polish iving in London

Dare to Dream

Paula is a bright, bubbly and beautiful soul. She knows courage and uses it to make her dreams a living reality.

Brought up in post-communist Poland, she had experienced challenges but she dared to dream. That dream meant leaving Poland and travelling to London at a young age for a new way of living and being.

Still, she faced difficulties until a new road opened up for her. As a brave and bold young woman she took it not knowing but she trusted.

You will be inspired by her decision to follow her heart and find a passion that is truly transformational for her clients.

Brenda Dempsey
Creator & Editor

Transformation #8

Dare to Dream

Paula Jarek

Business Owner Speaks Volumes

"Our experiences shape who we are. But we can still choose the direction this shape takes."

Paula Jarek

Our experiences shape who we are. But we can still choose the direction this shape takes.

My story is nothing extraordinary; I'm sure most of us have gone through similar experiences. I have found it difficult to pinpoint the one pivotal moment in my life. Bullying at school, harassment at work, unacceptably undermining remarks made by teachers and colleagues. It was more of a series of experiences that have shaped who I've become. A story of having had enough of people telling me what I can and cannot achieve in my life. Just like the saying: 'What doesn't kill you makes you stronger'. I now know I can be and do whatever the hell I want if only I am determined enough.

I grew up in a post-communist Poland, a patriarchal country where everyone is white, Polish and Catholic, and difference isn't necessarily welcome. I don't particularly miss my childhood, regardless of repeatedly being told that I would once it's gone.

Growing up, I was too stubborn and not precisely the crowd-following kind of child for most kids to like me. For a long time, I thought being a girl was somewhat a curse in comparison to how much easier and less judgemental boys lives seemed. Whether they were friends or not, they'd play football together, and everyone belonged.

I became sick with tuberculosis on my larynx at the age of sixteen. I wanted to be a professional singer and just before the diagnosis came through. Doctors warned me it was likely that I would never be able to use my voice for work again if the tests came back positive. My world had fallen apart. My parents suggested I shouldn't tell other kids as 'they might not understand'. I don't like ignorance and small-mindedness. If people wanted to move away from me because I'm unwell, even though I cannot pass the disease to them, they were not my friends in the first place. Things got pretty intense then: hospitals, doctors, tests, action plan, more probing and more doctors.

For a long time, I felt down, without direction, and I was not getting better, despite taking a 3-in-1 antibiotic every day for months. One day I woke up and I said to myself: 'No, I will not give up. I will fight.' I don't really know what was different about that day. I don't know where the power within me came from nor where I was headed, but I felt it so clearly for the first time. It was the determination to get better and start again. Suddenly my results began improving, and I made a full recovery. It was a life-changing experience I made happen for myself. I will never forget that feeling.

Eventually, I have learned I only need one real friend at a time to feel happy, accepted and loved. Without sounding cynical, people come and go, that's the way of life. But every each and one of them contribute and teaches us something along the way, be it a happy or painful lesson. They all leave marks on our hearts and impact our path one way or another.

I remember so well at the young and ambitious age of eighteen, the excitement I felt when telling people I'd be moving to London after final exams.

'You'll be calling your parents, crying and begging for money for the return ticket' they said.

'Your English is too 'life-like' to pass the advanced English Language exams' my class teacher said. What does that even mean?

I didn't listen.

Terrified, I sat on the plane with a one-way ticket to a new life, leaving everything I ever knew behind, including the only family and friends I had. I told myself I have to make this work. The beginnings were hard. I didn't know who I was or where I was going, all I knew is that I wanted to study for a psychology degree. As with the rest, I thought I should just take things as they come. First, I needed to find a job. But everyone wanted 20-year-olds with 10 years of experience. It is hard to describe the feeling of rejection when you are placed in an impossible situation like this, which is the reality for most young people now.

After sending thousands of e-mails with my CV, I finally received a phone call from the UK's leading hair loss solutions specialist inviting me for an interview. I didn't know what exactly hair extensions were, but I was eager to learn.

Despite not getting the memo about my interview being cancelled, I held myself together and was offered an assistant's job. 'Fate' I thought. Two weeks in, I was put into training to become a hair extensions technician.

I have read somewhere: *'if you know how to count, count on yourself'*. This was my chance to learn a valuable skill. It wasn't all great, the company did not treat us well, the girls I worked with were what I call 'Barbie-like' - shallow, hollow and lacked integrity. There was even visible exploitation and often bullying. This being my first real job meant I didn't have anything to compare it to. Naturally, I assumed the way we were treated was a 'normal' part of your work life.

I have learned a lot, not just about hair or without pains and tears, but I have changed rapidly. I have come across people from all walks of life, had to evaluate and adopt elements of British culture, learn how to be professional, read and understand other people's emotions, how to be more robust and compassionate at the same time.

I've always been an 'all-or-nothing' kind of person. Time gives you a particular perspective on things, and it seems everything others disliked about me while at school is what helped me grow strong and achieve my goals later in life.

Working three days a week meant I had enough personal space outside of work to concentrate on my university degree and to further my skills as a hair extensions technician. As time passed, I rose to the top of my game within the company, and I realised my worth. After putting my heart and soul into my work for over four years while doing my psychology degree, one day suddenly I was told I was no longer needed following a minor disagreement with a new floor manager. Apparently, I was a worker with no rights, not an employee who earned their respect. I was constructively dismissed in the middle of my studies with my student funding depending on me being employed. When collecting my belongings, the management even suggested, without any basis and proven otherwise, that some of the stuff has been stolen from the company!

What am I going to do?
Where will I find a part-time job that will fit around with my degree commitments?
What if I lose my funding?
How will I pay the rent?

Minor drama, you probably think. But it really hurt. I had done nothing wrong. How could they do something like that? I was not in a position financially or emotionally to fight back after investing so much of myself into a company which held no moral standards. Thoughts kept flooding into my mind, my heart was pounding, and I just went into a state of complete hysteria. For months after, I endured panic attacks mixed with mild depressive states. The all-consuming fury at the unfairness and the numbing sense of helplessness were utterly intoxicating. I was paralysed, unable to move on, filled with hateful feelings that were exhausting and pointless. I had to let go, or I would allow myself to be consumed by the vile emotions I so strongly felt. At last, I decided to refocus and re-channelled the negativity into strength.

I managed to secure a new job with my previous employer's biggest competitor. I soon realised I would not be sticking around as the owner was more concerned with the world of wealthy and entitled clients, luxurious brands and publicity rather than helping ordinary people or even treating their staff fairly.

My clients - their inspirational stories, the smile and confidence growing on their faces within a couple of hours spent with me enhancing their hair. There were often tears of joy at the prospect of a new life I could give them - I wanted to help people. I had enough. I would not spend my life being a push-over, shouted at for doing my best to build other people's dreams. I realised how much I love my job and that I have the knowledge, the integrity and the determination to achieve my own goals.

A year later, the following day after parting my ways with employment, I woke up in the middle of the night and 'Speak Volumes' was born - an independent hair extensions and hair loss solutions specialist who focuses on you.

Change is terrifying, the unknown always is. It does not mean one should hold back or be scared. We all come across at least one crossroads where we need to make decisions that can change our lives. Slowly, but steadily, I have grown my business and am now earning my living full time by helping women with hair loss problems. Listening to their struggles - which so often triggers their hair to fall out, stripping their confidence and sense of femininity - being able to lift that little bit of the weight off their shoulders, is incredibly emotionally satisfying. This entire journey has allowed me to keep my integrity, sense of ethics and find fulfilment while doing what I love and helping people.

We all have superpowers and something unique to contribute to this world. You just need to find your value and pursue your dreams. Take back control over your life and put it in your own hands. Do not fear to fail or looking foolish.

Because LIFE CAN BE MORE than what you have experienced so far.
Because YOU ARE MORE than what people have to lead you to believe until now.
Because YOU HAVE THE POWER within you to change things.

Believe in yourself and dare to dream. Be courageous. Be strong.

Dedication:

To all the people who have crossed my journey's path. Good or bad, still here or gone, you have all left marks on my heart and taught me valuable lessons that brought me to where and who I am now, so thank you all.

Paula's story unravels the challenges of young people, especially those who leave their homeland for a brighter future. When you have such a big vision and burning desire then you can, with determination, find a way to make your dream a reality. Be Inspired...

Brenda Dempsey
Creator & Editor

VOICES OF HOPE

Caroline Emile - Egyptian living in London

Red Lipstick

Caroline's story is full of joy, positivity and optimism for living life to the full. She spends every moment in gratitude, giving to others as a way of life. Her journey is very inspiring to anyone who is coping with a long term illness including cancer. The fact that she describes herself as a 'cancer thriver' tells you much about her Braveheart attitude and the beautiful soul that is Caroline Emile.

Without a doubt you will wonder and marvel at her infectious positive attitude towards the good and bad challenges that life sometimes throws at you. Caroline is very well equipped to support others find happiness in their lives as a coach.

A most precious butterfly is she…

Brenda Dempsey
Creator & Editor

Transformation #9

Red Lipstick

Caroline Emile

Happiness & Fulfilment Coach

"You cannot control what happens to you in life, but you can always control what you will feel and do about what happens to you."

Paulo Coelho

Wednesday 19th of April 2017.

I woke up early to get myself ready to meet him again. The eight days since I'd last seen him had been difficult for me, but it was finally time!

After washing and blow-drying my hair, I stood in front of my open wardrobe and examined it. I picked out the most vibrant blouse I had - a tribal African print in orange, hot pink, green, white and black, with a feminine drawstring neckline. I wanted to look and feel my absolute best on this significant day.

Satisfied with my attire, I put on the finishing touches; a glide of glossy red lipstick and my red coat. I headed out into a pretty spring day in London, with a blue sky and birds chirping all around. I made my way to our meeting place and took a seat.

Finally, there he was. He was even more handsome than I could remember at our last meeting! I started to feel butterflies in my stomach as we built up to the moment I'd been (impatiently) waiting for.

Sitting opposite me, he eventually looked straight into my eyes and said: "Caroline, it's as I suspected last week – you've got breast cancer."

You might expect me to have burst into tears at this point, but I didn't. I was actually relieved! After eight days of tormenting speculation since I'd last met Dr. Leff at Charing Cross Hospital and having a biopsy, I finally knew where I stood.

In this interim period, I had experienced a rollercoaster of emotions: shock that the lump that had recently appeared on my left breast had turned out to be highly suspicious of cancer; disbelief, fear, impatience to know if I had cancer or not; hope, dread, faithfulness, indifference and back to impatience.

The wait for the results over these eight days was rather unbearable. The more I'd read about breast cancer to try and console myself with the prospects of recovery should the lump turn out to be malignant, the more I'd freaked out! I tried hard to keep my focus elsewhere, but of course that was much easier said than done.

I felt like a defendant on trial awaiting the jury's verdict. I began waking up before dawn, trying to run through in my mind how things may play out. How spread out was the cancer (the ultrasound I'd had showed that it had already reached my lymph nodes)? Was I going to die? How much time did I have left if so? Was I going to lose my whole breast or just a part of it? Or would it even be both? What would that be like? Would I lose all my hair from chemotherapy? Was I going to become infertile and never become a mother?

The questions in my mind were endless!

It's not that I'm a pessimist – on the contrary, I'm an active advocate of positivity. But I'm also rather intuitive, and I unfortunately had a very strong feeling that I was heading towards a cancer diagnosis. So I wanted to be as prepared as possible for when I eventually got my results.

During this waiting period I eventually decided that I wanted to 'go out with a bang'. If cancer was going to be the end of my life story, then I was going to make sure that it was as inspiring and empowering as possible – not just for others, but for myself too. I decided that I didn't want to die a frail and broken woman, but instead one that was still smiling and wearing her red lipstick and bright coloured clothes to the very end; that would be my legacy!

Less than two months earlier, I'd done a personal development exercise where I'd written my life's desires. At the top of that list was: "To be used by God to fulfil his purpose for me - to maximise my potential and make a positive impact in as many people's lives as possible."

And here I was so shortly afterwards being presented with a potentially massive opportunity to positively impact others. I wasn't going to run away from it! I had asked, and here I was probably receiving – even if it was going to involve significant challenge and discomfort for me. Cancer now affects one in two people, and I felt that I had a responsibility to help normalise my experience of it for others, rather than continue to stigmatise it. And as a Happiness & Fulfilment coach, I also realised that I had to 'walk the talk' of how to remain positive in the face of my biggest life challenge to date so far.

And so when the day finally came to meet Dr. Leff again to get my results, I intentionally started as I meant to go on; I chose to show up as the best and brightest version of me (physically and non-physically), ready to embrace whatever came next.

Don't get me wrong, I wasn't fearless and would have of course preferred to hear very different words from him! This plot twist in my story was absolutely unexpected (there was no history of cancer in my family and I was only 42 – about a decade younger than the typical age bracket for breast cancer). But I'd had eight days to express my initial emotions to the news and I was eager to hit the ground running and learn what the treatment plan was. I knew I'd have plenty of time to cry later!

And the truth was - I was relieved to finally have back some control at my end! As with most people I know, passively waiting for things to unfold isn't the most comfortable of positions for me. I've always been more of a proactive doer, so being rendered an inert bystander for eight days in the face of such a bolt out of the blue had been surreal. And although a massive period of uncertainty now lay ahead of me, I was nonetheless finally back in the role of co-creator of my destiny. As a Christian, I believed that it's down to me to decide how I wanted to spend the next (and potentially last) part of my life, and up to God if it was indeed my last chapter or not.

I was of course anxious about what would come next: Dr. Leff recommended chemotherapy, surgery (a lumpectomy to remove the tumour with a safe margin from my breast and the lymph nodes in my left arm), radiotherapy and hormonal treatment for at least five years (in that order), none of which sounded appealing to me.

But my mission had now officially begun.

Within a couple of hours of leaving the hospital with my mum that afternoon, I had messaged my friends across the world telling them of my diagnosis, shortly followed by an announcement on my social media. As an introvert, this wasn't my usual style as I much prefer having time and space to comfortably process my thoughts and emotions, but as a woman on a mission, I wasn't going to hide away from the world!

That evening, alone at home for the first time, the full weight of the diagnosis began to sink in. I took comfort in my belief that God wouldn't have given me a challenge unless He was going to also help me handle it – if I chose to overcome it. I shared this online, as well as a "Keep Calm And Beat Breast

Cancer" meme (I had been a fan of the "Keep Calm" theme for a few years).

After praying, I finally managed to fall asleep, and Day 1 of my new life as a cancer patient finally ended.

In a way though, that was one of the easier days of what ensued! Over the following nine months, I underwent the recommended medical treatment: six rounds of chemo (preceded by an egg freezing procedure in case chemo left me infertile), breast and lymph node surgery, 20 sessions of radiotherapy and I started the hormonal treatment (a daily pill to minimise my oestrogen levels as the type of cancer I had was oestrogen-sensitive). These were interspersed with a plethora of scans, blood tests and injections (not just in my arms but also in the breast, stomach and thighs).

Amongst many other things, I lost around 90% of my hair, put on weight (courtesy of the steroids I was given before each chemo session), had decreased sensation across my whole body (a side effect of one of the chemo drugs), got blackened nails, experienced feeling like an octogenarian who was unable to walk due to piercing pains in the back, hips and legs, and had two scars (one on my breast and one near my left armpit).

There were days when I didn't recognise myself in the mirror. To say that this was very scary and unsettling would be a major understatement! And there were days when I just wanted to disappear into some black hole and for it all to just stop.

And yet, on the majority of days throughout my treatment, I was rather upbeat and went about my life almost normally. How did I do this? Because I was on a mission, remember?

One of the main lessons that I learnt from my experience of beating cancer is the importance of having a clear and compelling purpose or 'why' behind anything that we chose to do, otherwise we'll quit it when the going gets tough (which it undoubtedly will!).

Getting myself to sit in a chemo chair six separate times, for example, wasn't a one-off decision that I took at the outset only, but one that I had to renew prior to each session over the ensuing 15 weeks. As I experienced more painful side effects with each round, discontinuing treatment increasingly appealed to me. But my 'big why' was more important to me than the immediate pain and self-image challenges I was facing, and it fuelled me to return time and again to my sessions. Very simply, aside from my mission to inspire others to find happiness and fulfilment regardless of their circumstances, I refused to die on my parents! I wanted to do my utmost to eliminate the cancer from my body, for their sake more than mine, as I didn't want my family to experience burying me, and I believed that chemo was the best way for me to ensure this.

Of course, having a compelling purpose isn't enough to help us overcome our challenges - we also need to master the art of maintaining a positive mindset. As a life coach of two years at this point, I was already highly aware of how our mindset impacts our behaviour, which in turn affects our experience of the events in our life. I absolutely intended to do my best to triumph over cancer and so within a few days of receiving the diagnosis, I had designed my own artwork declaring this intention: "I am beating cancer".

Having such a visual reminder on my mobile and social media not only helped me to refresh my mindset when it inevitably eroded over time, but it also helped enhance the quality of my experience with cancer. I believe that we physically embody the energy of our chosen mindset, so I deliberately chose "beating" rather than "fighting" (the verb most commonly associated with cancer patients) as I didn't want to feel that I'm in an ongoing confrontation or struggle with the disease; this would have been very exhausting for me! Instead, I wanted to feel more at peace and settled within myself, and so I chose a word that reflects victory and celebration to always empower me to feel on top of the cancer, regardless of the circumstances. I also rejected "fighting" as this implied to me that there would be a winner and a loser after some competition, and I totally intended to defeat cancer, if not physically, than at least with my attitude! I didn't want to be remembered as yet another person who'd (bravely) fought cancer as is often said in such cases, but I wanted my legacy to be that I'd prevailed over the disease, despite of dying.

And so, for example, I continued to enthusiastically prepare myself before each hospital appointment. Even on the days where I was going for chemo, I'd still get up early, pick a brightly coloured blouse to wear and put on my glossy red lipstick. In fact there were times when I also especially painted my nails, as if I were heading to a night out on the town rather than to a chemo ward!

It was very important for me to continue having fun, no matter what was happening. I came to realise that some challenges, like cancer, take months to resolve. But that doesn't mean that we should pause our lives in the meantime. In fact, boosting our serotonin levels by having fun better equips us to face and overcome our challenges.

Before I started chemo, I felt like I was about to jump off a cliff into a great unknown (the consent form I signed listed a whole array of potential side effects, each more scary than the other!). So what did I do? I threw a party!

I love dancing and having fun, and I saw no reason to wait a few months until I finished treatment to enjoy myself. Plus, I was emotionally exhausted in the aftermath of receiving the diagnosis and doing all the staging tests to know how much it had spread.

And so I held my "Pre-Chemo & Egg Freezing Celebration" (it coincidentally turned out to be the day after I had this procedure done ahead of chemo, but at the time of sending out the invitations, it was only planned as a pre-chemo party). Choosing to have fun with my family and friends that evening didn't mean that I no longer had to face cancer and its gruelling treatment, but it replenished my mental, emotional and physical energy to better tackle what lay ahead of me.

Not only this, but I chose to inject fun (one of my top values in life) into each stage of my treatment. On chemo days, I'd take a photo at the start of each session, as if I were a tourist on holiday! I've always liked snapping photos to capture and share memories, and I saw no reason for things to be different while being treated. Plus I hoped to only experience cancer once, so these really were once in a lifetime events that deserved to be recorded in my opinion!

Some friends told me that I was really brave to continue publicly sharing my photos as my physical appearance deteriorated, but the way I saw it was that this was my life now. It would have been inauthentic of me to change one of my favourite habits to keep up a certain public image. And so I continued visually recording my journey on Earth as I had done before, also fuelled by my mission to de-stigmatise any shame or embarrassment still associated with having cancer.

But that wasn't all. At the back of my mind, I was conscious that any one of these photos could potentially be my last ever one. This is true for all of us at all times, but I had a heightened awareness of this given the risks of chemo. Should the worst happen, I wanted my legacy to be that I had fully LIVED (rather than passively existed) up to the very last moment, including during my cancer treatment. I wasn't going to postpone living to a time in the future when things were perfect.

Beating cancer has helped me to truly embrace my mission to inspire and empower others to unleash the best version of themselves. Whatever fears I previously had that prevented me from playing full out in all aspects of my life lost their foothold. Whenever I'm faced with a challenge now and my negative mind chatter and limiting beliefs come up, I'm able to quickly crush them with "If I could get through chemo, then I can get through this too!".

With this new-found self-confidence, I've walked on fire (hot coals), become an author and spoken on stage – and my journey as a cancer thriver is only just beginning!

Life will always surprise us with unexpected (and unwelcome) plot twists. Whether it's in the form of a shocking health diagnosis, a sudden job or business loss, the breakdown of a long-term relationship or other, we ALWAYS have a choice in what comes next for us. We may not always be able to immediately change the circumstances we find ourselves in, but we always get to decide how we'll travel through any challenge and how painful our experience is.

So choose to travel in style and learn to embrace any detour as an opportunity for your inner butterfly to mature!

Dedication:

I dedicate this chapter to my parents; Samir and Nancy. You always enjoyed my writing and encouraged me to get published. Thank you for EVERYTHING!

The Journey that Caroline has been on has not diminished her light, love or longing to support other people find happiness. She uses the symbol of the butterfly to represent not only her transformation but that of the other people she so beautifully serves. Caroline is now pursing a dream of speaking on stages, talking about happiness which is infused with a love that brings a warm smile to your face. Feel her presence...

Brenda Dempsey
Creator & Editor

The Art of Feminine Beauty

I feel torn and wrest asunder
A ship wrecked on a stormy sea
A stormy sea of mine own creation
How is it that I've let this be?

I'm in the dark, lost and uncertain
No lighthouse shines for me to see
How will I find safe passageway
To the truth inside of me?

A desire for wholeness pulls me forwards
Of how that looks I cannot see
And how to traverse these stormy waters
To the place where I'll be free?

These stormy waters black and oily
The shadows deep inside of me
My fears, my blocks, my hidden spaces
The parts of 'Self' no others see.

I feel so lost, so disconnected
No one to save or rescue me
Deep down, in truth the knowing that
The disconnect was done by me!

These stormy waters are created
By the battle for the truth in me
The black and oily stormy waters are
The veils of illusion that I now see.

So as I cling onto the wreckage
Created by my desire to be free
I realise this deep inner knowing
This too shall pass, this stormy sea!

And as I sit here in my knowing
That no-one "out there" can rescue me
The knowing that there is nought to seek "out there"
Indeed, the one I seek is ME!

I am the light that dispels the darkness
I am the lighthouse that guides me
I am the light that calm the waters
I am the light, the light is ME!

Louise Matson

VOICES OF HOPE

Charlotte Fitzgerald - London, UK

From Depression to Business Woman

There is a determination about Charlotte that has seen her follow her dreams. She has endured a rough road but knowing her mind allowed her to make decisions that were tough as a young mother of two children.

She had the courage to find a new career and not once did she allow her failure to stop her from achieving her goal.

Charlotte is a dedicated business woman who is keeping true to her vision of helping other women with their bodies, fitness and well-being.

Telling her story has opened new doors and given her a path that she can now follow to transform her life and that of her two children.

Brenda Dempsey
Creator & Editor

Transformation #10

From Depression to Business Woman

Charlotte Fitzgerald

Pilates Instructor, Health & Wellness Consultant

"You don't have to be great to start, but you have to start to be great."

Zig Ziglar

This is a story of how I used personal development, determination and resilience to battle my depression and anxiety. At the same time, I would build a Pilates business, as well as a health and wellness business, despite being a single mum of two small children.

For a long time, I thought this feeling of depression was a sign of weakness until I started to suffer from anxiety after my first child was born and then intensified after my second. My kids' dad was also suffering from depression, which didn't help, especially with all the stress and strain of raising two small children.

Time took its toll, and when my children were two and three, I separated from their dad. We moved into a new home away from my friends and family, setting out to start a new life for us. I was unemployed and on benefits. I had been with their dad for six years, so going it alone was a real struggle. I found myself in a new area with zero support, and I didn't know anyone.

We separated because we were both suffering from depression and couldn't help each other, which was only making things worse. We had battled for the last two years of our relationship trying to make it work, but we were never really on the same page. Treading on eggshells started to affect the children, especially as the living conditions were tense. Having no alternative, I had to make a decision.

A tell-tale sign of the inevitable breakdown also included that the intimacy had not been there for a long time to the point where we had not slept in the same bed for over five months.

When we did finally separate, I confided in an ex-partner, which if I were in the correct state of mind I more than likely would not have done so, as he was a manipulator and always knew what to say to me to get me hooked. He was toxic, and I was vulnerable. However, during this hard time, he made me feel wanted.

My depression and anxiety over this time had gone through phases that had seen me taking medication, going to therapy, having suicidal thoughts and sitting there feeling my whole body shake while I had this fog in my head. I felt helpless. I was frustrated and felt so out of control but had to keep it together for my two young children.

I began feeling like I needed to find something to focus on that was for me and would allow me to earn money flexibly around the children. My daughter was in part-time education at this time, and my son was full time.

A friend of mine had offered me an opportunity to work from home, but there was an initial start-up cost. Due to my anxiety and lack of confidence, this freaked me out, so I said no as being on income support gave me no additional funds whatsoever.

I then started to consider becoming a Pilates Instructor as I really enjoyed the classes and had attended them weekly before I split with my partner. Due to a change in location and in need of a babysitter, it was no longer convenient for me to go along regularly.

With determination, I set about finding a Pilates course as I believed that it would be a career that I could work flexibly around my children while they were at school. I had even joked to my Pilates instructor, whose business it was, that in the future I may be teaching Pilates. Little did she know that one day I may be telling the truth!

Being on benefits was challenging, leaving us just affording to live. I knew I wanted more for us. I had always worked and was determined that this was not the kind of life that I wanted to lead.

Motivated, I found a weekend job that would allow us to have a few extras in life and give me some disposable income that I could use towards getting my Pilates qualification.

Within a couple of months of working, I was asked again if I wanted to be part of this work from home business and seeing as I was so set on giving us a better life this time I said Yes.

This favourable decision allowed me to build a business flexibly around my children so I didn't need to pay for childcare and could be there when they needed me. It was low risk and, in the health and wellness sector which fitted in nicely with what I was already working towards.

So there I was a single mum of two very demanding children; studying a subject from scratch, starting a new business, holding up a part-time job all while battling with my inner demons.

It was going to be challenging; however, I was willing to commit and immersed myself in it all. I have no idea what was going through my head at the time; I knew that things had to be better and I was willing to try anything possible to make things work out; little did I know what my future was going to hold.

When it came to my studies I had to use my evenings once the children were in bed, as I only had one child in full-time education. My daughter was still part-time, so I spent my mornings in playgroups and afternoons running errands.

The only issue was that by the evening, I was absolutely exhausted; nevertheless, I tried my best to work through the online material, attended the weekend workshops and started to revise for my first exam. I passed my Level 2 exam the first time around which was great.

A few months later I would take my Level 3 theory exam. This one was a real struggle for me as it was more in depth and I had to do all of my revision in the evenings. As a consequence of my exhaustion, I kept falling asleep, which meant I wasn't retaining the information.

The day came for my Level 3 exam. I really felt that I struggled with this one. I stayed positive and eagerly awaited my result. They were not due to arrive for another two weeks. I took this time to slow down a bit, recuperate and focus on my business.

By this time, I had been introduced into the personal development world, and it was helping to boost my emotions and change the way that I thought about things especially when it came to managing my anxiety.

I still remember receiving the email and being really disappointed that I had failed my exam, but I had to keep going as I was a busy woman and 'thought I will pass the next time'. I went back to revising again, which after failing, was not an easy thing to do. This truly tested my resilience.

Due to my weekend job, I was unable to reschedule my exam straight away. I had to wait for four months between resits. I felt this situation was dragging it out longer than I wanted when I was already finding it a struggle to fit everything in. If it wasn't for the support network I had that encouraged me to keep going, I more than likely would have quit.

I then went on to fail my Level 3 exam for a second and a third time. It was the third time I failed that really broke me as I had made many changes to accommodate my revision.

I had changed my daughter from afternoon to morning nursery so that I could have two hours of revision (without being disturbed) a couple of times a week. I thought the extra two hours were making a difference, but it turned out that I had received the same result for both failed exams! Something wasn't working, and I started to doubt myself and became extremely frustrated, my confidence was at an all-time low, and I didn't know if I could continue like this.

Adding to the depth of despair I found myself in, my ex-partner was not sympathetic at all and just tried to brush it off. He seemed to have a knack for that and more often than not, left me feeling deflated instead of supported.

In my loneliness, we had been seeing each other on and off for almost a year now, and things were not improving. I was always left feeling empty and was receiving minimal effort from him due to his obsession with his own business.

I felt like I was living two completely different lives; I felt like I was going insane. Monday to Friday I would spend with my kids with very little support. I was struggling to maintain everything. At the weekend with a sense of freedom, my Saturday nights were filled with too much alcohol and sex. Consequently, I was suffering from stress and felt overwhelmed, so it took me a long time to realise that this was not healthy and was most certainly not doing me any good. All I craved was love and support.

I was becoming more aware of the issues within our relationship and decided that I wanted to focus on myself, but he would never give me the space that I needed to clear my head and focus on my business as well as my studies.

Trapped, I started to feel helpless as he always made me think that things would improve and I believed him, which began to make me feel so low. All I craved was head space to figure out what I really wanted. The lack of head space made me feel suffocated, so I decided to keep on working on myself and started to realise that this was not the life for me. I wanted more from the relationship.

Despite making the decision that I wanted 'us' to be over, he would tell me all the things that I wanted to hear simply to keep me around. Instantly, I realised that I had been manipulated yet again and was stuck in this vicious circle of uncertainty, broken promises and wild weekends, all wreaking havoc on my anxiety.

Not only was I dealing with my anxiety, but I was also looking after two young children, studying for a qualification, building a business, dealing with a toxic relationship and trying to keep it all together. I was overwhelmed with this massive challenge, and it was making my anxiety worse.

Listening to daily motivational speakers was the only thing helping me through my mess and stopping me from falling back into depression, which I honestly believe at times was not far off. It allowed me to put things into perspective and keep moving forward, as well as making numerous calls to my friends for reassurance that all would be ok if I just kept pushing.

Personal development was a new concept to me that was only brought to my attention when I started my health and wellness business. If it wasn't for working on myself and taking the time to read books and seek advice from already successful people, I don't think that I would have overcome most of my challenges.

So with my battered yet growing confidence, I kept pushing and working on myself and kept revising for my exam. To say that I lacked motivation was an understatement, but I knew that I was going to pass it eventually and I had come so far that I owed it to myself to make it happen. I tried everything possible to retain the information and went into my fourth exam filled with so much anxiety.

Two weeks later, I received my result, it was a positive one, yet I felt deflated. Although it was a pass mark, it was the exact score I needed, I thought I could have done better as I had put in the extra effort. I was harsh on myself for some time, but thankfully I have some amazing friends who tell me when I am being too hard on myself and to remind me that a pass is still a pass. Passing my exam was the last piece of the puzzle for my qualification as I had achieved my practical assessment and portfolio a few months before.

With everything I needed it meant that I could upgrade from my student insurance and start the add on courses which were Pre and Post Natal Pilates and small equipment. It was notable for my well being and sanity, thst I reward myself, so I took some time to recover before beginning these courses as I felt that I deserved it.

I was already teaching two mixed ability Pilates classes which helped me to gain confidence in my abilities and helped me to speak in public, something for a long time was a huge fear of mine.

With my courses under my belt, I was excited and started teaching Pre-Natal Pilates classes. I only ever had one client at a time, who sometimes was unable to attend consistently due to still being at work.

I was also trained in Post Natal Pilates, so I decided to change my direction and run a class where mums could bring their babies along and get a chance to have some focused time for themselves.

This idea was better received and included some challenges; however, my marketing efforts brought me a more regular clientele and allowed me to get some more recommendations for my classes.

At first, I wasn't keen to teach pre or postnatal Pilates due to the different approach needed, but I later realised that I was being drawn in that direction and was getting queries and potential clients, so I took the risk, and it's been progressing as word spreads through word of mouth and marketing. It's about listening to your inner voice and being open to receiving what the universe sends you. It knows what you need when you are following your purpose.

I still had my retail job, but it had reached the point where I was too comfortable; I no longer had the desire to spend my weekends in retail when I had my own businesses to promote. I used the knowledge that my bills were covered and fear of the unknown as an excuse for staying. But once I had become aware of the fact that I was holding myself back due to comfort, it started to weigh me down, and I realised that I was not working to my full potential.

As a single mum, teaching five classes a week, when it came to the weekend, I would send my kids off to their dad so I could go to work. I never really had time to focus on what I wanted for the future and doing a nine-hour shift on my feet was not my perfect idea of how I wanted to spend my Saturdays.

I had made the decision that I wanted to teach Pilates on a Saturday morning instead but didn't know how I would make it work as my weekend job paid my bills and it was an uncomfortable risk for me.

I started to look for venues where I could host my Saturday morning classes. I was not having much luck; then one day by chance, I found a room enabling me to teach a class of five with two lessons back to back. How strange that I had never known the room was there, yet I was fully aware of the venue. It was the sign I needed to start taking this idea of me having my own business seriously.

This all happened in September 2018. Despite receiving confirmation that I could use the room, I couldn't bring myself to believe that I could actually pull it off as it was entirely out of my comfort zone. After some thought, I decided that it was up to me to make it happen.

I revisited my financial situation to see if it was viable, along with all my other classes. It turned out this dream could actually work, so I started to spread the word on social media and received a few enquiries about the lessons helping to put my mind at ease.

I then confirmed the day that I intended to start but had not told my manager at my retail job yet. When I spoke to my manager in person and informed him of my intentions, he was very supportive. All of that worrying for nothing! It's funny how we make stories up in our heads that have no bearing on the reality.

I couldn't believe that I was actually going for it and embarking on a venture that would give me so much more free time for my Saturdays, something that I had never had, and to think that it was all made possible by me believing in myself, my abilities and merely taking the risk.

With my new sense of belief, I found my courage and disposed of my toxic ex-partner so that I could completely invest my whole being into this venture without any distractions. I no longer wanted to feel like I was trapped in a life that only made one side happy.

As the date grew ever closer, I became nervous, but I knew in my heart that I was doing the right thing. My soul finally felt aligned. I continued to promote my classes and started to get confirmations of attendance, which was such a great feeling, it was happening.

The day of my first class came around, and I had managed to book five out of the ten places that I had available, four of which were from my marketing and one place was a mum that I had met through my daughter's drama class.

The feeling I experienced when I soaked up the atmosphere for a second was immense, and I felt insanely proud of myself that I had made it to this point.

I had proven to myself that it was possible, that taking the risk and believing in myself and my capabilities had allowed me to pull it off and actually get people attending.

I now had proof that despite being held back time and time again I just had to keep working hard and be true to myself when the going gets tough, because at the end of the day, if it's going to be it's up to me.

The development that I have seen within myself has allowed me to build my own Pilates classes, and have the confidence to develop my own business while showing others how to do the same.

My journey has not been straight forward, but it has given me the courage to pursue bigger and better things. If it wasn't for my personal development and the resilience I gained during my personal and business challenges, I may have never known that there was a higher purpose and I believed I was capable of more.

My past experiences will always be a reminder of how far I have come, and I will use their lessons to guide me towards the best future for myself and my children.

Let the next chapter begin...

Dedication:

I dedicate this chapter to Oliver and Lily, my beautiful children. They have shown me that life does not always have to be so serious, live in the moment and have fun.

It's apparent to see that Charlotte has great tenacity. Despite a number of hurdles she was determined to achieve her goal. She learned quickly that failing is part of success.

Charlotte is a great role model for her young children who undoubtedly witness their mum going after what she wants to improve her life; she believes you can too... Be who you want to be...

Brenda Dempsey
Creator & Editor

VOICES OF HOPE
Sue Ritchie - Derby, UK

Your Life Transformation Starts With a Single Decision

When existence becomes overbearing it takes courage to do something about it. Sue is that woman who screams no more. Fed up of people-pleasing and living her life on everyone elses's terms but her own, she had had enough.

Like many women faced with a hopeless situation of having to bring up children single-handedly she digs deep to do whatever it takes to keep her family together.

For Sue it took until her health was up against the wall before she paid any attention.

When the darkness descends, is when the human spirit fights to find that glimpse of light that leads them to a better world. Sue knows that road so well that she now helps others to find the light sooner rather than later.

Brenda Dempsey
Creator & Editor

Transformation #11

Your Life Transformation Starts With a Single Decision

Sue Ritchie

Coach, Mentor, Speaker, Author

"First comes thought: then the organisation of that thought into ideas and plans; then transformation of those plans into reality. The beginning, as you will observe, is in your imagination." Napoleon Hill

Imagine living a life where you are trying to please everyone. You are driven to make sure you give more than 100% in all that you do. Everything has to be perfect, but actually, in reality, it is more than excellent. You spend many hours when you should be sleeping and resting, going over and over what you had done and said, "This is wrong!" You are continually beating yourself up.

Your life is like being on a perpetual treadmill. You are just pounding away every day. You are always looking for and craving approval from others, but even when you receive support and praise, you don't really feel deserving of it. Your job or your work is what defines you. You are just living to work.

That was my life for more than 40 years. From a career point of view, those years had been successful. I worked myself up to the ladder in the corporate world to a very senior level in marketing. I worked very hard, always working long hours, and was always stressed, but I wasn't really living. I was existing.

My personal life did not work out the way I would have liked. I found myself in an abusive relationship, had two lovely children and eventually found the strength and energy to walk away.

I moved a long way away and set up my own business. A lot of people have said to me that it was a very courageous thing to do. Move home to a whole new area as a single parent with two young children and set up a new business at the same time. But it all felt like the right thing to do, and everything just seemed to flow. There were a few challenges, like finding out that the people who sold me their house were doing a runner from debt, and having bailiffs knocking on the door, threatening to take my contents!

Everything worked well for a time, then the business started to grow, and the old patterns of being on the treadmill started to reappear. I met a man who is now my husband, and have a great supportive relationship.

Then in 2009, I found myself always tired, I couldn't focus, I couldn't concentrate; my memory, which had always been brilliant, was playing huge tricks on me. There were days when I thought I was going mad. I had a lot of other health issues - digestive problems, recurrent cystitis, and joint pain. Then I received the diagnosis that I had Hashimoto's disease. This is an autoimmune disease that affects the thyroid gland, making it under-active. When I suggested I could get myself well again, the doctor's response was to tell me in no uncertain terms, that it was impossible and that I would be on the medication for the rest of my life.

I felt as if my whole life had been written off. I was 52. Was that it now? Was I now going to have to curtail my dreams of travelling the world, being able to chase my grandchildren (when and if they came along) round the garden, and not being able to do all things I wanted to?

For someone who had always lived a very active life, this prognosis was unacceptable. So I started doing a lot of research about Hashimoto's and autoimmune diseases in general.

I then hit what I can only call a black hole. I was fat, sick and tired! Despite being on medication, my energy wasn't right. There was nothing I could do that made an impact on my weight. I tried everything. I was feeling unfulfilled, the business started to go pear-shaped, the money stopped coming in because I was hiding away. I had always been independent. I had brought up two children as a single parent, but now I was earning very little. I prioritised paying my employee, and I didn't get paid. Not being able to contribute financially and feeling that my husband was judging me just added to the burden on how useless and helpless I felt.

Then someone suggested I go to an event. It felt right to go, so I did. Then the challenge arose. I knew I needed to do the programme the coach offered, but how could I pay the £2,000 to do it when I had no money? My head and my heart argued for several minutes. Thank goodness my heart won, and I took my credit card out and paid.

Had I not listened to my heart and made that investment in myself, I would definitely not be in the place that I am today, enjoying a healthy and fulfilled life and helping others. From this experience, I learnt that when you invest in yourself, you are validating to both yourself and the universe that you are worth it. But it is also a critical moment, because I don't know about you, but I have always had a big problem asking for help. I always thought that if I couldn't sort something out myself, then I was a failure. However, the truth is quite the opposite as I now know. I am not saying I am now brilliant at always asking for help when I need it, but it does become a lot easier.

You see, when we ask for help, we solve the problem a lot quicker, and it is a lot less painful, but we are also being generous to others in allowing them to feel appreciated by helping us. I know that when I help others, it always makes me think I'm making a difference. What about you?

Having completed the programme, where I learnt all about that negative voice in your head and how it controls you and tries to keep you small and safe, there came a huge realisation that my life needed to change big time. I realised that I could choose to create the experiences I wanted to live, and I could wake up every morning and consciously decide to have a great day. It was time for me to start living my life in a way that served and honoured me, rather than living it on other people's terms.

Undoubtedly, I knew that I did not want to live a compromised life. I had to get myself well again. To do that, I needed to step off that treadmill, take time out, get quiet and be kind to myself.

Stepping off that treadmill was a big decision to make. There were so many things I had to let go of to do that - busyness addiction, approval, what would other people say, what would my husband say – not earning money. (Interestingly enough you will learn later on that my belief about the money didn't happen). I had always been independent, and I had also been a single parent and that negative voice in myself would tell me that I had to support myself. I couldn't trust any other way.

After much deliberation, feeling very guilty about the effect my decision would have on my employee, as well as feeling scared, I made the decision to shrink my business. Once I had made my decision, there was a feeling of enormous relief. It felt like a load dropping from my back. My husband also asked, "Why didn't you do this ages ago?"

I decided that I would focus on just working and supporting my current customers and let go of the pressure of trying to get new customers on board. I made my employee redundant, but she got another job very quickly, so I needn't have worried, and I cut my expenses by taking the business back to my home.

Through my research, I discovered that the root cause of my health issues lay in my gut. I went through a process to get my gut health back into a healthy state, made changes to my diet and within a couple of weeks, my health and energy started to improve. Within 3 months I was feeling great, I lost 2 ½ stone - the weight just fell off, and within 18 months I was medication free and feeling healthier and more energised than I had in years and it has remained that way.

So in all of this, what happened to my business? The reality is that I doubled my turnover and almost doubled my profit. It was actually a lot more successful. I bet you are wondering how that could have happened if I wasn't working all the hours God sends any more?

Let me share with you some of the critical things that were a significant contributing factor.

Firstly, I put in place some healthy work/life boundaries in terms of the time I would work, and when I would spend time focusing on me. I made sure I stuck to them. I am not saying it was easy and letting go of the guilt was tough, but my "WHY", in terms of looking after me and getting well again, was big enough to make sure that I achieved it.

As a result, I became more productive and focused in the allotted work time. I made sure too that I "Ate my Frogs". There is a brilliant book called *Eat that Frog* by Brian Tracey which tells you to do the tasks you hate doing and the most important ones first. It was crucial too that I wrote down goals for all areas of my life, not just money and business, because that also helped me to stay focused on what I wanted for myself and how I wanted to live my life.

I also took time out during the day to go for a walk in nature. When you are feeling overwhelmed, and you have a to-do list a mile long, it is tough just to stop and take time out. I discovered to my amazement that it is the best thing you can do. When you create space in your head, you become more creative and more productive. The exercise also gets everything going in your body and being out in nature releases those endorphins. Just half an hour out makes a big difference. It is beneficial for your health, and one of the things we tend to neglect when we are always busy is to look after our health.

The third thing that I put into practice was a daily nurturing routine that I would do every morning. This included 15-20 minutes of meditation when I woke up. I would start the day by telling myself what a brilliant day it was going to be and that no matter what challenges came up, I would be easily able to handle them. I also made sure that I had "me" time every day, and I started bringing back into my life some of the things I loved doing, like photography and singing.

I would write my to-do list for the next day when I finished work. But my to-do list was divided up into Urgent and Important, Not Urgent and Important, Urgent and not Important and Not Urgent and Not Important. The next day I would prioritise working on the Urgent and Important. These were all the things that were aligned with my goals. At night, I would end the day thinking about all the things I had done well and all the things that I was grateful for in my life.

I also invested time on healing emotional traumas from the past and on my personal development. Forgiveness is a hugely healing experience.

One of the biggest "Aha" moments for me in the process of turning my life and my business around was the realisation that through my mindset, thoughts, beliefs and behaviour I had created both the good and the bad in my life and that was a totally game-changing moment.

By taking responsibility for my life and my health, I was able to get out from being stuck. From then on, I knew that I could choose to create the experience that I want, and it is possible for everybody. Life does have its ups and downs, this is inevitable, but we can choose to view the downs differently. Instead of playing the victim, we can take the learning and move forward.

I would love to say that this is an immediate process, but the truth is, it does take commitment and practice, and you will falter at times along the way, but that is totally fine and normal for everyone.

If you feel in your heart (because that is what we ought to be listening to, not our heads) that the life you are currently living is not serving you, then you can change it for the better. All it takes is that one first step - making the decision that things need to change. Reach out and ask for help; you are not alone, and you deserve the best.

Love and blessings, Sue.

Dedication: *I dedicate this chapter to all those amazing women who are caught up on a treadmill, stressed, constantly busy, that never take any time to take care of themselves, but know that there is a little voice deep inside crying out to them "I can't carry on living my life this way," that they are constantly ignoring. Let me tell you there is a better way to live and you are deserving of it. Just take the first step today.*

Sue is one of a number of women who found a road to freedom. She makes no excuses for wakening up to the realisation that we are responsible for much of our darkness. She recommends that it takes commitment and practice to find the light at the end of the tunnel, but once you do take that first step, your life will never be the same again. You become the creator of a life you deserve.

Brenda Dempsey
Creator & Editor

The Art of Feminine Beauty

Tawny Owl

Sally Wibrew

Sally Wibrew is a multi-talented artist and sculptor. She loved art at school and went on to study Computer Visualization and Animation. She had aspirations of working at Pixar as an Animator. However Sally soon realised she didn't quite have the temperament to be an Animator as it took two weeks work to produce two seconds of animation.

Every artist has their struggles. Sally found herself working as a chamber maid in a hotel just to keep a roof over her head. She worked there for 18 months. She calls it her 18 months in purgatory! She hated it, but it made her determined to succeed when she found a new path.

Sally attended a country show with a friend who was a tree surgeon. She was hooked, especially as she saw a female tree surgeon give the men a run for their money. Sally booked herself on a course and can still be seen doing a spot of Arboriculture alongside her sculptures.

In the future as Sally grows her business, she is planning to build a pottery studio so she can make different priced items to sell alongside her beloved wooden sculptures.

Find out more about Sally's work at www.maytree.me.uk or drop her a line at Sally@maytree.me.uk

VOICES OF HOPE

Judy Feldhausen - Chicago, USA

Life is a Journey

With a whole range of experiences around motherhood and health, Judy knows only too well the importance of being a good mom and looking after your health.

When you find something in life that is life-changing you develop a conviction that sets your soul on fire. It becomes the driver of your life because it has such a profound impact on you. This is what happened to Judy who now devotes her life to helping others.

She has a big vision and travels around America sharing her message to others including the Medical Profession. She is determined to share this message around the world too and intends to extend the impact she is making as a woman in business on a mission to make a difference.

Brenda Dempsey
Creator & Editor

Transformation #12

Life is a Journey

Judy Feldhausen

Founder, Cardio-Wellness Group

"The end of one journey
is the doorway into
another."

Judy Feldhausen

I was six years old when my dad was taken from me. They said it was a fatal heart attack. He was 39 years young.

Being so young, I accepted what happened. My dad was in the Air Force, so my mom got a pension; therefore, we were not affected financially with his death. But it was an emotional journey.

My mom never wanted to talk about my dad. It was such a big hole for her; subsequently, she closed herself emotionally to many things, even though she was always laughing with her friends.

We never had that close conversation, that intimate relationship with one another. I think in my Mom's mind she felt that when you get close to somebody, you die. Consequently, I've learned that too. Although I had lots and lots of friends and was in many clubs, I did everything, I went everywhere, but I never developed those tight relationships with people.

My goal in life from that terrible day was to reach 39 years of age. It was a massive goal for me. Everything I did during those years was to live a good healthy life. What a celebration when I reached that milestone! It seemed that I had climbed my mountain and so now I could let go.

As I reached adulthood, I had the same dreams as many other people; a good job, marriage and children. Like a dream come true, I was married, and I had children. My role as a parent was reflected in my own upbringing. In the early years, the same patterns happened with my children early on. I was a perfect mother. I was a great disciplinarian. I wanted to do the best for my kids. I wanted to be there for them. And one day I woke up and just figured that the best way to be there for them was not to be the disciplinarian, but to be the loving mother, and to be there for everything.

My mom never went to one of my events. I was a singer. She never even went to my scholarship, try-outs. I was a gymnast. She never went to any of my gyms meets. In fact, I was in a play and in a gym meet at the same time, and she decided that I didn't need to go to the gym meet. She let me sleep the day off until the phone rang and it woke me up. Everyone at the meeting was waiting for me. My friends and trainers waited an hour for me and I slept through the alarm; and my mom wouldn't let me go.

I was 16 years old, and she wouldn't let me go to my gym meet, despite being the best gymnast in the area at the time. I was devastated.

This experience haunted me, I had to break the pattern, so when my kids started to join hobbies and do things, I knew that I had to be there for them for everything. I went to practices with them. I was there cheering them on, wanting to let them know that I loved them and, whether they won or not, they were terrific.

This change in my parenting occurred when my daughter was born; my son was six. I was working, I was doing the right things all the time. Before my daughter was born, I felt I was two people. I was the professional; a manager in the electronics industry. This position allowed me to travel around the country. I was viewed as this 'big wig'. I would move and go to the other salespeople's homes who were reporting to me. I never spoke about my family. I never spoke about anything.

I remember a husband and wife were taking me out to dinner one night after we worked, and the husband was the salesman. I asked if I could use the rest-room. She looked at me and said apologetically, "Oh, there are toys in the bathtub. I'm so sorry."

The way I dressed affected what and how people thought about me. I wore a suit and was seen as this high powered woman. I looked at the lady and thought, 'Oh my gosh.' I couldn't even say what I was feeling; instead, I just replied, "Oh, that's okay." The emotion arose in me because I was thinking, but I'm a mom too! I've got toys in my bathtub. I've got a lot more than that in my bathtub!

I was wearing a mask. When I was about halfway home, I was able to leave my professional persona behind. Now I could go back to being a mom.

The day came when I turned 39. I felt free because that's when my dad had died, and I had made it. I reached the goal. When you make the goal, you celebrate. I celebrated by not taking good care of myself as I had been while working towards my goal. Now I was not eating as well, not exercising, not even growing with my business. At that time, I was not in the industry I'm in now. I thought, 'Oh well, I've arrived, I don't need to study anymore. I'm in management. I work for a Fortune 100 company. I can just have fun.'

I was self-sabotaging; I was on self-destruct.

This is no way to behave, to make choices and to live. I had a wakeup call when I went to a meeting. There was a gentleman there who had a new Food and Drug Administration (FDA) device. The approved medical device actually worked on checking the state of your cardiovascular system. As it was FDA approved, I could consider it reliable. He was giving people free screenings because he was just learning how to use it, just trying to work with it. I was jockeying back there and thought, 'Oh well, this is fun. I know I'm really healthy. I'll just help him out.'

It's three minutes long, non-invasive, and really simple. After I had my screening, I found out that my arteries were 25 years older than my chronological age. I was shocked. How can this be? I looked really well. I had no signs of disease. I didn't have high blood pressure or high cholesterol or any of those markers for disease. Maybe it's wrong, I thought. After all, it was only a medical device, however, it was FDA! He turned to me and said, "You can change this."

It was time to set my next goal. I was going to change this reading. I didn't exactly know what to do, but I knew that I could be in charge. After all, I was in charge of reaching 39 years of age; why couldn't I be in charge of getting to 99 years old?

This was the start of my journey into natural healing therapies.

I was introduced to nitric oxide therapy, which won the 1988 Nobel Prize in Physiology and Medicine, for the reversal and prevention of heart disease and strokes. This therapy was back in 2011. Nonetheless, 13 years later, no one knew about this Nobel prize. Now here in 2019, every day I talk to people that have no idea that there's a natural way to prevent and reverse heart disease.

Regardless of the reasons for others not knowing this information, I do know that I now have a responsibility to share what I know through my messaging. Nitric oxide therapy is as simple as drinking a glass of water once or twice a day with powder, which contains nitric oxide therapy. My husband calls it 'Kool-Aid' because it actually kind of tastes like 'Kool-Aid'! It took him four years to start taking it, and now his cholesterol has been reduced. It is just so simple to do. I just used it once a day, and in no time at all my scores reduced. I was so impressed that I ended up buying the device so I could share its success rates with other people. A while later, when I tested myself again, my arteries were 20 years younger than my chronological age. I had gained 45 years!

Given my level of success, I started my business. I used to share my findings with friends, family, business contacts. I practised using the device; I gave a lot of free screenings. I discovered that the insurance companies will pay $110 for one of these screenings.

I started screening people just to get the message out that, if you are not healthy, there is a way for you to renew your health and get back to where you should be. Now I'm not only working with individuals, but I work with the medical community. I do screenings in doctors' offices for them. The doctor just supplies me with their patient base. I carry out selections; 15 minutes for each patient all day long. I also sell the device to doctors, and I help the doctors with a protocol to help reverse their patients' high blood pressure, diabetes and high cholesterol.

The doctors I speak to, absolutely buy into natural healing. I do not go and see a doctor unless they do. Does the medical community in the United

States overall, buy into it? It absolutely does not. It's dependent upon each doctor, where they are and where they're going. Some of the doctors do not participate because of the laws and licensing. They cannot promote anything except what the Food and Drug Administration say they can encourage.

There is too much red tape to get through. What I do is work with doctors that are working outside the system. I tend to work with Naturopaths, Chiropractors and Homeopaths; those doctors who believe in healing and not a disease.

I love what I do. I travel all over the country. I also teach people how to use the device and suggest other ways of natural healing. I am going to Houston soon, and I'm looking forward to it. More importantly, I have a big Vision. I'm looking forward to expanding globally.

My big goal is to make the product that I represent a household name. I want everybody to say, "Have you had your ProArgi-9+ today?"

That's what I want because I know that it's going to help so many people. I've had people able to get out of wheelchairs and walkers and back to a healthy life. I talked to a guy who said that within 15 minutes of taking the drink, his blood pressure reduced. I've had people who have been sent home to get their affairs in order, and five years later are climbing ladders at their ranch.

My Vision includes the "Million Lives Project." The first Vision is to heal a million people from the devastating effects of cardiovascular disease. That's what we're doing now, and that's why we're in discussions with doctors and nutritionists and personal trainers. These are people who are seeing many people daily, so that we can spread the message faster and broader.

It is also important to consider giving it to younger people as a preventative measure. We manufacture nitric oxide in our bodies until we're about 19 years old. The product also gives you more clarity of mind and energy. For some people, it helps them sleep better. My seven-year-old grandson loves it.

One of the first things we want to do is raise awareness that people have a choice. I believe people have to understand that they don't have to do what their doctor says. Too many people allow their doctor to be their God. I know this because almost every day when I talked to them, they say, "Well, my doctor says this and my doctor won't let me, and my doctor..."

I want to be an advocate. I'm a consumer wellness advocate. I'm a certified consumer wellness advocate. I want to be there to help you look at other options, not necessarily to go against your doctor. I would never say to someone, "Stop taking your medication or don't listen to your doctor." I would encourage them to look at other alternatives and maybe make additional choices. With my additional choice, I can help them start to reduce their medication. If that's the only goal that they have, then I've still won.

My dream is to leave a legacy of responsibility. We are all responsible for our own life. This perspective doesn't discount my belief in God. I remember a joke I heard years and years ago about two little boys waiting for the bus and the bus doesn't come.

So Jimmy says to Joey, "Joey, the bus isn't coming, what are we going to do?"

"We gotta wait, we gotta wait." Then Joey looks at Jimmy and says, "You wait, I'm running to school."

It's just the opportunity to take responsibility. You can wait for something to happen or you can make it happen.

Dedication:

This chapter is dedicated to my children and grandchildren who have an amazing life ahead of them.

HOPE

Be the Light

Never underestimate the power of your experiences, they shape who you become. Judy has found a purpose in her life and she shows great determination to spread her beliefs with her family, the USA and a global audience.

When you have been so gravely ill, something spiritual happens inside and it changes you forever. The change is so profound that you feel like you have been reborn.

Judy now spends her time sharing her message with others. What drives you each day to leading a life of purpose?

Brenda Dempsey
Creator & Editor

VOICES OF HOPE

Jane Scanlan - UK

Freedom from your Personal Prison

When you meet Jane you can see she has a steely determination. She knows what she wants and has learned the magic of turning her wants into desires.

Her story has many twists and turns. She has fallen, risen, fallen and risen again. She knows the power in her mistakes and like many other women, there comes a point - which I call a Pivotal Moment - when she screamed "ENOUGH"

Jane is one such inspirational woman. With a new conscious awakening, Jane is in the driving seat, creating a life for her and her family on her terms. This is living.

Let the story begin...

Brenda Dempsey
Creator & Editor

Transformation #13

Freedom from your Personal Prison

Jane Scanlan

Coach and Healer

"Emancipate yourselves from mental slavery. None but ourselves can free our minds."

Bob Marley

My story tells of different life chapters and the struggles I endured as a result of always trying to escape the imprisonment I placed upon my own mind, thoughts and behaviour. Once I realised that my old ways did not serve my life purpose, I found a new path that has taken me on a journey of self-discovery, love and adventure.

Like many young children, starting school was an exciting and worrying time. I did not want to go to school, I was quite happy at home with my mum, so in the first week of school I decided to run away from school and go home to my mum! I got as far as the gates before my plan was foiled! My school life continued to sour because I was not making the progress that was expected of someone my age. This was the beginning of noticing I was different. Within a year of starting school, it was discovered that I had 75% hearing loss, needed glasses and was later diagnosed with dyslexia, which I took on as a label. As a result of these findings, I had an operation for my hearing, a pair of glasses for my poor eyesight and transferred to a more understanding school. I was soon flourishing, although I was never thought of as being highly academic.

I would be the child at family parties who would massage people's shoulders and make them feel good when they would say that they were tired or were in pain. I was even told that I had healing hands. I had a profound caring nature and knew that by my actions, I could heal others. Around that time, I began to notice that I felt different from other people. I was able to use my intuition and could sense things before they happened. These feeling used to scare me sometimes. I took comfort in being close to nature and animals as it helped me feel grounded, even at a young age.

I loved being around animals as I felt in tune with them. The animals never gave me any bullshit, they made me feel safe, and they did not judge. They simply are what they are and give back what you give them. They do not wear any masks, whereas, humans wore different masks for lots of situations, many of which I didn't understand and quite frankly it confused me. This love of animals fostered the idea of becoming a vet when I grew up.

I was like many other young children. I loved freedom. I used to play in my large garden in London and would love to run around in the family farm when I visited my dad's family in Limerick, Ireland. This feeling of freedom is something that shaped my life, my decisions and my behaviour, even though the choices and practices were not always in my best interest or served my higher self.

My family shaped my life; my mum was an academic, my dad a farmer and my older sister creative and intelligent. Although my mum was academic, she was interested in alternative ways, creativity and healing was part of our lives. As my dad was bought up a farmer and became a builder when he moved to London, working on the land, being with nature and being practical was something fundamental to my family.

By the time I was a teenager, I had encountered more freedom when my mother, who was studying to be a teacher, entrusted me with my own house key. This 'grown-up' situation fed my need for independence as I could now let myself into the house and be in my own company for a short time.

There was a downside to this new freedom, which on reflection, makes me realise that with it comes a sense of responsibility. I started choosing to eat whatever I wanted when I got home from school – crunchy nut cornflakes, toast and other foods that were high in sugar and wheat, which was not good for me. Consequently, I started putting on weight around this time. Up to this point, we ate sensibly as a family; the usual three square meals. I was not the sporty type, so I had no real outlet for the extra food I was feeding myself.

Many things contributed to this new angry teen emotional state. I was fuelling my body with carbs and sugar, and as a result, becoming more lethargic. My body was raging with hormones and I felt hard done by because I was always the youngest... youngest of the family, youngest of the class, youngest with my friends, I was an August baby and fed up with it! I felt like everyone I hung around with were older than me and had more freedom. Having pretty strict parents, who I thought were "Victorian" at the time, meant I was unable to join my friends out having fun. This added to my anger and frustration; after all teenagers are notorious for pushing boundaries. I was no different.

As I gained more freedom and frustration in my life, I began to push all sorts of boundaries. I started smoking, smoking weed, drugs and generally trying to fit in with the 'crowd'. This impacted on my college work, and I just scraped through with a pass as I preferred to smoke weed in the park, and play pool in the pub instead of going to lessons. After college, I didn't get a job straight away; I still didn't know what I wanted to do anyway. I still would have loved to become a vet but was told with dyslexia, it would be pretty much impossible to get through the seven years of training but perhaps I could be a veterinary nurse instead! This just fuelled my anger. My self-esteem and self-worth were on the floor, my frustration and anger through the roof and as a result, I thought 'F**k it' and signed on the dole to do nothing.

About 9 months later, I bumped into an old friend; I used to go to his club nights back in the day. He was an IT Engineer. He was in a spot of trouble for being caught speeding too many times and was about to lose his driving licence. He told me he could not lose his job and if he lost his licence he would need a chauffeur to drive him around so he could continue working. Seeing as I had no job, loads of time and loved driving, I put my hand up for the job! I went to court with him the next week where he was banned from driving for six months. When we left the courtroom, he turned and handed me his keys and said, "You've got the job Jane, and you start today. You're working for me now, and I will train you as an IT Engineer in return."

I loved it. I learned how to fix laptops, computers and printers. I had a sense of freedom again as I used to drive around the South East of England repairing IT equipment for so many different companies, no day was the same. It was like being your own boss. I walked into offices, sorted their stuff and walked out again.

The universe has strange ways of putting people together just when they need each other most.

We had such a great six months together; everyday was filled with laughter and when the six months were up, I was taken on full time by his company. At this time, I entered into an abusive relationship for nine months with someone celebrated at the start, then I realised he had massive mental health and addiction issues. He became very controlling, emotionally and then physically abusive, which caused me to stop smiling and going out. The only freedom was my job, the car and the road.

When I found the courage to leave, I knew life had to be better than this, so I started saving up, and I decided to go travelling for a year. Adventure and escapism called me! I went to Tahiti, New Zealand and Australia. On my return, I got my old IT Engineer role back for 18 months before I then failed an IT exam, was made redundant, and dumped by my boyfriend all in the space of 3 days! So I had another "fuck it" moment and I went travelling for two months, this time to West Africa. I had escaped once more and found freedom. Interestingly I never did or missed drugs whilst travelling; you see I felt alive, I felt free.

My next job was working for an insurance company as an IT Engineer. Only 25% of my role was spent travelling, and I was beginning to feel trapped again. I received a promotion but soon found myself feeling stagnant within the same office day in day out. This I did not like and felt stifled. It was during this job I decided to go to night school and study massage and holistic therapies. This idea associated with natural therapies came up as a result of my travelling and childhood.

I knew that being back in London; being in with the same crowd, meant that I had access to drugs and a life that was not allowing me to feel free. In fact, I was imprisoning myself with my patterns of behaviour. I was easily influenced by the people I was surrounding myself with, and now looking back, I was also a big influencer to others. This was a repeating pattern.

I knew deep down I had to break free as I was on a self-destruct cycle.

I hated myself for this. I was consumed with guilt and my friends would often comment, "Oh Jane, you always feel so guilty afterwards! Don't worry about it!"

Following on from learning massage at night school and the desire to get out of the IT world, I had applied for a role at the London Ambulance Service as a paramedic. I still wanted to help people but I knew I wasn't ready to set up my own business, nor did I want to feel trapped doing massage in a salon.

Again the universe gives us signs. I failed the Paramedic test three times and each time for a different reason. Yet it was the encouragement from the staff who told me to apply for a job as a Call Taker and Dispatcher. I sat those tests and passed with flying colours, they actually called me up to tell me they were some of the best results they have seen. I remained in the Ambulance Service for eleven years, the first three years as a Call Taker and Dispatcher doing 12-hour shifts. I also found myself another role within the Control Room as a Loggist, which allowed me to pretty much be my own boss. I was responsible for pairing up one-man crews for the ambulance when there were absenteeism and holidays. I also made sure that all the vehicles were on the road.

But it was a case of working hard and partying hard. My drinking escalated as a result. Ironically, I liked the community and the laugh of this job, even though we were stuck in an office for 12 hours, but as soon as the regulations became stronger and stronger, the laughs became less and less, I found that I didn't like it so much.

During this time, around my 30th birthday, I was engaged and had the wedding planned to perfection. It was a time also when I was earning the most money. For my birthday I decided I wanted a classier affair with wine and cheese at home with a few friends. I tried to keep it clean; no drugs.

Despite being clear on my desires, my fiancé and friends showed up with drugs as usual. Before I knew it, food was out and drugs were on the table, and while I resisted at first, I soon found myself being caught in that cycle again. The party lasted until 8 am the next day. This event left me feeling so disgusted and depressed. Two weeks later I had another "fuck it" moment - I split up from my fiancé and the wedding was cancelled for good. I applied for a three year homeopathy course and started within six weeks of my 30th birthday. And I applied for a Deputy Managers' position within the service, which I was in within 8 weeks of my 30th birthday. This allowed me to hang out less with certain groups of friends, which reduced my drinking and drug taking.

Two years later, I found myself in a relationship with a friend I had known for 10 years and subsequently, my daughter was born. Unfortunately, her father left as soon as I told him the news, (the happy news is we are friends again and he does see his daughter). I knew that I was destined to be a single mum from day one! Despite this, I was happy and excited about my new adventure. Another great situation to come out of my pregnancy was that it further removed me from my now dwindling circles of friends. Moreover, during this time instead of gaining weight, I lost three stone because I was eating healthily and looking after my body.

My daughter was a gift from God, the Universe, the Divine.

After she was born, I went back to the Ambulance Service job. I then fought to go part-time. It seemed to me that everything was a fight. After six months, I was left wondering, why on earth did I fight for this job?

The old story of 'should've, could've, would've' came up again. I was still feeling trapped. It took me a few more years to find my COURAGE to do something about it, which, of course, was to leave.

I began working with mums who were binge drinkers like I used to be. At that time, I still did the odd binge drinking (I don't drink anymore). I then realised how can I authentically coach these women when I was just like them? Not only that, but I spent a lot of money marketing, advertising and creating programmes. I soon discovered the women I was attracting weren't ready to actually take the action to transform their lives. The pivotal moment came when I heard a coach say that your clients are just three steps behind you. I now realised that binge drinking was way more than three steps behind me. This insight resulted in me stopping coaching for a year as I was put off by the whole experience.

I found myself going back to my massaging skills. I was beginning to create a business massaging for me and my daughter, and at the time I decided to leave, I was only making around £500 per month. This did not stop me from sticking to my intuition and leaving my job. I gave up an excellent job with a pension from the London Ambulance Service after eleven years.

I was now working with mums with back pain. Within three email campaigns, I had ten clients. I then started going round mother and toddler groups. It was easy to get clients. As I began to get more clients, I realised that I didn't want to spend my time massaging. While I love it and love healing people, I didn't want to feel like a conveyor belt.

As you can tell I have had many 'F**k it' moments. When I realise I am not living a life aligned to me. When I realise I am doing something every day I hate. I say F**k it, you can to do something better!

Consequently, I looked at what my dreams and goals were. I knew I didn't want to live in London. I always wanted to live outside of London, but I had never found the right place. I also knew that by building up my face to face clients in London, I was creating an environment and business I felt stuck in.

Working online gives me freedom. I knew I could do it, but I didn't know how. I want to work with people who want to transform their lives, who know what they want but they don't know how to get there, and I can teach them.

This insight made me look back at my life of being stuck and fighting for freedom, I knew that I worked through seven steps to transform my life. This allowed me to create an excellent programme out of my experiences. I taught the programme over 12 weeks. This was a significant point for me as I was now being paid for coaching. At first, the clients and income went up and down, but now it is a steady flow.

For me, there is always hope that what you truly dream of is there waiting for you. You can create your desired life when you have clarity and are clear with the steps you're required to take. There are still choices. I made many decisions, some good and some not so good. Now, I am living a dream life. I have my online coaching business, with fantastic programmes, which I fit around my daughter and myself. I am living consciously and where I want to be with easy access to the beach whenever we decide to go there.

My big vision? I want to be doing TED Talks, have a thriving membership programme with huge numbers and helping thousands of ladies achieve their dreams.

Dedication: *To all I have loved and who have loved me, we shaped each others lives unknowingly!*

Jane is a young woman on a mission. She has a clear vision and continues to take steps to make them her reality.

Facing her demons head on, Jane decided to use her learning to benefit other women just like her. She understood them. She could empathise with their situations and knew what they would have to do if their desire was to change.

Jane is at the precipice of change for herself and her business. Jump Jane, you are ready to fly...

Brenda Dempsey
Creator & Editor

The Art of Feminine Beauty

Connecting with Nature
Feeds Our Soul

Sue Ritchie

The Art of Feminine Beauty

Pelican

"Be still. Allow the world to flow around you. Let its beauty and grace envelop you. Only in the present can we find this state of grace."

VOICES OF HOPE

Carol Wachniak - Chicago, USA

Big Things Don't Come to Small People

Carol is a remarkable woman with beautiful and colourful experiences of life. Her accomplishments are awe-inspiring and although she has eight children of her own, she can still find time to put others first. Carol is a precious and rare breed of divine spirit living in a human body and experience.

In her chapter she reveals many tales that would have broken others.

Her resilience and fortitude stand out to show us a woman who knows the secret of acceptance. Through letting go many of her situations, you will read about a stronger, wiser and more powerful woman than I have ever known.

Her Doula skills are to be admired as she shows great compassion towards others who have been rejected by society.

Be ready to be inspired.

Brenda Dempsey
Creator & Editor

Transformation #14

Big Things Don't Come to Small People

Carol Wachniak

Coach and Entrepreneur

"In the darkest moments do not FEAR – go out and find someone to help."

Carol Wachniak

As a result of my experiences, I find that my faith is stronger; that I am more supported than I am willing to receive sometimes. I know that God is there, and others are there for me if I'm more willing to open my heart and know that I'm worthy to receive the gifts that are available to me.

My faith has evolved, especially after my mom had passed away. My mom was the first of five family members to pass away, and the most devastating. I lost a total of four women and one man within two years: my mother, my grandmother, my mother-in-law, my grandmother-in-law, and then my murdered brother. At that time, I was 25 and a mother of four children as well as taking care of my two nieces. So, I became the matriarch of the family.

During this time, I had done a lot of grief work. At our church, I was on the suicide prevention team, so I had a support system. If someone experienced suicide, our church would go and minister to the school or whoever needed our support. This experience was invaluable to me.

In 1986, the death of my brother was tough to bear. Everything was 'normal'. Then I received a phone call from a mutual friend saying that my brother had gone missing. We could not find him anywhere. Consequently, I started to call him too. I was concerned as we spoke regularly every week; up to three or four times. He lived in a town about twenty-five miles away. He even missed Thanksgiving; that was when the alarm bells went off. I was going crazy. I had no clue where he was.

As he was an adult, reporting him missing to the police was challenging. The thing that was more devastating to me about my brother was that I thought the search and rescue dogs would come running in. I thought the knights in shining armour, so to speak, with the white horses, would go and care as much as I did. They didn't. It was disappointing that the police didn't take me seriously because he was missing. And it's challenging to get a missing person's report on an adult because they're an adult. Adults are free to go wherever they want. But we finally were able to get a police report done.

To add to my devastation, I found out that there were no search and rescue dogs available in our area to go looking like you see on the movies. They sniff the clothes and off they go. The lack of this service made me feel even more vulnerable. What got me more than anything is people are afraid when something traumatic happens, they're scared to get close because it might rub off on them. Even my other brothers and my dad had a hard time dealing with the situation. I thought, if they're not going to look for my brother, they wouldn't even look for me. That's hurtful.

That fateful day arrived. We discovered someone he knew had murdered him. He was dismembered actually and buried in a cornfield in a town called the Aurora. He was found in a field by some surveyors. This discovery occurred after I was able to get a missing person's report out. As they were surveying the area, they saw something odd at the bottom of the field. It turned out to be my brother's hand sticking up out of a shallow grave in the cornfield.

Death is just one area of life that we talk about and find the conversation uncomfortable. We learn how to cope and move on.

It is individuals who just come and befriend you; they love you, and they nurture you. The first group of women who helped me was La Leche League. I was pregnant with my third child when my mom died. I believe the shock of her death resulted in my waters rupturing, which left me on bed rest for three months. Every day, they brought me meals at lunch and dinner for my husband. They helped watch my other kids. They wrapped themselves around me; I didn't really know these women. I have found that when we reach out, we can receive what we request. We learn to do that for each other.

It feels like God's angels come just at your most vulnerable and desperate moment.

I want to share another experience in my life. It is not about people but possessions; more importantly, my home.

It was 1999, and I was living in Chicago when they dug a deep tunnel underneath the houses. It was a mining project for the sanitation department. This work had been carried out over 20 years. Ultimately what happened was the groundwater that hydrates was syphoned off using hydraulics. This procedure resulted in air pockets forming. So instead of water under the houses, there were air pockets. Consequently, when they dug the deep tunnel, those air pockets caused the house to fall into the hole because the water was no longer there underneath it.

Thankfully there was no one at home as we were all in Salt Lake City. I felt that was like Divine Intervention.

What's interesting is that I didn't know the signs of the settlement. No insurance company takes on that type of house. This chain of events all happened after only living in the house for twelve weeks before it sank. We were instantly homeless. When we went to the city council, they too wanted to levy us. They tried to punish us for not repairing the house right away. They didn't want anyone to know that they had been keeping the information a secret. These houses were above the air pockets. They did not want us to go public with the information and what had just happened to us.

As a result of this situation, my husband and I walked around the neighbourhood. The public was on our side. We registered a letter to the council for public disclosure. Also, we went to the historical society to figure out, with aerial photographs, what the situation was before they constructed the neighbourhood.

It turned out that we were on an old farm, which they had tunnelled underneath it. Any further digging in that area was going to have trouble. I thought I had bought a home that was going to be our security.

My biggest lesson was your home is not your security. It's not a building that gives you protection; it is within yourself. The fun part about this whole lesson concerning the house was, I was doing a Bible study with Nehemiah and building the walls. I kept on saying, focus on God and not the walls, focus on God and not the walls, because my house walls were gone.

I have eight children, so finding a house is not an easy job. Ironically we still owed the money on the old house. That doesn't go away because the insurance doesn't cover it. So we have $250,000 that just literally went into a sinkhole, and we're homeless, and we have to find another house. Ultimately, I'm praying. I wanted a super large kitchen. Now my kitchen is 24 x 14. I wanted a full basement, and the list went on. Do you know what I learned about this whole thing? I received everything I wanted in that prayer - Pray bigger!

All the things I manifested is the Law of Attraction working at its finest.

The lesson connected to this whole experience was that we were always protected. We stayed in people's homes. The first week we were in our car, but after that, we went to the Salvation Army summer camp. So for the whole summer, we were at a park with the kids and had fun doing lots of activities. After that, we were staying with a friend who put a great big sign on her house saying, 'Welcome home.' We lived in her basement for months as we were trying to figure out the legalities of everything that happened to us as a result of the sinkhole.

The fire in my belly.

I have been a 'Doula' for thirty-nine years. I help women give birth. After all, I have eight children! My biggest lesson is when life hits you, I find a way to go out and help somebody else. That is my biggest life lesson.

Right now, my daughter is fighting cancer. She is my oldest; she's a midwife. As I've mentioned, I have eight kids and sixteen grandkids, so there's never a day that's typically 'normal'. My healthy might be someone else's hell.

Recently, I have been a little bit down. One day I met a woman at the doctor's office who was in a lot of pain. I invited her over to my home, and I said,

"Janet, why don't you come on over, and I'll give you a BEMER session." A BEMER is a medical device from Europe, from Lichtenstein, that you lay on and it increases your micro-circulation. You don't feel anything. She accepted my invitation and came over. Talking to her helped; it hugged me, and it hugged her.

NASA is using it in the space program. It moves blood flow in the micro-circulatory system. When it does that, you decrease inflammation, you increase in oxygen, and you grow the body's ability for the immune system to improve.

Speaking with people inspires me to keep reaching out to others; that is the last life lesson I gave my kids when I thought I wasn't going to be here anymore when I was sick, really sick.

One day, all of a sudden, I became ill. In the beginning, I didn't know that I had become very acidic, hyper acidic. So much so that if I ate anything, my blood pressure would go to 290 over 190 and then I'd go into anaphylactic shock. They took me to hospital, and all the major hospitals here that I had turned to, never looked at acidity. The medics never checked that. All of my tests would go crazy because the acid was changing the results. Eventually, they gave up on me, and they sent me home to die. They said, there's nothing we can do for you.

The Pivotal Moment for me was when I was in intensive care. The account I am about to reveal really happened. I was the only one in intensive care. I'm looking through the intensive care window; looking at my eight children, waving back at me. I was praying, "God, don't take me; don't take me." My youngest was four years old at the time. I heard these words, "Coach at the cellular level," audibly, with only me in the room, nobody there, and it was a deep resounding voice. When they sent me home on January 4th to get my paperwork in order, I believed the doctors when they said that I wasn't going to live. I lived 96 days on only water and prayer.

On March 22nd, I thought to myself, I've got to find one last life lesson to teach my children before I die. I asked, what is that? I gathered all of my children in the room. I said, "Y'all have to go out and find somebody to help."

The very next day I heard on the radio, "Coach at the cellular level." They read out a phone number which was for an alternative health clinic. It turned out to be a couple of towns away from me.

At that time, it was $1,200 to talk to this particular doctor for 30 minutes; now it's $18,000 to speak to him for 30 minutes. That was a light bulb moment for me when I found out about the benefits of being alkaline and foods with bio-electrical charge are suitable for our electrical cells. Our body is electrical, and our heart is 90 millivolts of electricity. So what do we eat today that has an electrical charge to recharge our battery? Hello? Most of us don't. So dead food is dead people, living food is living people.

Finally, your experiences don't define you. It's what you do as a result - knowing that despite your challenges, there are always people who need your help.

From your challenges, you build strength, resilience and will power that keeps you going. Death, Murder, Sickness and Being Homeless are no excuses to throw in the towel. The best way to get over anything is to help others.

Dedication:

I dedicate this chapter to my children and grandchildren. No matter what it looks like at this moment in time, never give up on your dreams.

HOPE

Be the Light

What a journey Carol as been on! Sometimes when life throws you curve balls you learn how to roll with them. This is Carol's lesson in life. Her acceptance of her situation and looking for the silver lining is what helped her cope with the difficult and challenging times in her life. I do love her philosophy - when you have a problem go and help someone else with theirs.

Brenda Dempsey
Creator & Editor

VOICES OF HOPE
Tiffany Hinton - Chicago, USA

My Test, My Testimony

When Tiffany was a young woman, she experienced what many women dread to hear, that they may never be able to have children.

Having endured many medical procedures, she found within her a determination and tenacity that meant she would never give up on enjoying life and living in a healthy state.

Tiffany was heaven blessed as she turned to God to help her through her battles.

Using the gifts of her infinite intelligence, she began to see herself as a whole and not a person who had issues with certain parts of her. In adopting this perspective on life she was able to turn herself from misfortune and pessimism into someone who was fortunate and optimistic that she could turn her life around.

Be inspired as you read how this woman was able to bear her burden before turning her life around and using her story to support others who are walking a similar path.

Brenda Dempsey
Creator & Editor

Transformation #15

My Test, My Testimony

Tiffany Hinton

Business Owner, Best Selling Author, Speaker,
Functional Medicine Certified Health Coach

"Hope is knowing God has something for you bigger than life."

Tiffany Hinton

"The test will become your testimony." I heard this growing up, along with "God will never give you more than you can endure." I have questioned these two phrases many times in the last 20 years, at times, even asking God's path for my life.

My health started to decline when I was 14. I began to experience constant stomach pain, acid reflux and menstrual periods in length of 60 days and sometimes more. I was removed from school physical education classes and told to take an acid reducer. I remember carrying antacid or chalk tablets around in my pocket.

As my health continued to decline, by the age of 18, my intestines were bleeding. Living with this condition is no way to be as a senior in high school who makes up excuses when asked out, through fear of farting blood. I also had the not-so-lovely opportunity to have two colonoscopies by the age of 18. I would never wish this on my worst enemy. The preparation is horrific. In case you have never had the pleasure of a colonoscopy, here is a peek.

You start with drinking liquid magnesium flavoured like bad lemonade to flush your system. Consequently, you spend a few hours on the toilet, followed by an enema to ensure your digestive tract is clean. You are giving yourself nausea plus vomiting, diarrhoea and stomach cramping intentionally. YUK!

I was diagnosed with IBS and Crohn's Disease, told to eat more fibre, along with avoiding nuts and seeds. Looking back on that advice, I could be furious, which I was for a while. Then I realized that what the doctors learn is what they know, and have little time to continue their studies once they begin practising. Lately, they seem to have only about eight minutes to see each patient. This is one of the frustrations that propelled me forward.

I lived with this diagnosis, for the next 15 years, taking up to 25 pharmaceuticals a day, taking naps and continuing to feel worse. One of the medicines I took was to line my intestinal tract to prevent irritation while eating. In reality, it did such an excellent job at prevention, that it also stopped my absorption of food and nutrients. This anomaly caused me to be nutrient deficient and unable to heal. On the plus side, I could eat a whole large pizza by myself and not gain a pound.

One of the setbacks was that I suffered from infertility for over 14 years, leading me to choose a lie when asked when I was going to have kids. I would respond that I did not want kids to avoid having to talk about my health. All the while, I was an emotional wreck and spiritually disconnected.

In 2007, I rushed to the emergency room with the belief that my appendix had ruptured. During this traumatic time, my parents met my husband for the first time, at 3:30 am. HA!

I remember waking up from the surgery and told my appendix had not ruptured although it had strands growing all around it and was being squeezed. I asked if it was cancer, and the ER surgeon said no, he had not seen this before, and the tissue sent to pathology. The results came back as endometriosis. My results indicated stage four endometriosis, which means the tissue from inside my uterus was growing outside my reproductive area.

A similar tissue was growing on my lungs, appendix, intestines, kidneys and ovaries. It now even become apparent in my skin. By 2010 we owed the university hospital over 680,000 dollars, and they were refusing to see me as a patient any longer. I came home and cried on the bathroom floor. The resulting vulnerable conversation with my husband was a turning point in my health and forced me to take another approach. I turned to Mr Google. I know I am not the only one to do this for health questions. At last, I found a board-certified endocrinologist who practices in infertility and holistic medicine. I later came to realize this doctor was a practising Functional Medicine doctor at the core.

This new doctor repeated tests and ran an additional 200 tests, resulting in an accurate diagnosis and root cause. He discovered that I had Celiac disease, along with endometriosis and several food allergies. Following his treatment plan, which started with food and lifestyle change, it brought us three beautiful miracles. I received the heavenly gift of having three girls in three years. Yep, we have two sets of Irish twins! They are each 14 months apart. I thank God each day.

When I was pregnant with my last daughter, my colon and uterus had fused to become one organ as a result of my autoimmune disease. I went into labour with Josi at 3:30 in the morning. We finally arrived at the hospital around 5:30 am after getting childcare for the other girls. By this time, I was in extreme pain. Josi was born naturally by 6:30 am with the help of an epidural. I was still in acute pain and completely exhausted. I was scheduled to have a tubal ligation later that evening.

God had another plan, and I am very grateful. It was the cancellation of one of the planned C-sections. They took me back for the outpatient procedure at 7:15 am while my epidural was still active. I remember laying there with the mini blue curtain expecting a 15-minute operation. With the first incision, blood squirted to the ceiling. The OB-Gyn began paging additional nurses and an extra doctor. He called for anaesthesia and told me to breathe. They reopened my past C-section scar and started to vacuum the blood. What they found was the ruptured uterus and colon, something they had never seen before.

I remember the doctor pulling the organs out to examine and saying they reminded him of shrapnel wounds from his tour of duty. Accordingly, he cauterized both organs to save my life. The smell of burning flesh was disgusting. The anaesthesia showed up just in time for me to be stitched back together. This in-the-nick-of-time surgery gave me another chance at life. God had given me a second chance. What I learned was that I was about 1 1/2 hours from bleeding out internally.

Fast forward one year, and I am back at the gastro because of blood in my stool and extreme pain. It turns out you cannot singe a colon and expect it to operate correctly. It had died in a small section, which would require a colon resection. It was a minor surgery compared to the rupturing, and I was home the next day.

By this time, I was familiar with Functional Medicine and using food to heal. I refused to fill the prescriptions, and the gastro refused to let me go home. We agreed to seek the help of the Functional Medicine doctor at the hospital for a treatment plan and a 6-week window to see results without the use of pharmaceuticals. It worked! Within six weeks of using the elimination diet, I was healing, the blood had stopped, and I had a normal bowel movement. One year later, I was back to cardio works at the gym with no pain. My love for Functional Medicine forged through my health challenges and triumphs.

Beginning in 2010, I started a blog as my way to deal with the emotions of chronic disease diagnosis. Moving to a gluten-free diet in 2007, challenged me to create and cook my food. At the time, the gluten-free food options were very limited. The limitation of these food products was the beginning of my business, GF Mom Certified. I wrote and published gluten-free and allergy-safe cookbooks around foods that I missed and others needed. It was simple and great-tasting food that my soul remembered: cakes, pies, holiday cookies, pastries, and family comfort foods. I was asked to fill in for a keynote speaker in 2005 at the most extensive Gluten Free Expo in the United States, two days before the event. I fell in love with educating and giving hope to other women who may never find a cure.

I reflected on my story of hope and can see the triggers of my health. At age 11, my dad went to federal prison; this stress triggered my Celiac to become active. In my mid-twenties, my first marriage fell apart, triggering the auto-immune diseases to flare and grow more. With functional medicine, the treatment is not about just fixing one system or organ; the treatment includes food, nutrients, root cause, environment and mindset.

I went back to school to complete a degree in Functional Medicine, giving me more wisdom to help other women find healing. We have begun to take the Thrive Clean program and build local groups to bring more healing. My mission is to hear 1 million stories of healing through food in the next ten years. I will achieve this by building a community and giving women a platform to share from their healing.

Functional medicine is a combination of using science and holistic medicine together to achieve more excellent health. I believe health is not the mere absence of disease; it is the continuous seeking for better health with the use of wellness strategies. In school, we are taught to envision the body as a tree. The top of the tree with the leaves and branches are the many systems of the body: systems that include cardio, neurological, gastric, lymphatic and many more. The trunk and core of the tree are our DNA, heritage and ancestry. Next, consider the roots of the tree as our environment, then the environment as our physical location, water, activity, stress, supplements and other external factors.

When you begin to see the tree as a whole unit and connect the symptoms, you can treat the root of the issue, an approach based on root cause treatment and functional medicine. Unlike traditional western medicine, it is very specialized and only looks at one system, which results in finding the root of the symptom.

Functional medicine uses a five-step process to begin the process of reducing inflammation and gaining health. The first is to look at food and increase the amount of nutrient-dense food. You can accomplish this process by increasing the amount of fruit and vegetables consumed each day.

The next step is to remove any allergens or foods to which you are sensitive. The third step is to remove toxins in the environment. The fourth is to add supplements, vitamins and minerals as required, following a comprehensive blood panel. Finally, the fifth step is a detox, if and only if still needed.

The Thrive Clean program includes all five steps; some essential details of my own, along with a plan to help us make it actionable. I believe the future of medicine is rooted in a functional approach with individual care for each person. We all need a team who will listen to us and understand our full tree. By adopting a more holistic approach, it will bring each of us healing. With God's help and my vision of hearing stories of one million women, healing will take place.

Dedication: *For my husband and greatest support Will, who challenges me to be more every day.*

Without a shadow of a doubt, Tiffany is a super mom and woman. She drives herself each day to create a world that transforms lives. With her experiences and lessons she is ready, able and willing to show others just what it takes to turn your life around. Her tenacity to find a solution is a great testimony to her purpose and today she still strives to create change in others on a global scale. Thank you for your contribution to making the world a better place.

Brenda Dempsey
Creator & Editor

The Art of Feminine Beauty

Emma Greenslade

VOICES OF HOPE

Mira Warszawski - Polish, living in London, UK

Bizarre Dreams in Margaret's House

If you are ever blessed to meet Mira, you will feel her beautiful soul from the moment you see her. Despite her adversity, she chooses to see only good.

Mira is a natural storyteller and you are soon brought into her world with her narrative. She is determined to see the rays of sunshine through whatever adversity she faces. This optimistic view of the world has enabled her to accept the hand she has been dealt and face her fate with courage.

Be humbled by this charming tale which in fact is a real life story.

Brenda Dempsey
Creator & Editor

Transformation #16

Bizarre Dreams in Margaret's House

Mira Warszawski

Nurse

"When you follow the path of opportunity, it can lead you to finding yourself."

Mira Warszawski

When I found myself in Chocholow – a small village on the border of Slovakia and Poland, I realized that life had pushed me to the edge. This beautiful village lies in the bottom of the valley, divided by the main road leading from a Zakopane to Slovakia, with breathtaking views over the forests and the Tatra Mountains to the south and hills to the north. Although the surroundings brought lots of joy to others, I felt like a failure. All my passions and desires fled my body, leaving me hopeless. I couldn't stop asking myself, how this all happened to me?

I came with big hopes to Zakopane - the winter capital of Poland and popular tourist destination for skiing, climbing and walking. I was offered a job as a manager of a small boutique hotel where I was later residing with my teenage daughter, Klaudia, a beautiful and sensitive girl. There were only two of us since her father had left us when she was little. I was hoping for a better life for us; saving money for a dream home, meeting amazing friends and even finding true love.

We felt ecstatic leaving our hometown of Debica where for some people we never were good enough; an overambitious divorcee and her rebellious daughter. We took our dog and a few belongings with us for this life-changing adventure. We felt alone at times but full of hope about the future, open to meet new people and connect with them.

After one happy year, the hotel was sold to a new owner, and underwent general refurbishment. A lift and a few disabled bathrooms were added to raise the standard of the property which aimed to become a 3* hotel. As a Grade 2 building, it required individual permissions for renovation works to be carried out, and I obtained them from the local authorities. Shortly after, the hotel returned to its regular business; the guests were flowing in.

Nevertheless, the new owner decided I was no longer needed. I sensed something terrible was going to happen. One day, the big boss approached me in the spacious lounge, handing over a paper with a cynical smile on his face. "You are fired," he said without a blink. I felt shot in the heart and almost collapsed from the shock it caused me. I felt physically sick for a couple of days, lying in a bed, a lifeless body, not being able to digest 'a failure', not to mention a simple meal. My heartbroken daughter was taking genuine care of me. We had no choice but to leave Zakopane.

It was the end of March 2004 when we moved into an abandoned house in Chocholow, which was available for rent. Winter was at its peak, with heavy snow and temperatures dropping to minus twenty overnight. The house was located close to the main road and a river which flooded during springtime.

My first impression of the building wasn't right. A few steps led to the ground floor of the house.

There was a grey carpet on the storey of a spacious living room, the windows were draped with brown curtains, and there was an overwhelming odour of decay. It was freezing cold. I felt shivers all over my body just thinking how we were going to manage here and keep it warm?

The locals called it haunted due to its tragic history of a woman who ended her life here, overdosing on sleeping pills. Her dead body had been found in the kitchen, the same kitchen that we were using for making our meals. The navy tiles on the floor made it look even more unwelcoming. They said it was due to her being unhappy in her relationship with her husband, our landlord. She was a beautiful mum of two boys and was too young to die. Her name was Margaret. My daughter and I decided to name our new residence, Margaret's House. We had loads of sympathy for the poor woman and wanted to honour her memory. We even visited her grave in the local cemetery to discover a shocking inscription: "Because this was God's will."

Have I been called to this place for a reason? It was a four-storey house with seven bedrooms, once used as bed and breakfast. It was dark and drab; however, Klaudia and I knew we could bring some light to this home with our love. Despite all the obstacles that life threw at us between 2004 and 2005, the bond between my daughter and I had never been stronger. The odds were all stacked against us, but we felt content exploring Margaret's House;

discovering old photographs, and all the beautiful nature that surrounded us. We had two dogs living with us at this time, gentle Gaia and aggressive Killer, who you could say was our bodyguard. While we felt grateful for the shelter, I had no job and little money.

I was applying everywhere for a job but was getting no responses. I reached out to friends with no luck. They were all too busy; I felt forgotten. Klaudia then fell ill with a severe chest infection, and our money had run out. I was forced to sell jewellery and my valuables to buy medication, food and other necessities. My beloved mum was worrying terribly about us so she sent me some money to help us survive this difficult time. Feelings of gratitude but also of shame, fulfilled my heart. I knew I must do something, but I didn't know what.

My brother Dariusz came from our hometown, Debica to visit me. He was shocked with disbelief, seeing how my life had been totally turned upside down. He looked around at old furniture and begged me to leave this forbidden place and run away from it. The invisible attraction to the enigma of this house kept me stuck there. I didn't feel I had the power to change anything. My self-esteem vanished, and my soul was shaking like an injured butterfly.

I started having crazy dreams. One night I woke up in a sweat because it all seemed so real. I rang a friend in the middle of the night in despair because I needed to talk to someone. She said that I was disturbing her! I burst into tears and smashed my mobile phone against the wall losing the last point of connection, as there was no internet access in the house and no land-line either.

I took Killer for a walk. I stopped on the bridge of the river flowing nearby. The moon shone on the snowy trees, and the dark water was sparkling in the night. The water seemed so inviting, I felt as if it was calling me. I wondered if this was all still part of a dream. Or was I being led to follow in Margaret's footsteps? Suddenly, the dog started pulling me back. This really had shaken me up. As I reflected on the moment on the bridge, I felt something awakened within me. My love for my daughter recalled me to action. I knew that I still had the power within me! Not all had been lost! The time to change was now. I knew if I stayed there one week longer, I would have never left that place.

I managed to find a job in a pleasant restaurant in Zakopane. The owners were supportive; customers liked me, and I slowly regained my sense of being. I was able to provide for my little family.

I had finally spotted the rays of sunshine striking through that time of darkness, and I made a life-changing decision. I decided to leave Poland and go to England.

I had been walking alongside River Thames at Fulham, with the view of Hammersmith Bridge to the right and Putney Bridge to the left. The day was perfect, sunny and bright with a light touch of a summer breeze. I fell in love with this part of London, where my new story had just begun. I was buzzing from excitement caused by a massive jump from the edge of my life in Poland to this new chapter of my life in one of the biggest cities in the world! Wow! Everything was magnificent! Everything seemed to be possible! I felt like a superb adventurous person climbing the mountains, and all because I made that decision.

I didn't know what to do and where to start. All I had was £300 on me and a suitcase of belongings. I experienced a high level of endorphins flowing in my blood from the excitement and fear.

On this memorable walk, I was watching seagulls floating on the surface of the water. The noisy birds appeared to not bother about the current, which was taking them with a flow, turning them around at times like plastic toys. This got me thinking that maybe I shall trust that the Universe has my back; let it happen; let it be and believe in a positive outcomes.

Having come to the UK, I took a plunge into the unknown. What is waiting here for me? Where will I sleep, and what will I eat? Where will I find a job, moreover how will I find a job? Currently, my

English wasn't good. I could ask a simple question, but I had a problem asking more complex issues. So why did I choose to come to the United Kingdom?

Only a year before my arrival to London, Poland had become a member of the European Union and, as I have always loved the English language, I assumed this was a perfect place for me to come but after arriving in this cosmopolitan city, I quickly realized that I was far from fluent.

I stayed in the house of an elderly man through my Polish connections. He was an extraordinary person, and during many talks we had together, he shared his passionate love for books and history.

I didn't come to London with my daughter Klaudia, and I was missing her terribly. I felt pressurized to get any job as soon as possible, to be able to rent a room and bring her over. It wasn't as easy as I thought it would be. It took seven months of being in London before my she was reunited with me.

After a couple of weeks, I had moved to my brother's place in Greenford, and I managed to find a job in a nursing home as a tea-time lady, just because I put cooking as my hobby on my CV. I attended an interview and got stuck when I was asked questions about the meaning of equal opportunities; something I never came across in Poland. Equal opportunities became words of great importance in my new life in the UK. In Poland, I saw jobs advertisement reserved for people who were no more than 35 years old. In London, I started to grow in confidence with assurance that I am not too old for anything; being already 39 years old.

New decisions bring new challenges...and sometimes...new love. This was an extra bonus that I never dreamt about.

I met Kris during my brother Anton's birthday party, on the fourth day of my stay in London. During this time, I could not have known that within a year, we would be a married couple. We bonded quickly, and our friendship evolved beyond my wildest expectations.

There were U-turns caused by Kris' illness, something which we both didn't have a clue about when we first met. His diagnosis came as a shock to both of us: epilepsy triggered by a brain tumour. I felt devastated by the news.

My new life in the UK has given me lessons in being non-judgemental, humble, polite, respectful, diversity and aware of equality, not discriminating against others. It felt at times, that I was on my knees, forgetting about the Master's Degree I achieved in Poland and leaving behind ambitions. Not to mention starting everything from scratch, being separated from my daughter for a few painful months, and being challenged by life to help Kris find a reason to live.

Where in the hell, did all that courage come from? Was it coming from prayers or maybe from beliefs that faith and determination will be rewarded? Well, Yes and No. I believe that this strength came from inner resilience, guiding me intuitively to that higher purpose in my life if only I dared to call it.

Hope was always my inevitable friend, and everything that I experienced in my life has made me stronger. Not everything smelled of roses in my garden. There were dark times, not because I chose them but I let them pick me: not loving myself enough, putting others first but never me. I have commenced on a personal journey, doing my best to improve my life by creating it through positive thoughts, visualization and openness to new opportunities. Also, I learned the importance of 'going with the flow' as seagulls do.

I've totally changed my career path, becoming a registered nurse at the age of 47 as well as passing all my exams in English. My job creates a swell of pride in my heart and fills it with great satisfaction. I feel grateful that I can help people in need, holding compassionate space for them.

Despite the enormous satisfaction that I feel from being a nurse, there is a voice screaming inside me, longing to be heard. I know that this is the voice of an inner calling, begging to activate my dreams.

I never gave up on my dreams, and I never will! I uphold a passion for writing, humanitarian work, and networking. I can feel this burning desire to fulfil my life purpose, bringing more happiness to myself and others. I have made this promise to myself that as long as I am alive, I am willing to be loved and I want to spread love, believing that love is the highest vibration and has that miraculous power to make this world a better place to live in.

Margaret's house seemed like a distant dream, but it is still embedded in me. It taught me that life can be like a long, dark tunnel. We don't always see the light at the end of it, and if we do, the light may feel too out of reach. However, the little tiny cracks in the tunnel allow the light to peek through like small candles of hope. Those flames, those little glimpses are what will lead you out, even when it feels hopeless.

Yes, I was led to Margaret's house for a reason. It has taught me lessons of resilience but also how easy it can be to get caught up in moments and situations. Everything that happened has led me to where I am now. I am surrounded by people, my dearest family and friends who always inspire and encourage me to be my best self.

My love for my daughter and her love for me has helped us wade through the darkness, bringing so much hope to Margaret's house. I will never forget the light that seeped through the cracks and will forever be grateful for both the sun and the cracks.

Dedication:

I dedicate this story to mum, who showed me the power of resilience.

∞

I am sure you are left feeling in awe of the depth of love that Mira radiates not only to her beloved daughter but her family and in fact the world.

This is the charm of Mira as she gives gratitude for everything that she experiences in her life good and bad. This acceptance of the cards one is dealt reveals a secret to a happy life.

Mira continues to extend gratitude, love and acceptance of everything she is now enjoying in the UK. She is the epitome of the meaning of life and how we should live it in the journey to be the best version of ourselves.

Brenda Dempsey
Creator & Editor

VOICES OF HOPE

Trina Kavanagh-Thomas - Nottinghamshire, UK

I Refuse to Give Up on Myself

Trina is one of the three co-authors from Voices of Courage to join me and the other courageous souls who have taken the plunge to be part of Voices of Hope.

When you read Trina's story you will feel the power of her vulnerability as she bares her soul. In her truth, she sets herself free from the limiting beliefs that have haunted her most of her life.

You will be truly inspired by her honesty and will experience a sense of permission to reach inside your own soul to find the blocks and the sense of overwhelm that keeps you from being who you truly are meant to be.

As a woman, mother and wife, Trina refuses to give up on herself as she continues to battle the demons inside. Knowing Trina I believe that she has come so far and is on the cusp of realising her dream for her and her family.

Brenda Dempsey
Creator & Editor

Transformation #17

I Refuse to Give Up on Myself

Trina Kavanagh-Thomas
Intuitive Personal Trainer & Health Coach

"I refuse to give up on myself while following the path to freedom."

Trina Kavanagh-Thomas

Freedom is an important value for me. What does freedom mean to me and at what cost?

My story from Voices of Courage evolved around money, and that money story didn't end there.

Did it get better? No, it got worse; much worse. However, the end is now in sight...

Take a deep breath as we plunge into the depths of mental health, through my own anxiety and depression. My focus is to learn how to let go of the past and move on to a brighter future.

We start again, with everything seeming well; you know, like that 'Happy ever after' Disney movie. Just like my childhood days when I had it easy; everything I wanted, needed and more. I was overfed, and by the age of 13, I was a size 16.

Never did I know that I would have to revisit the abandonment of my father, clear my own self-punishment and self-pity. I call Brenda Dempsey, for advise while in Ibiza.

At this time, I participated in a branding challenge ran online by Sammy Blindell. It is 7.30am, I am still in bed, congratulating the other participants in the challenge who had won one of her prizes. Unexpectedly, I hear Sammy say my name!

Before I know it, I am in floods of tears. My husband comes running upstairs. "What's wrong?" he asks.

"I've won! I can't believe it, I've won!" I scream with tears rolling down my cheeks.

The next few days are a whirlwind. However, my mum is dubious.

A few days later, I decide to create a video, one that is emotionally challenging to make. The reason? I realise how much I do not love myself, and I need others to love me to feel validated.

Honouring myself, I quit teaching my personal training classes. I feel I have to leave my clients even though I never want to lose them. I am giving away my work, my reputation and my ego. Yes, my ego! I quickly realise needing validation feeds my ego, which makes me feel happy about myself. Leaving what I've built is the start of moving away from the old and rebuilding something new.

The prizes awarded from Sammy are life-changing. My prize is a one day coaching session followed by 5-days' branding event in her farmhouse in France, The day with her aids me in getting to grips with the wording of my business. This is only the start. We work all day, I'm genuinely grateful for her guidance. Without her (and Brenda), this significant step forward, would never happen.

By the time the retreat comes round. I travel to the West coast of France in the car (by myself). It is an adventure which is much needed. I have time away from the turmoil that is keeping me stuck.

Reflecting on this situation, I know my intuition had guided and saved me many times. It is time to look more into my intuition and trust it.

How can you trust life, when you don't trust people?; when you've been let down so often and when your parent abandoned you? I remember a time when I was left at the park by myself as a child. How can you come back from a time when the one you love abandons you?

At the retreat, I begin the much-needed work on healing the abandonment I so strongly feel. I need proof that there's something bigger than we've ever known or realised. Spookily enough, it all comes up. From regular electrics sparking out, showers turning on before stepping in, banging and so on.

During these episodes, I work on my new ideas and venture. *I am apprehensive and afraid, yet refuse to give up on myself, on my path to freedom.*

Here's a tale of serendipity. Driving back to the U.K., I happen to miss the ferry. Having extra time gives me the opportunity in Normandy to read about the history of D-Day. Little do I know that D-Day is not just about the war. It occurs to me it's about starting or ending something so you can have a clear pathway to possibilities that are exciting and new after great sadness.

As I sit on the beach, watching the swimmers in the sea, I contemplate a new future. The journey, however, is going to be on troubled waters.

The bailiffs have been around again, but this time my husband lets them in. I take action and call a debt relief company. This is the first step to recovery and freedom.

At this point, I am afraid to be at home, afraid to answer the door, I just want to be away, so I do not have to face the truth. I feel shame, judgement and disgust at myself while having a smiley persona. I am genuinely wearing a great mask.

I cry to my friend Jackie, I am at breaking point. I feel like a clock is rewinding to my psychosis times. I want out. I want not to be here. I feel everyone is better off without me.

What happens when you ask for change? You get it. Only if you let go and trust the journey.

Do you ever ask? Have you ever experienced serendipity when something pops up to lead the way?

Another stepping stone appears. This challenge allows me to look into the way I think about life and how money can appear in different ways.

At the time we need heating and my beautiful parents-in-law gift us with the means to buy a much-needed heating system. I'm genuinely thankful for them and my mum. They've aided us to get through the bad times while moving forward.

Tasha Chen, Money Attraction entrepreneur, guides me to see the real power of gratitude. Being grateful for where I am now and what I do have. I'm truly blessed to be writing this for you, now.

As little things start to appear from this challenge, I begin to delve into Tasha's money program with excellent results. But something is missing. Another phenomenal woman, Kezia Luckett, enters my life, and I have a wonderful call with her. Her words will always mean so much to me.

"It's generational Trina; look at your family lineage. How can you change this? Break that cycle?"

Kezia connects me to Etta Mae for a planetary reading. Thoughts of my dad arise from her words. There is a 'masculine dominance' over me. The negative energy manifests in the way I act out, with anger, cutting people out my life and no words.

From October through November, my feelings of rejection grow stronger. I want to see my dad. I ask a friend how I go about finding him. Dark thoughts enter my mind, and I decide to leave it because I don't want to upset my mum. Here I am again putting others before me. I am learning that my feelings are the ones that have to come first.

My friend Yvonne invites me to a pub I used to go to as a child for her 'spirit night'. My intuition just says, "You are here for another reason." I push the thought away and enjoy the night.

As the night goes on, it is amazing to hear what the readings mean for all the people there. You may not believe in spiritual things; however, certain times in life are unexplainable. "Why do you need an explanation of everything?" says the Spirit Guide. Her words are spot on.

At the end of the evening, my friend says: "I'll meet you outside." As I walk out of the pub, I see him. He is sitting down. He has glasses on, and his black afro hair is flecked with grey, over brown skin. He holds a walking stick and wears a blue coat. My heart yearns. It is him!

I carry on walking outside; however, I look back to see him watching me. I decide to speak to Yvonne, so I go back inside the pub.

.

Seeing the look on my face, she knows.

"It's your dad, isn't it? "Then she says something profound.

"You don't have to speak to him" she reminds me.

I do not want to speak to him yet, there is a pull, and I decide to walk out. As I glance through the window, I see it, for a split second, I see vindictiveness on his face. There is something not quite right.

For the next week, I drink seven to ten bottles of wine. I have a deep self-hatred and loathing. I feel pain in my mid-back muscles, which are connected to rejection. I am hurt. I decide to write a Facebook post about this; the support from everyone is unbelievable. However, I am hurt.

A beautiful soul, Penny Bryant, reaches out with a few NLP (neuro-linguistic programme) sessions. Who knew that this connection would lay to rest something that has been with me for such a long time? Deep-rooted anger.

Penny teaches me to connect and speak to my inner child, so I can explain to my younger sense (as an adult), that when adults become parents it can change people. At the same time, my husband provides further insight from the male perspective of parenting that it's not always easy when people are young and become parents.

It is like a massive weight off my shoulders. My pain stops. My drinking drastically reduces overnight, and the break away makes me realise how much I have been hiding inside.

No one knows what I am experiencing, except those who are close to me. The real impact of getting outside into nature and fresh air always does me the world of good. All that monkey chatter, all that mind chatter, comes out. It can only hide in my head the more I stay inside. I feell a massive shift. I say to my husband, I could give up everything I'm working for, just to be outdoors.

He suggests, "Why don't you take your work outdoors then? Show others the benefits it has on your mental health and well-being."

As being outdoors had always helped me. I start to trust and listen to my intuition more.

The more I hear those words in my head and acknowledge them rather than ignore them, the more the right people and the right places come into my life.

This injects a new lease of life into my attiude towards my work. Everything has brought me to my biggest challenge yet - my own darkness, my own shadows.

I have been the bully, the controlling person, the liar, the person of pity. How can someone love me when I've done these things?

What have I learned? It is vital that you love yourself first. Leave everything behind from childhood, all the abandonment of life and start anew. Start a brand new relationship with yourself and with others. People and opportunities will turn up exactly when you need them.

Three things come to mind; forgiveness, awareness and beauty of self. Be aware of the self-doubt, self-talk, self-pity and take action. You may find that you move forward one day and take a step back the next. It's all about moving forward and refusing to give up on you, while on the path to freedom. That journey begins with healing yourself first, lighting the road with hope not only for yourself but for others.

Dedication:

I dedicate this chapter to my mum, in-laws and everyone who aided us with support. I am truly grateful and blessed to have you all in my life.

∞

With a sharp intake of breath you have finished reading Trina's story.

She has detailed her roller coaster journey since Voices of Courage with great humility and honesty. Trina knows the power of letting go those feelings and experiences that do not serve you as you strive to reach a higher dimension on this earthly journey.

With a new found philosophy and responsibility to herself, she continues to show to others the significance and power of honouring yourself. She is learning to put her needs first so that she can better serve her family and those who are blessed to work with Trina.

She is a woman in business on a big mission to make a difference in the world. With great tenacity and persistence I know that Trina will achieve her goals sooner than she thinks.

Brenda Dempsey
Creator & Editor

HOPE

BE THE LIGHT

The Art of Feminine Beauty

SELF OF ALL

We are all One. The same Self is in all. So start with your Self.

You deserve to give your best, to be your best, to do your best and to have the best.

Put your Self first and you will be vibrant, healthy, wealthy, happy and fulfilled. Your purpose will unfold and your life will have greater meaning.

You are only ever in competition with yourself. Focus on letting your light shine through. Do what it takes to go beyond all negativity and disempowerment.

Others benefit when you are at your best. Live your Truth and aim for greatness. Live the Sacred and live Love.

Kindness in words creates confidence

Kindness in thinking creates profoundness

Kindness in giving creates love

Make Yourself Great, Others Even Greater

Stand in your strength, clarity and power and allow others to do the same. Aim to assist them so that they are even greater. Let the world evolve into the positive and abundant place it is meant to be.

Your life is your legacy. It is the gift of your life's purpose. A native American belief says that anything we do now has an effect for seven generations. What effect will you have?

Women Of The World

We are all connected. We are all of the same Divine Essence. Unify your intention with the flame of love in every woman's heart. Be a beacon for other women to reach their spiritual goals.

SPIRITUAL PRACTICE: Plan your legacy for the next generation. How can your life contribute right now to a better world? What would you like to leave behind for the next generation and beyond? Take the first step towards this legacy. Reconnect each day with that intended legacy and act on it.

SPIRITUAL SECRET: 'I am that that Thou art'

Excerpt from 'Gorgeous all Over - a daily guide for women with spirit' by Indira Kennedy

VOICES OF HOPE

Emma Greenslade - Gloucestershire, UK

I Am Good Enough
Just as I AM

Emma Greenslade has enjoyed the finer things in life. She travelled and lived overseas basking in the fruits of her labours.

Sometimes in life we are dealt a bad hand and turmoil and challenges walk into our lives to teach us a lesson.

Emma's determination and resilience to create a better life back in the UK soon was the battle she would win.

One of the lessons we can all benefit from, is the realisation that Emma experienced that we can only live life for ourselves. This is a tale of such understanding and the gifts that we are given as part of the despair we can face on our journey of life.

Brenda Dempsey
Creator & Editor

Transformation #18

I Am Good Enough
Just as I Am

Emma Greenslade

Business Mentor

"Learn to get in touch with the silence within yourself, and know that everything in life has a purpose. There are no mistakes, no coincidences; all events are blessings given to us as a lesson"

Elizabeth Kubler-Ross

Imagine a country that is really hot most of the year, then add layers of different smells – perhaps cooking, vehicle fumes, incense, dust, now a mix of sounds and sights, hooting horns, people shouting, cows mooing, dogs yapping, motorbikes, rickshaws, lorries, cars, buses; now the final sense of knowing you are in your spiritual home. This country is an assault dance of the senses and one that I enjoyed for eight exciting and challenging years. This chapter is a story of my time in incredible India.

I arrived in Mumbai on Gandhi's birthday in 2007 with my only daughter at the time. At the airport, my ex-husband and his friend came to meet us. Having decided to move to Goa so 'he' could be the main-bread-winner, I could now do my 'job' of being Mum to our child while I escaped capital gains tax back in the UK. We had chosen Goa on a whim due to the expat community, Christian faith, fantastic food and a place where we could do what we knew best – refurbishing property. Unfortunately, that was soon to be a non-starter, the rules around foreigners owning property were changing!

The husband insisted we take all our belongings to India. We managed to find a large house, a run-down sprawling, old Portuguese property that would accommodate all furniture from our five bedroomed coaching Inn back home.

While we were waiting for our container to arrive from the UK, we stayed in an apartment in Panaji, the central city of Goa; here we found I was expecting our second child.

This pregnancy was the first of many challenges, as I felt sick for its duration. Nausea in itself was rather debilitating, the sight of food, let alone the smell had me feeling sick; added to that the heat saw a reduction in weight at a terrific speed. With C-section births fashionable and costly, finding a doctor and nurses that spoke my language, physically and emotionally this was difficult, but finally, with six weeks to go, I was led to a German midwife who owned the Natural Birthing Centre. Fortunately, daughter number 2 arrived with ease, while her older sister looked on; a treasured moment that she still talks about today - the baby stuck her head out, made a funny face and licked her lips - during the monsoon of 2008.

I felt blessed as I had a maid for cleaning, a nanny for the eldest and a chef for cooking – being Mum to my newborn was a doddle compared to my first experience in the UK.

I mentioned that I was in India to avoid paying CGT (capital gain tax). I needed to be non-resident of the UK for five years. I had an extensive property portfolio of which half had been sold off.

There is a lot of back-story to this entire tale, however, for the main point of this story, in short, is to remember the Credit Crunch of 2008.

Due to having funding with an Icelandic Bank, I remember in 2008 I required a large sum of money to 'get-out-of-it'. Cast your mind back to my feeling sick, with a 5-hour time difference to the UK, I found myself often working till midnight, managing the remainder of the property and juggling money in the bank accounts. Finally, I found a new mortgage for a bulk of estate; rents were not covering the mortgages, we already had a deficit, so the money I had 'saved' from CGT avoidance was quickly dwindling.

As a result of not buying property 'he' decided to do something outside of his expertise, something he only knew of, by us frequenting some of the best establishments in the world – he decided to open a restaurant!

I gave him a budget of £35,000; this convinced him it was going to work.

While I had my eye off the ball, he maxed out my credit cards, spent three times the budget which resulted in me having several properties re-possessed; I needed to sell investments quickly for under-market valuation. The upshot of this serious squandering is I lost my business and culminated a multiple 6-figure debt – ALL in my name.

Our marriage ended. And my ex-husband flew into the sunset!

This story is not about me being a victim; although it occurred many a day, it's about strength and resilience; when we fall so low, the steps we take to empower ourselves, our children and our community are most important.

I started taking small steps and addressing the things I could change while letting go of the things I couldn't. Now, this didn't all happen immediately nor according to the list but for months, even years. I could do nothing about the bailiffs. I couldn't pay my UK phone bill, so they naturally stopped. I could do something about the furniture shop aka the home; therefore I created piles of stuff that wasn't needed, wasn't beautiful, or I didn't like (probably the first sale consisted of everything to do with my ex-husband!) to sell in a series of 'house and yard sales'. My belongings proved popular after named 'imports', and the sales were extremely well attended; by keeping the prices low I was able to clear the majority as well as making the much-needed income to feed my children.

After a trip to the UK to buy new visas, I had an epiphany one morning 'I don't want to feel like this anymore'; the night before I had only drunk a couple of bottles of beer, but I felt lousy, I woke up on my eldest's bed in the cool of the air-conditioning. The girls were watching TV, the voice was so distinct,

255

'I don't want to feel this way anymore' - it was the day I stopped drinking alcohol, coffee, smoking cigarettes and taking drugs. It was the day that I decided to get clean on the inside, and I had spent so much time looking outside that now was the time to look inside.

We know that we are here for a purpose, we know that life happens for us not to us but in the depth of our pity-party, it's genuinely challenging to start finding the light to guide our journey.

You see, I was adopted, I was always told how lucky I was: I didn't feel it; I thought I must be so unwanted, unloved and unworthy that I had to be given away. Now I can rationalise these feelings and thoughts, but as I grew up, there was a series of making friends and then running away from them before I got too attached. It was the same for my boyfriends, keeping them at arm's-length, not letting them in too far but co-dependent on being good enough for them, people-pleasing to be accepted, as well as approved.

I am good enough, just as I am.

No one can tell you this, you have to feel it, believe it and live it.

Embarking on the journey of 'operation clean-up' I learnt more about myself, about what gives me pleasure (and pain), who I needed to surround myself with, and how I desire to feel. I set about making all these things happen, and when I became true to myself, my self-worth began to flourish, my net-worth improved as my spiritual gifts began to re-establish and I listened to the quiet voice inside (my intuition). I manifested teachers into my life that helped me along my path. As my body and mind cleared, I could ask questions and answers would appear, I became in-tune with nature.

During the monsoon, to cool off, we used to swim in the local quarry, we had to walk across old foundations. As I was walking one particular afternoon I wondered to myself if snakes were in the water – seconds later a giant water snake swam past me just to let me know he had heard me!

It was this same monsoon, after a three-month sojourn to Himachal Pradesh, that the children's father came in August to take them to the UK for a holiday; they were due to return at the end of September 2012.

The next morning, I received an email from the children's father informing me he was not bringing them back to Goa. He had registered them in school and told the school I was coming to live in the UK! He gave a plethora of terrible excuses and wouldn't let me speak to them. They were 4 and 8 years old. The day after this, divorce papers arrived with horrible reasons for him divorcing me. I was stunned. I was in shock. I had been nervous about letting him take them, but he had assured me there was nothing to worry about, and he would bring them back! It was an anxious wait for businesses to open in the UK, and as soon as 9 am GMT arrived, I spoke with my solicitor who informed me it might take years to get them back and cost in the region of six figures.

I didn't have that sort of money, let alone the resources to stay in the UK while we fought in the courts. Not being able to see my children was excruciating. He was telling me I was a bad mother, and that awful feeling of not being enough came back with wrecking-ball force, I didn't think I had any more power to fight him. I resigned myself to the fact that I may not be able to get my children back; what would my life look like not being a Mother? After a couple of hours, I reached my senses – no way! I set about devising a plan to get to England and into court.

I was fortunate to be guided to a lady who arrived back to Goa after experiencing a similar situation with her children; she told me what I needed to do, she gave me the name of the judge along with the solicitor she used.

Within a week the plan was set. I left in the afternoon for a short flight to Mumbai, then overnight to Heathrow, arriving into the UK early morning. With no-sleep I trundled my flight-bag across London to the court and booking into having an audience with the Judge of choice. The next stop was the solicitors to prepare my claimant documents with its 26 exhibits. I was set for my court appearance two days later. Within ten days, I had my children back!

During this time, I was staying in South London, travelling between north and south. I noticed how the majority of citizens were zoning-out, escaping, stressed, oppressed, even depressed, uncaring and rude. They looked trapped in a life of surviving not thriving. I have also been that person!

My intuition guided me to learn a new way of helping and serving people, so I used the next few years to learn many healing modalities. I became certificated as a business coach, money coach, health coach; if I were interested in making something better for myself then I would undertake training in it - I still do.

While growing-up we experience unpleasant events, perhaps trauma, people may say negative things that upset us. Experiencing being at school for getting the question wrong or even just for our surname; these circumstances force us to dim our lights, and sometimes turn-off all together; so as adults, we want to escape from the low-vibe feelings inside.

Negativity can manifest in a plethora of ways, just as it did for me: overeating, binging on alcohol, exercising excessively, watching TV, taking drugs as well as working too hard. The escapisms are endless.

My passion is to free my clients, so they lead a high-vibe glowing life with all the success they desire. I have the hindsight from marriage; I was following my ex-husband's dreams and desires, which were different from mine! Although I was successful, I wasn't in alignment with this type of success. Success is so different to everyone; it doesn't require fancy cars or loads of zeros at the end of the savings account. How do you rate your success? It could be having a nice car, a good career and a holiday each year. Or it could be travelling the world. Perhaps yours is helping people with an NGO or charity?

If we are not aware of our dreams and desires, how do we know we have arrived? What is it YOU genuinely want? What is the big why of your desire? What would you do if money was no object?

My big why is to empower women to be the best version of themselves they can be while accepting themselves just as they are – perfect! They learn to be willing and able to acknowledge their self-worth! To give themselves approval and permission to be all of who they are! To let go of fear to be ruled by love.

When women recognise their greatness, they can transform their family, their community, their business and the ripple keeps going on and on. Especially to the next generation. All it starts with is a desire and a decision to make a change.

Dedication:

I dedicate this chapter to my beautiful daughters, without their support this journey would have been very different.

∞

Emma's story illustrates that we can never take things for granted in life. Even if everything seems perfect, if we do not live for us then lessons are learned the hard way.

With great resilience and determination, Emma found a way to overcome the hurdles she faced as her marriage fell apart when she lived in India. Unafraid, she found a way back to the UK to create a new life for her and her children.

Her lesson is never to be afraid of losing everything for the universe has a way of bringing you more and better riches than before when you live in a world as you.

Brenda Dempsey
Creator & Editor

VOICES OF HOPE

Aviv Ortal - Israeli, living in USA

Life Isn't Worth Living in Fear

From the moment Aviv shared her story I was captivated by her inner beauty. Her journey to saying 'yes' to becoming a co-author is a story in itself.

It wasn't until I received the manuscript from Aviv that the extent of the trauma she endured came to light. Despite the pain she suffered, like all beautiful souls she would seek to find an escape from the life she was living.

It was during this quest that she found her strength to stand up for herself and grasp the spark of hope that presented itself to her.

Having reached the point of 'enough is enough' she found her voice and from that day has never looked back. She has used writing as a medium to help her heal and reach out to other women who find themselves in her shoes.

Brenda Dempsey
Creator & Editor

Transformation #19

Life Isn't Worth Living in Fear

Aviv Ortal

Author and Mentor

"Times are changed, we are also changed with them."

Latin Adage

A very smart friend of mine told me that in my past but I didn't understand it until now.

I grew up in the Middle East in a conservative family. In general, life was good for me. My parents gave us all we needed; food, clothes and money, but we never talked openly about sex, nudity or our body. We didn't even speak about the big world out there; for some reason, it was taboo. We were expected to keep quiet. I believed being forbidden to talk about so many things as part of our religion and society that they wanted to keep us in a safe bubble.

I married in 2008. I was very young, inexperienced and innocent. Our marriage was a match between our parents; they met first, then we did. Initially, we didn't like each other at all. We weren't right for each other, but on the second date he didn't leave me for a second. My mom told me, "He is from a good family, and you can't buy that in the grocery store. You have to try. Love disappears after a few years, but friendship can build with time."

We started dating; in the beginning everything was perfect. This man was very nice to me; he told me that he worked in real estate in a different country. It all felt magical to me. It felt like I won the jackpot. I had found a good guy from a good family with money. What else could I ask?

I gave up a good government job and moved to another town where he decided we would live. It was not the same. I felt that I was giving up my career for him but for us, I was willing to give up everything and change my profession.

Slowly he told me that my childhood friends did not fit my lifestyle and that I was better than them. He told me that it was not right for me to go out alone with my girlfriends because other guys can talk to me or look at me cheaply. As we were now together, this lack of respect was unacceptable as I was his girlfriend. He even made me believe that my family was against me, that my brothers and sisters were jealous of me. Step by step the isolation began - the removal to another city, the exclusion from the family and friends; total isolation from what I knew.

The isolation and the brain washing continued. It felt good in the beginning to know that someone needed me so much and that I meant the world to him. Today I know it all was a lie.

After about a year we were married. When I told him I was pregnant he started to change. I thought he would protect me but he didn't. After I gave birth to the baby, and it was a difficult delivery, I felt like I went to the hospital with one husband and came back home with different one.

I was in my early 20s when I had my first child. I felt like a little girl myself. The pain, the hormones and the changes in my body left me very weak, physically and mentally. It was a challenging to realize that I'm responsible for another life.

The mental abuse worsened. I had no voice in my own home, no opinion or decision. He started to yell and treat badly. I was so afraid. I felt like I was walking on egg shells in my house and that every wrong word triggered him. He would tell me that I was nothing, that I was worthless.

As the years went by things worsened, and after the second child, I started to realize that I did not exist in our marriage, that it was only him. I was there to please him, but as a person, as a wife, as a human being, my feelings meant nothing. I was begging for someone to hear my voice.

I was married but felt so alone most of the time even when he was with me.

After nine years of marriage I had had enough. I was fed up with waking up in the morning and feeling nothing and everything I did was not appreciated. I was screamed at, cursed and humiliated. I had no close family, no friends, nothing. He had turned me into nothing.

My mom was the first person to create a change in me. We started to talk more on the phone and she asked me to get rid of the hair cover and buy a lipstick. My mom told me, "Every morning when you wake up brush your teeth, wash your face, fix your hair and put lipstick on then look in the mirror and say "I am beautiful!" she insisted. "DO IT! Even if you feel ridiculous DO IT! No matter what, don't stop."

I started to make a change from the outside but I didn't know what impact it would have on my inside. When the kids were over a year old we put them in to daycare. Finally I went to work where I met other parents and quickly began to understand how unhealthy my relationship was.

I asked for a divorce; he did not agree. Our families did not agree with us and asked us to try to "Mishna Makom - Mishna Mazal" which means that when you relocate, your luck will change so we moved to a different continent. A fresh and clean start, I thought to myself; maybe we'll start again I can forgive him if he changes for our children and for the sake of the family.

I remember on the plane I took a deep breath and said I was leaving everything behind, that I was flying to a new place with fresh air and a new beginning.

We were supposed to be in his parents' house for three months. In the end we lived there for a year and a half, during which for the first time in my life, I was exposed to his family. I suffered disrespect in this house in all kinds of ways and my husband did nothing to protect me as a woman and as his wife.

One day, I decided to fill myself with dancing. Music was always part of my childhood house especially belly dancing, as the music goes through my soul and fills it with life.

I remember I had a show; I was so nervous. For me it was a very big deal because I had a fear of performing but I told myself it is a chance of a lifetime so I went with it. I invited him and the kids, I was so excited so I bought tickets and told him to be there at 6:30 pm when the show started.

All the time when I was backstage he kept texting me to say how terrible the music sounded. I remember sitting there looking at my phone feeling all those mixed emotions and said to myself, "He will not ruin the one thing I had, the one thing I worked so hard and I am worth it." There was something extremely scary about it but also empowering; for you and the audience.

The loud clapping brought me back to reality. I'm there on stage breathing heavily after dancing for three and a half minutes –posing, looking, searching but no husband, no kids, only disappointment!

It was the last show, all the dancers came up on stage receiving flowers, hugs and taking family pictures… and me? I was standing there alone wanting to cry. I'm so alone, surrounded with people but feeling so alone.

I went to the restroom and looked at myself in the mirror "You did it! I'm so proud of you, you got out from your safe zone - you broke the rules - you are a winner! " This moment was my little victory.

That night when I arrived home, I didn't sleep in our bed. I went to sleep with the kids. Finally, I understood that no matter what I did or happened, he would never understand.

I asked for so long to go to therapy and he said that nothing was wrong with him, that the only problem was me. I started therapy by myself. In the beginning I thought maybe I can do it and work on our relationship by doing it alone but as the therapy kept going I realized that I didn't want to fix "us" because there's no "us" and there never was - it was always and will be "Him" only. It dawned on me that I was in an abusive relationship with a narcissist and emotional sociopath that no matter what I did, he would see only himself.

After I received notice of the death of my grandfather I realized how far away I was from my family. I felt so hopeless that I couldn't do anything. I experienced some emotional breakdown. I remember sitting down looking at the tree in my backyard and thinking I could be dead tomorrow and my life has just past by without living, breathing only. I told him I was sad and I asked for his understanding but his reaction was unbelievable.

I was shocked and I understood that he didn't care about me as his wife or even as a person. During these moments of good or bad, sick or health, life of death, I was alone! That is when I knew I had had enough. I started to think about a life without him or not next to him. We barely talked after this occasion. When he came to the house at 6:30 pm I would go out to the gym or see friends that I met and he didn't liked them of course. If I stayed in the house it would usually end with him yelling, screaming and insulting me, then him wanting sex.

After I discovered I had contracted HPV, the doctor said I needed to have surgery as soon as possible. He didn't believe me when I told him. Again it was all about him - he said to me, "You're just saying it because you don't want to have sex with me! That's an excuse!" At that moment in my life I wasn't afraid of him anymore and told him, "I don't want to have sex with you. You see me as an object to use when you need. You don't love me; you never did it really was a convenience for you that I'm with the kids, working, cleaning the house as well as doing the laundry, a babysitter and provide you with sex!" He demanded that I get a letter from the doctor explaining my situation.

That day I moved all my stuff to my little son's room. I slept there until I left the house.

After the surgery, my two best friends took care of me; I don't know how I would have survived without them. When I went back home barely able to walk, he didn't even look at me.

Shortly after the surgery I became stronger, found a job and looked for a house without him knowing. I acquired a driving licence and opened my own bank account. I started for the first time to be independent.

One day when he was barking at me like a dog I noticed my kids' faces. I knew that it was not healthy for them anymore; it's not just about me but them too. I took some clothes for them and went to sleep at my friend's house. That day I put the kids in school and went to claim for a divorce at court. He freaked out when he received it but from that moment on, five months later, it was over - I was free!

For the first time in my life I had choices in life - I chose me first! Finally I had a voice even to decorate the house my way, with my voice!

The first morning I made myself a coffee and sat outside on the rocking chair. The sun was warm and the birds were singing. I took a deep breath and I smiled my first real smile in a while. I felt free just like those birds around me.

My journey of a life filled with mental, spiritual, sexual and financial abuse made me who I am today. I am a really strong woman who knows to say NO and does not please anyone. I am who I am, and I love myself with all my flaws.

My kids are happier as I showed them a mom that does not compromise on anything less than good, a mom that was attentive to her emotions and walked away when she felt that it was not okay; that she deserved better.

Now my kids and I have the most amazing conversations which are open and able to talk about bodies, sex, life, and emotions. The most amazing part of my journey is I found a new love in my life. I found out that when you meet the one you don't need words to communicate, but when you do talk it's the most amazing deep conversation ever. I found out that I'm very sexy women and I didn't know about making love until I met my new guy. I found out that to have someone that raises and supports you whenever you need it that true real love can heal even the most broken soul.

I learned to say "I love you", I learned to appreciate myself as a woman, as a mom, as a person - that I do matter, that I am good and that I can affect other people's lives.

Today I'm helping other women in my old situation. I was amazed to see how many women there are out there who are afraid and don't know how even to start to break free. I'm always telling them ,

"I'm living proof that there is a better way and there is something good waiting for you out there."
I know that every journey in this life, starting with one little step, will start a wonderful journey.

Remember - We came to this world to LIVE not only to breathe.

Dedication:

I dedicate my work to the most important people in my life- my mom, who was an important part of my awakening - my kids and my love. It is with the help of them I found my voice and my way- I love you guys more than you ever know.

As a young naive young woman shaped by her culture and up-bringing, Aviv unwittingly subsumed the limiting beliefs of her family and heritage. Deep within her stirred a longing for something more when she realised that life is not meant to be lived in pain but rather it is to be lived in joy.

This deep intuitive knowing enabled her to find a new way of living and now free, she uses writing to allow her to connect with other women who are walking in her shoes.

Brenda Dempsey
Creator & Editor

VOICES OF HOPE

Janet Groom - from Ireland, living in Switzerland

Power of Words

Janet's warmth greets you from the moment you meet her. Undeniably, her love of books radiates out from every pore hiding a painful secret that she is coming to terms with.

She embraces her joy of writing books and now works with others to inspire them to connect within and find their story.

Living in the mountains is a great place to let your creative side loose and from her log cabin, Janet reaches out to the world with her podcast show 'The Write Word'.

In her powerful story, Janet finds the right words to express her shock at finding out life changing news as a young woman. Having worked through her trauma, she is ready to reveal her story to you today.

Brenda Dempsey
Creator & Editor

Transformation#20

Power of Words

Janet Groom

Author & Book Coach

"Words have the power
to both destroy and heal.
When words are both
true and kind, they can
change our world."

Buddha

Words have always been important to me. Words shape us – the wrong words bring us down, while the right words raise us up. The tales we tell ourselves impact our lives in so many ways. Sometimes for good, yet sometimes they hold us back from following our dreams, leaving many of us stuck in a rut of self-sabotage, low self-esteem and lack of enthusiasm for the joys of life.

I used to be like that, with a torrent of anger and hatred directed at myself. I allowed fear to keep me in the small box the world had put me in, suppressing my dreams and shutting down my heart to numb the pain. There were periods of depression when the darkness would swallow me up, and yet I managed to keep struggling on. Forcing myself to drag me through the daily grind of life as I felt I owed people something. In reality, never thinking for a second of what I owed myself. At these times, my self-talk was critical and self-destructive.

I was an expert at admonishing myself, allowing any external criticism to re-enforce my lack of self-worth. My head was awash with negative thoughts and a never-ending critique. I remember a boss once told me I was my own worst enemy, and now I would agree. My personal thoughts and beliefs were indeed destroying me from the inside out. I was never good enough. My healing journey is an on-going process, peeling away the layers and working through the limiting beliefs that hold me back. It is a step-by-step approach to healing the pain, transforming my mindset and shifting ideas which no longer serve my highest purpose. I am a 'work-in-progress'. With each new layer of healing, I move forward with clarity, stepping into my truth. To me, it is a similar process to removing the outer layer of carbon to reveal the diamond hidden within.

Allow me to share two of my 'old stories'. Stories which I had clung on to for far too long.

Old Stories and Traumas

I grew up in Northern Ireland at the height of the civil unrest, known as 'The Troubles'. It was a time when the news was filled with daily shootings and bombings. It was a war zone with police checkpoints and armed soldiers on the streets. This was the norm.

As a highly sensitive child, it was genuinely confusing and terrifying. I could not make sense of the world around with messages inciting hatred and violence. It was too much for my young mind to cope with, and I turned to books for comfort.

Books and stories really were my saving grace. They would allow me to escape the horrors of the real world and transport me to realms of majestic beauty filled with wonder and magic. Fantasy adventures were my sanctuary.

Any chance I got, I would disappear with a book in hand, often I could be found sitting up a tree reading, or hidden away making up my own stories in my head. I devoured books. Books provided me with a sense of security that I found lacking in the 'real' world. Engrossed in a story was my safe place, and I often wished that I would wake up and find out that the 'real' world has been a bad dream and my actual life was one of a courageous princess adventurer, sword in hand, on a quest to rid the realm of evil monsters.

It is only in recent years, I have come to recognise how traumatic my childhood was, and I suspect that I suffer from mild symptoms of Post-Traumatic Stress Disorder (PTSD). There have been times over the years when loud bangs have triggered that deep-seated fear, casting me back to being that terrified child again. Fortunately, for me, I found my way to alternative healing techniques and now have a 'toolbox' at hand to help me cope. With my training as a Neuro-Linguistic Programming & Hypnosis Practitioner and Life Coach, I have found several ways I can support myself when the next level of healing is required.

Growing up in Northern Ireland is only one of the stories which affected my life for a long time. In my mid-twenties, I was hit with another massive blow, one that severely impacted my life for almost three decades.

At the time I was living in London, following my return from an overseas posting to Paris with the British Foreign & Commonwealth Office. My time in Paris has been filled with friends, parties, Champagne and a role I really enjoyed at one of the most prestigious embassies. Paris was a fabulous city, and I had loved the experiences presented; from meeting HM The Queen to strolling through the leafy boulevards by the Seine on a balmy summer's evening. My new role was back in Whitehall, and I had earned promotion to a junior diplomatic position, which was demanding. All was going well, and I was coping with the stress. Unfortunately, I ended up in a relationship, which turned unpleasant, with a guy who ended up threatening me.

Balancing the demands of the job and the on-going threats were exhausting. I am not proud to admit I was so petrified that I slept with a kitchen knife under my pillow.

Around this time, I was referred by my GP to investigate my lack of periods. Personally, I had considered not having periods a blessing, one less hassle in my life.

It feels like yesterday, sitting in the consultant's office, waiting for the results of the various tests. The lady consultant shuffled into the room with a nurse hot on her heels. She was brusque with her delivery of the results and diagnosis and avoided eye contact. Amongst the onslaught of medical jargon, one word stood out. A word I recognised, but yet it was alien to me – MENOPAUSE.

The consultant then got up and left the room, leaving me bewildered and confused. Surely menopause was something to do with older women. At this point, the nurse moved her chair closer to mine and slowly explained what the consultant had failed to say. She had kind eyes and spoke softly with great compassion.

As I struggled to make sense of what she was telling me, she explained that I had suffered 'Primary Ovarian Failure', which meant my ovaries had stopped working. They suspected that a viral infection had triggered my autoimmune system to overreact and attack my ovaries. Basically, I had gone through puberty, then menopause in my teens.

My ovaries were dried up – dead. I was barren. I was offered no psychological support to deal with the impact of this news.

I went home to my empty flat and tried to put a brave face on, forcing myself to get up every day and face the daily routine of life. I told no-one as I grappled to make sense of it all. I was in shock. I would never have the family I always wanted. I hated my own body for letting me down. I didn't feel like a real woman. I was angry and hurt. A short time later, I suffered a breakdown. Between the stress in my job culminating with the abuse from my ex-boyfriend, it was all too much. The pain and grief were unbearable. I spiralled down the rabbit hole into the black abyss. How do you come to terms with such news? I didn't – for a very long time.

Family and friends tried to be supportive, but it was difficult as there was just no precedence. I quickly learned it was not a topic I could openly talk about as it made people too uncomfortable.

After a period of recuperation, I returned to work in London, discovering the only way I could carry on was to shut down my feelings. I numbed the pain by building a wall around my heart. My zest for life was crushed. I was a zombie living a half-life.

Over the ensuing years, it was tough to watch as my friends and siblings had their own children. Each time I would hear the news of another pregnancy and birth, it felt like a knife stabbing me a little deeper into my heart. Again, I adapted to the demands of the outside world and wore my 'happy Janet face', as no-one wished to witness my pain.

Time to Heal

When I met and married my wonderful husband, we embarked on living an expat life. It was a period of fun and excitement, exploring new lands and new cultures. We began married life in Singapore, where I love the exotic melee of East meets West; returning to London for some years before jetting off to America. What only supposed to have been an eighteen-month assignment in the US, turned into four years. As our time drew to a close, we had planned to return to the UK to put down roots. It had been a great adventure travelling the world, and now we agreed it was time to settle down; to put some roots down.

As we neared the end of our time, we set about making our arrangements to return home, the world was rocked by the 2008 Financial Crisis — it rocked our world too. My husband no longer had a job in the US, and there were no more extended job opportunities in the UK. As an expat spouse, I also had no job and no income. A lifeline was thrown to us with the offer of a role in Zurich, Switzerland. Not part of our plans, but we really did not feel we were in a position to turn it down, and so we set off to begin life, yet again, in another foreign country.

I kept telling myself it would only be for a year, everything would quickly sort itself out and we could move back to the UK and build the life we yearned for; to be closer to family and friends, as well as being back to a familiar lifestyle. And more importantly, our chance to grow our family with either IVF or adoption.

A year into my new life, there was no sign of us returning to the UK. It was a harsh realisation for me, and as much as I tried to fight it, I suffered from my second major breakdown. In Switzerland,

I was too old for IVF treatment, and adoption was also out as we were not Swiss.

Once again, my heart was crushed, and any hopes of motherhood slipped away. It was at this point I finally received the counselling support I so desperately needed. This was the turning point in my story. It only took ONE question for me to find the glimmer of HOPE to carry on. The sympathetic psychologist smiled at me and asked:

"What small thing can you choose to do today to make yourself feel good?"

It was a question that made me sit up and think. I never really thought about my own needs or doing things for my own happiness. I was too wrapped up in my own pity-party, and when I wasn't, I was too eager to please other people. It was a question that got me thinking about how I dwelt on my past and worried about my future. It hit home that I never focused on the present moment – the here and now.

I allowed myself to be tied up in the chains of my old stories of pain and suffering, and when I dared to think about the future, I was fearful and anxious.

What a shock to realise that I live through so many moments of my precious life not really being here. As part of my healing, I found my way back to reading and enjoying books again. I fell back in love with the pure pleasure of searching for a quiet spot to enjoy a good book. I read book after book, from fantasy to self-help. Through the discovery of self-development books, a new world revealed itself to me. I was hungry to learn more about mindset and healing, and this led me to study Neuro-Linguistic Programming, Hypnosis, Life Coaching, Energy Healing and many more great healing modalities.

As I mentioned, I now have pulled together my own 'toolbox' which I can delve into whenever another layer of healing is required. I have my own daily rituals to help keep the darkness at bay, and when I stay on track, I feel so much better in myself and the world around me is a more harmonious place.

One of my greatest blessings has been finding my way to fulfilling my dream of writing a book. A dream that has been in my heart since childhood, and I had been sitting with an idea for a fiction novel for over fifteen years, nurturing it in the back of my mind. Finally, giving myself permission to write that book and become a published author, was one of the most liberating decisions in my life.

My first foray into writing fiction was a cathartic experience, drawing upon my old stories and allowing them to be told in a way I could disassociate with them. They became someone else's story in a book. This was a significant step in my healing process – releasing. Opening the door to my creativity allowed my heart to heal and the walls to come tumbling down.

I have now birthed two books, one fiction and one non-fiction, with lots more to come. Writing is my passion. I derive great satisfaction weaving words together like an artist wielding their paintbrush. Another excellent side-effect is the thrill I feel being able also to support other amazing people to share their own incredible stories and books into the world.

I'm not saying that every day is perfect and there are no wobbles – I am saying that I feel so much brighter and when the heaviness starts to descend, I have help at hand to find my way back to the 'light'.

The world can be scary, dark and lonely; and equally, it can be bright and happy. I believe it is our own words and the stories we tell ourselves that make all the difference.

Here are a few of my favourite words that uplift me: Peace, Joy, Love, Compassion, Delight, Calm, Honour, Celebrate, Truth, Healing, Happy, Gratitude, Kindness, Forgiveness, Rest, Wonder, Creativity, Open, Fun, Harmony, Value, Shine, Laughter, Oneness, Abundance, Ease, Flow, Bliss…

What words resonate with you and make you feel lighter and brighter?

I leave you with this thought – are your words and stories serving you in your own life? Do they inspire you to shine?

If not, perhaps it is time to change them and transform your life – allow your words to help you grow wings and soar.

Words have a transformational power – so I implore you to choose your words and stories wisely, after all, they can be life-changing.

Dedication:

To everyone who has found their way through the darkness back to the light, and dares to share their uplifting story into the world; shining a ray of hope out into the darkness, leading lost souls back home.

∞

Having read Janet's story, it is easy to see why she attracts so many incredible people to her podcast.

When you overcome adversity, trauma and life changing news, something deep and meaningful is revealed to you. This 'knowing' creates a hope for a new life. A life that you can express as hopeful and reach out to others to create a ripple effect opening to them a new way of thinking, doing and being.

Janet has turned to the power of words to help her express gratitude for everything she has and experiences. As a Braveheart, she found her courage to take new action and unashamedly sees it through so she can experience a sense of achievement and worth.

As a Book Coach, Janet inspires others to find their words and helps them to use their new-found words to create a new life. After all, words have the power to inspire transformation.

Brenda Dempsey
Creator & Editor

The Art of Feminine Beauty

Mandala Magic

Jaswinder K. Challi Sahiba
Mandala Therapist

Mandala Magic

Dear Mandala,

You are hope and inspiration to my life in so many ways.

Through your creation, I find myself, I lose myself, I surrender myself, and in all of myself you are HOPE.

I create that hope through you in so many different ways, using the elements: stone, flowers, for Earth, water, shells, for emotions and femininity, feathers and incenses for Air, candles for fire. Colours play such a significant part too.

The size, is the Space, the Akash, the circle, the beginning and end of all things, alpha, omega.

All of these are just a glimpse into your uses, and your creation!

Let's not forget the centre, the Bindu, the gateway to the universe, infinite realms, the spirit world, dimensions, galaxies and other universes.

So when I have this rich abundance through you, my magic mandala, I have all the hope for me and others.

Jaswinder K. Challi Sahiba
Mandala Therapist

VOICES OF HOPE

Fiona Clark - Surrey, UK

Hope Was All I Needed

In today's world transition is becoming a common experience. Sometimes it's through choice and then there are those times when it is thrust upon you.

Fiona Clark experienced the latter a number of years ago when her marriage suddenly ended whilst living in the Philippines. After a time of recovery she decided to pack everything up and return to the UK with her two young sons. This was the story Fiona told in Voices of Courage and now is keen to show others how to be resilient and pick yourself back up and create a whole new life even when you feel a foreigner in your own country.

Charting her journey of getting back in the saddle of being a woman in business, Fiona shares her ups and downs of wondering if she will ever enjoy the leve of success she had enjoyed in the Philippines.

Brenda Dempsey
Creator & Editor

Transformation #21

Hope Was All I Needed

Fiona Clark

The Zenergiser, Coach & Healer

'Hope is not something
we do to escape the storm.
Hope is what we hold fast
to endure each wave.'

Fiona Clark

This part of my life's journey begins on my return to the UK from the Philippines after a traumatic marriage breakdown; I was emotionally and physically burnt-out. I had no hope or expectations because I had no idea what was going on. I also had to settle my two boys (aged 14 and 16) into a new way of life.

I felt completely alone. I had moved into an area where I only knew one person. I had no friends, the boys had no friends.

It took me about a year and a half before I began to feel I belonged. I felt like a foreigner. I had left very secure foundations in many ways because I had an excellent network of friends and people around me. I had a successful business which people knew, and it ran on word of mouth. In the Philippines, I was doing workshops, reflexology, coaching and EFT. I was working with anybody and everybody from 17-months to 60, male and female.

I am now back here and have to start all of that all over again. I soon learned that the market here was very different. I soon learned that I HAD to Niche. I didn't know anything about niching. I didn't know anything about funnels. I didn't know anything about online marketing; I didn't know online anything.

It was like walking into a different language, let alone a different country and a different culture even though it was my so-called culture. All of this left me feeling incredibly stressed, empty, numb. I felt very numb as I was still getting myself together. I had my son saying he didn't like his school. My boys were fighting all of the time.

It was now about me finding a new path; a pathway that I didn't have any idea of what direction to take. The first thing that came to mind that I had to do was meet people, so I joined the Yoga studio. I had researched all of this before I moved back to the UK. I joined an excellent health club and met people there. Then I realised that I had to go online. So this is what I did – go online. I started to meet people.

Being online allowed me to connect with different groups, where I joined with more like-minded people, and I started to meet people. I did all this while I found out more about this online world - a world that everyone seemed to be engaging in. Forget about meeting people, although I did take on some workshops at the Yoga Centre, which were okay. It was not my first love, so I wanted to find something more meaningful for me.

As I was not familiar with all of this, I employed a coach from America. The world becomes smaller and being online makes it possible. I worked with her for about six months and it cost me a fortune. I was left feeling befuddled by what she was talking about with Online Programmes, Videos and how to do Facebook ads. I felt out of my depth as it was a completely different language. As I did not fully understand, it left me feeling stuck, overwhelmed with no direction. I was unclear and uncertain, despite all of my years' experience and success. Now I felt entirely like a fraud.

I found myself in a stressful situation and knew that enough was enough. I'm done feeling out of control, and I knew I have to do something different to turn things around.

I would say that it was more of a gradual process than any one thing. It was discovering and beginning to understand more about the online networking, understanding more about funnels and understanding more about Facebook. It seemed to be more about how to do videos. I remember a significant impact on me was joining Peri10K. Joining this group encouraged you to use video to grow your business land; it pushed me outside of my comfort zone. You had to do live videos. It meant you had to have a topic, and be structured, and that terrified me.

The turning point that I undertook was making live videos my focus. I did this for a whole year, which demonstrated my commitment to succeed. I made a lot of live stream videos. I was so committed that I earned my Bronze Badge in using Periscope. This success meant I had achieved doing three videos a week with over 200 views each. Sometimes I would sit there for over an hour and a half to make sure I reached my 200 views. I often told myself, 'I am not leaving this until I get my 200 views.' There was a determination that I was not going to give up until I earned that Bronze Badge. I achieved that goal!

I believe that having experienced everything that challenged me returning to the UK, being determined to succeed in Peri10K, help boost my confidence. I now knew I could make better decisions, use a sound structure and select topics to speak about on video with ease. Peri10K gave me the idea of using the theme with three bullet points about which I could happily talk. This experience was of great value as I had something to guide me. I now knew I could speak on video with high confidence instead of speaking a load of crap. I had more focus.

Another benefit of being part of Peri10K was it allowed me to meet a lot of great people from all around the world. Some of these relationships I built up, continue today where I regularly keep contact.

All of this new online experience, coupled with my years of experience in Manila, allowed me to realise that I have so many skills and techniques. I had started in 1991 as a Kinesiologist, then went on to train in Reflexology, Reiki, Coaching, Theta Healing and Emotional Freedom Technique (EFT). Most people know this as Tapping.

295

It didn't matter who the client was; the main thing was to use all of my skills and techniques in a way that they could then go on and use these themselves. I used to put on workshops in the Philippines for children. I love working with children. It is about how I can inspire them to understand how they can be in control of dealing with their emotions positively. Providing them with the skills and techniques to deal with any future challenges, is my purpose and passion. It's about inspiring people to take responsibility for their health and well-being by using a skill-set that I used to share with them. This understanding started me on the path to discovering how I bring 30 years of experience, training, skills and techniques together to balance body, mind and soul as energy BEings.

Born out of this challenge, came the Energy Balance Approach, through an inspiring mentor called Brenda Dempsey. She is a magical lady with words. She helped me phenomenally with structure, systems and strategy. It is always important to find someone who understands you and can inspire and encourage you when you want to retreat into the cocoon from which the beautiful butterfly emerges.

During the last few years on this journey, I have come to realise that now everyone is talking about 'energy'. I had been working with energy since 1991 when very few people were talking about it.

The vision conjured up was a person with a big flowing gown, looking a bit odd and 'woo woo'.

I had not been talking about energy, and I felt like a closet queen of energy healing. I realised this was a vital part of my work and so I decided to bring it out into the open. Now I talk openly about energy. I even use my Pendulum for spiritual guidance in front of people, something I would not have done a few years ago. Both the Pendulum as well as a movement from my kinesiology, which I call the "Wonder Wave", are easy to share with clients which they can then use for themselves.

The Energy Balance Approach is for anyone who wants to start living more consciously. Living with more awareness of your energy enables you to connect to your Zenergy, instilling a high vibrational state which creates more inner peace and conscious living.

Part of my passion is to encourage people to be free to live a happy life. Happiness is what people want, and I intend to enable them to do this for themselves. It's not a matter of them coming to me once a week while still living in stress

The Energy Balance Approach allows you to connect to your inner knowing, your heart space as opposed to your negative mind chatter, which I call the committee having a conference. This journey enables you to re-vitalise, rejuvenate and renew your energy for your mental health and well-being, including your relationships.

I also know the value of being in the same space as others, and this has allowed me to create a retreat for people who are ready and want to develop their skills to a much deeper level so they can feel happier and freer as a result. It allows them to take a few days out of their busy lives to concentrate on themselves. It gives them the luxury of time to think about themselves and not worry about anyone else. After all, you have to look after you first and foremost before you can effectively care for and give to others.

My story, where I had no hope on my return from Manila, encountered a new language and had to readjust to life once again in the UK, is now where I have once again found a more exciting way of being and living that is full of hope. This knowing puts me in a strong position to share with others who have lost hope and are hiding behind masks, that there are always possibilities, something different and something new. We have to have that curiosity and courage to delve a little bit deeper and never give up.

As many of my clients are entrepreneurs, who can often find themselves stuck, overwhelmed and on the treadmill which creates stress, engaging with the Energy Balance Approach can help them reconnect to their limitless selves and find their Zenergy

Chest of skills and techniques so they can be more energised, happier and free. In this re-vitalised state, they can be more successful within themselves and of course, in business. Zenergy describes perfectly a high-vibrational state of calm, to have free-flowing energy when you can do and be who you are meant to be.

Dedication:

I dedicate this to the beautiful women who have lost all hope, lost a sense of who they are and what they want out of life. Never give up, tomorrow is always another day!

Fiona's story demonstrates how you can find light at the end of the tunnel when you have hope. After having her confidence and self-belief battered and bruised, Fiona is find a way of re-inventing herself.

She has put all of her twenty-five years plus of experience to good use and crafted a new concept of the Energy Balance Approach. Fiona is passionate about sharing her Zenergy Chest of Tools and Techniques to empower others to use them to self heal in times of stress, anxiety and when life just seems to deal you lemons. As she lives using these on a daily basis, she is steadfast in their effectiveness to change people's lives.

Brenda Dempsey
Creator & Editor

VOICES OF HOPE

Indira Kennedy - Australian, living in London, UK

Gorgeous All Over

Indira Kennedy has a calm energy that you can sense whenever she speaks to you.

On reading her story you will see why she lives in this beautiful state which many of us aspire to.

As an Intuitive, she has an inner knowing that allows her to see deep into your soul. You will not be surprised therefore that she has crafted a book called 'Gorgeous All Over' which is also the title of her chapter in this book - Voices of Hope.

Unafraid, she has left her homeland of Australia behind to create a new life for herself in London. It is this trait that motivates her to step up and stand out as she brings her own indomitable spirit to the business world of London and beyond.

Brenda Dempsey
Creator & Editor

Transformation #22

Gorgeous All Over

Indira Kennedy
Author - Speaker -
Conscious Leadership Coach

"I am a child of God, and all is well."

Indira Kennedy

When I was 34, I decided I had to leave an unhappy and unproductive marriage. I believed we would all be happier. I was also determined to raise my children with the standards I desired for them. For me, this meant that divorce did not necessarily have to be difficult and that we would be able to move on to live a very abundant life. As a determined woman, I knew this had to be. At this time, there was still much judgement around divorce because of the sacredness of marriage vows and the guilt and challenge of breaking them. The view around this was brought home to me when a 'close' friend said, "How dare you be happy; you are breaking up a marriage and you have no right to be happy about that." I found these words to be extraordinary.

I know I have always been a bit of a left-field thinker. I tend to go for untraditional things, but I deeply value happiness. We deserved a good life.

The other thing too was that I was raised in an unconventional family, in that we are all incredibly intuitive with the belief that there is another part of our world that we can't see. I trusted my intuition.

I had a Scottish grandmother who took me out to talk to fairies in the garden. She would quietly take me out to the bottom of the garden and say, "Can you hear the fairies talking here Dear?"

Frequently, my mother would wake up and open the local newspaper and say, "Oh my goodness, that has broken my dream." She had dreamt what was on the front page. My father was intrigued by anything to do with magic and UFOs. Do you get the picture? I grew up with these sorts of things, as a very normal conversation.

It wasn't such a stretch for me, to move into spiritual growth and what I do now, which is where my story leads. I was always had awareness as a child. I realise as an adult and even more so as I grow older, that I have innately strong intuitive powers. I am very connected with the spirit world.

I remember around the age of four or five I was playing in my cowboy tent; I was by myself – my sister was probably sleeping – and I was not feeling all that happy. I felt a little bit lonely. I remember a male voice speaking to me and saying something reassuring to me. I can't quite remember what it was, but I had a sense about my life, and I'm getting it now as I write this chapter. He was telling me something reassuring about my life. At that moment I knew there was someone secretly looking out for me.

When I started my spiritual healing training and met my Guide, who is male, I remember saying, "Oh my goodness, I've been listening to you all of my life." I had thought that I was thinking in a male voice.

By the time I divorced, I already had a lot of skills that allowed me to understand how to manage myself, my energy, and what was 'right' at a spiritual level. We deserve to be happy, loving and kind people who do good stuff in the world. The only way I could see myself living these qualities while managing a five-year-old and a seven-year-old as a young single mother, was to be brave and strong. This situation makes me think about my daughters now. What would I have thought if they were single with two young children? As a grandmother, what would I feel for them?

I remember at the time my ex-husband thought I was incredibly brave to be doing this. He never thought I would follow through and have the courage to do it. Perhaps this says a lot about how he saw me as a woman and a person. However, determined I decided that I needed to find a way to restore and stay connected to my inner strength, and that was through meditation.

In the past, I read a book by Ainslie Meares, "Relief Without Drugs" on natural ways to manage stress. As a Drama Teacher, I had learned Creative Visualisation and Deep Relaxation as innovative tools. What you bring to the theatre is a massive process of self-awareness and personal development.

So I have known from an early age that I have unique gifts and power to share with the world.

There are two parts to this gift. One appeared during my separation. A spiritual crisis dawned when I was coming home alone from work one day. I had gone back to work part-time to keep building on my talents, serving and earning, yet I was feeling quite empty. I remember coming to an intersection, and stopping at a red light. I looked across, and noticed there was a Christian Church on one side; there was an Uniting Church on another, an Anglican Church opposite and a house on the fourth corner. I had been reading Shirley McLean's books at the time, about her heightened intuitive states of awareness and unusual out of body experiences and they resonated with me. However, it felt like a veil was covering everything like a fog I couldn't see through. I looked at these three churches and thought, "I need a belief, but not a religion." I was raised a Christian and I still sincerely believed in God and I knew for me with all my unusual ways, my uniqueness it was not going to be a conventional. one.

That belief system came to me in the form of yoga with its profound spiritual laws, teachings and understandings. I discovered it was way more than doing yoga poses. Inspired, I went on to learn meditation in a deeper, more controlled and meaningful way to get me started. Meditation led to many profound experiences that are now part of who I am. I was given the gift of deep spiritual connection and insight beyond what I had previously known.

The second gift came, after having taken up all those practices and going through all the changes from the divorce. For a long time I had felt a tremendous heat pouring out of my hands. I had so much heat coming out of my hands that I felt like I should put them on people. Sometimes I drove along the road with the windows open just wanting to put them out and cool them down. I didn't understand what was happening, so I thought I would learn Reiki as a form of hands-on healing, but that still wasn't quite it.

Next, a friend from the ashram, who was training as a spiritual healer, asked me if I would let her practise on me. It was at that moment I was introduced to the whole system that I now work with and underpins so much of what I do.

I was given the gift of healing. Mostly my life is two things now; spiritually, what I practice from yoga about Consciousness and what I have learned and practice about the spirit realms to lift my vibration and lead a meaningful life. As a result, the calling I am now following has so many tools, techniques and skills to support it, some innate and some learned.

Subsequently, I wrote the book "Gorgeous All Over" - a daily guide for women with spirit. I am a systems thinker, and I broke down everything into a process of what I was doing, the way I was doing it, and what was working for me. I had been through a healing crisis myself and used much of what I had learned to heal myself. I had also used to the Western approach, but ultimately everything I experienced was tied into the process I set out in the book.

Let me tell you how I came to write the book. Creatively I was feeling extremely stifled, I decided to have a coaching session with a woman who was using a particular profiling system, and I came up sharply as a Creator. Going through that process with her and talking about what that meant and all of the things I needed to do uncovered a fury in me. Thank goodness there wasn't anybody around at the time. The energy that was unleashed, I can only describe as absolute rage. It was like someone had opened Pandora's Box and set my creativity free.

I rang my coach and asked her, "What has just happened?" I had another timely session with her. The next weekend, I sat down and wrote, "Gorgeous All Over".

I wrote that book in two days. It was the most joyful process I have ever experienced. The words poured out. With all the rage dissolved, all I had to do was get out of my way and launch into publishing the book to share with other women.

I know I will never allow myself to be held back from my creativity ever again.

The book is one thing I use to stand in my power and model to other people to do the same. I believe that is what we are here to do. It's our birthright. It's something we can't allow anyone to take away from us. It's our absolute Freedom with a capital 'F'. I want to use "Gorgeous All Over" as a spiritual approach for women to evolve and underpin the way I work with my corporate clients in conscious leadership.

Ask yourself powerful questions like: "Who am I at my core?", "What's my life purpose?", "What are the values I want to live by?", "How will I do that?", "How will I tap into that inner strength and guidance that I have as a leader?" In my work in the corporate world, I use a set of Eight Elements that help answer these questions. Spiritually the core principles are the same no matter where we are. We are just talking a different language in the corporate world.

There are those individuals, and we're talking about women actually, who want a more private conversation around their intuition, a sense of purpose and spirituality, in wanting to make a more significant difference in the world.

My hope for "Gorgeous All Over" is that women can adopt this approach as a way of life. It's a conscious way of being; it's processing how we respond, the choices we make, and how the impact raises further questions.

Did it work? Did it not work? What do I need to change?

Asking compelling questions allows, through various processes, to expose these more profound answers. There are yogic contemplation methods you can use that layer through and get beyond the mind so the heart can speak its wisdom - you will know the right thing to do. I use it regularly as my guidance system.

Journaling, deep relaxation, attuning to my Guide, making sure my energy is high, are essential to my way of living. I hope that women will embrace personal rituals that give them the ultimate life they seek. When they do, they will evolve spiritually and find that they become influential leaders in their world. Others are already looking towards them to help raise their vibration and have a more positive impact on the planet. They need to model it.

My message, for women, is don't wait for permission to be all you can be. Some people consider it will take one hundred and thirty-five years until we get to fifty-fifty equity between men and women in leadership. All I care about is that men, women and children are here being everything they are meant to be – right now. They are unique, and they need to be themselves.

My purpose is to help women find their way of being their very best. I've seen too many women fight this inner rift - for too long. They don't know how to shift from where they are to where they want to be, and I intend to help them do it.

"Gorgeous All Over" is the vehicle that can take you from one level of existence to the next and live the life you were born to live. Be who you are in mind, body and soul. Be brave and be gorgeous all over.

Dedication:

Thank you to all who have shown me the true Power of life and how to use it for our upliftment. I continue to learn and have fun on the way.

From a young age Indira was attuned to the spirit world. She knew she had an acute awareness of her intuitive powers.

Her dilemma was revealed when she developed her Conscious Leadership business without acknowledging the strong spiritual aspect of her very being.

Gorgeous All Over has been catalytic in carving a new path for Indira where she embraces all of her. This truth is something we all have to face within ourselves. Working with someone special like Indira will reveal a deep inner beauty and peace that we seek outside of us. Look within.

Brenda Dempsey
Creator & Editor

The Art of Feminine Beauty

A Little Malawi Magic at Sunset

Photograph by Brenda Dempsey

VOICES OF HOPE

Leah Adhiambo - Kenya, Africa

My Candle of Hope

Thank you for Social Media. Without platforms like Facebook I would not have encountered the beautiful soul that is Leah Adhiambo.

The world is full of serendipity and sometimes magic happens and when you try to recollect how you connected with someone the reason evades you.

Leah's story will tug at your heart strings yet you will feel the force of a lioness who looks after her pride. Despite her own drastic challenges, Leah always puts other people first, especially the children and young people in her community.

This is a story that has touched my heart so I have decided to support Leah through Voices of Hope. When you read her story you will understand why.

Brenda Dempsey
Creator & Editor

Transformation #23

My Candle of Hope

Leah Adhiambo

Mentor and Jewellery Maker

"Empowered Women Growth in Society Beyond Measure"

Leah Adhiambo

My name is Leah Adhiambo from Kenya in Africa. I am a young single mother of two little boys who grew up in a humble background. After my sons were born I lost my father, and I am now left with my mother to look after too. We are a family of three ladies and three men wherein I am the fourth born.

For us to get the basic needs as a family was a real struggle. As a result, my mother was doing second-hand clothes and bags sales job. Food, house, home and school fees were a problem. No one could support us. I remember when I joined my high school, I was the last student to be admitted in Form one. To add more pressure, when I joined the exams of first term were to start in the next two days. That was the beginning of the toughest thing I experienced in my life. I needed someone to give me courage during those days.

Being sent home, for lack of school fees, became a habit, and I could even be off a month at home without going to school. What I used to do during this time was sit on the side of the road waiting for my classmates. I would request to see their books then I would rush home to copy the notes to help me read. Then very early in the morning I could wait aside near the school to give back the book to the owner. The good thing was that I could still be on the top ten list of the course; the best girl regarding the Performance list.

Inwardly, I was completely down and full of worries, but my mother could work no harder for us until I finished high school.

Now life became much harder after high school; I joined the community organisations in the village where I used to live with my uncle, my mother's brother. Then my mom took me to the college and took a Diploma in Business, Information, Communication and Technology (DBICT) First semester was okay, things became worse in second and third semester when my mother became sick for more extended periods and no one was able to pay my fees. I went through the whole course but was denied to sit my Final Exams for graduation.

I left college; started hustling doing different jobs in the city until I landed in the Kibera Slum and became a Volunteer for the Adolescent Girls. I knew what I went through and was still going through with the struggles, that I could help them. I know that for a young child, it is much more painful and full of worries hence I am here to give them hope; provide them with courage. I lend them an ear to listen to their stories and struggles. A shoulder and an arm to lean on and I have seen a significant change in them. We love each other! We have strongly bonded, and they are free to call me anytime they need me. The times they are depressed, and so down emotionally hence I find myself doing this job even without payment!

During the moment I left college to hustle, I met a young man just like me. We dated, and I decided to have kids with him as our plan was to get married and stay together, but I rushed into love with the wrong person. I saw the signs of my life ruined yet it's hard, it was going to be the Worst!

I decided to live alone with my kids - it's now almost five years being a single parent and I had the idea to make jewellery using mostly beads. I would make necklaces, earrings, wristbands and hair bands as a way of sustaining my life and my children's lives. I do share this skill to the jobless, young mothers and also the disabled who can do this bead-work when they are sitting down.

Our family is still struggling. We both have no jobs, just hustling to pay our bills. We are homeless in the village and my mother, who is not doing well health-wise, is staying in the slum in the coastal part of Kenya.

If I had the opportunity to have a well-paid job, I would like to build a house for my mother and take her home, because I have questions running through my head. Every time I think, "If, just suppose, my mother dies today or any of us, her children, where will we be buried?" We are scattered as a family because we have no home to unite us! Every night I wet my pillow with tears due to deep thoughts.

Also given I have a well-paid job/support, I will go and do a course on Inner Healing Education Approach to help my community with their inner Wounds, healing adults and children with wounds who struggle daily and no one is there for the Healing service. It is a gap I have noticed, and I am a reliable witness!

I have a lot of struggle that I have experienced, and I am still facing, and that's why I give Hope to the children who are the Leaders of Tomorrow. That's why I run a small program known as Prior Needs, providing support to a child by providing what he/she is highly in need of, the priority, basically for the essentials of life.

The greatest challenge I am facing is that no one wants to hold your hand. People don't come close to those who are struggling with life and who are impoverished. Others are full of jealousy when you appear to be doing something to improve your life. It seems as you have nowhere, you can go for help and support, but my candle of HOPE has never waned, it still flickers brightly.

And if you are the heaven-sent Brenda to me, then please walk with me, be my mentor, be my therapist, share the opportunities. You see I can fit into a vision of hope for others who need the light. Share the scholarship opportunities for my little boys and me as right now we don't live together because life is not sweet with us.

I try to send shopping from the little money I have and try to make regular visits.

Although I am not happy, I am just too Strong. That's why you can still see my smile.

Dedication:

For all the girls and children who are looking for hope. Look inside to find your light.

It is with great gratitude that I take up the beacon of light for Leah and the work she is doing in Kenya within her community. She tirelessly gives of herself always and despite not being able to travel and see her own children, she finds time to nurture and support the young people within her village.

Not content with spending her time helping others, Leah knows the value of education and continues studying to give herself the best opportunity so she can rise up and make something of her life in such adverse circumstances. It is for these reasons that I am delighted to share with you the vision of bringing to Kenya, Healing Houses of Hope, where Leah will be able to work with the children and young people in educating them from the inside out.

Brenda Dempsey
Creator & Editor

VOICES OF HOPE

Joyce Osei - Born in Ghana, living in London, UK

Living Your Truth

The first thing you notice about Joyce is her beautiful smile. It lights up a whole room. The next thing you become aware of is her passion for all things Inclusion and Diversity. This has been born through her story but more importantly children's literature.

Like many women today, Joyce is no longer willing to accept things and challenges the status quo to impact change in her unique way through her belief in the power of networking.

During her journey Joyce has learnt to honour herself and answer her calling and chooses to step into the exciting world of becoming her own boss and an author.

This takes courage and as a mum to two gorgeous children she is prepared to do what it takes to be an excellent role model, showing them that you can go after your dreams and in what you believe.

Brenda Dempsey
Creator & Editor

Transformation #24

Living your Truth -
An Assured Path to Success

Joyce Osei

Author

"You can't have a testimony, unless you have been through the test."

Joyce Osei

I was born in Ghana and raised by my mum, grandparents and her extended family. I moved to London at a young age. Most of my time growing up was spent with my grandparents as my mum worked. Equally, my aunts and uncles filled in the gaps developing my knowledge when my mum couldn't. As a child who did much thinking, when I reflected on this I coined the term 'conscious collaboration' because even though I didn't know it at the time, all those people were genuinely contributing to my upbringing and supporting me.

Grandma is from Barbados and Grandad was from Ghana, and they would often tell me stories about growing up in their respective countries. Hearing their tales birthed my love and joy of stories; it gave me a sense of identity and allowed me to see the importance of growing up with family. One of the stories that I most remember is how they met at Woolworths on Holloway Road when they both came to England to study in the 1950s.

Growing up, I was surrounded by a lot of love, even though my biological father was not part of my life.

I always had a yearning to know my biological father. Over the years I saw him a few times, but it wasn't until I was 29 that I reconnected with him properly when he told me his story as to why he couldn't be a part of my life. This connection and his story gave me an insight into his perspective and the complexities and decisions that adults make when faced with challenges. Sometimes these choices result in sacrifice of what others may consider being 'right'. As a consequence of this discovery, it enabled me to finally forgive my dad for not being part of my life as a child. The feeling of relief was immense as I had completed the puzzle and experienced closure on this part of my life.

My mum met my stepdad, who was a doctor, when I was eight years old, and he had a significant and positive impact on my life. When I was thirteen, he found a new job, and we moved from Hackney to a small town surrounded by quaint villages in Hertfordshire. As you can imagine the setting was at the opposite ends of the spectrum; Hackney was urban and multicultural whereas Hertfordshire was full of lush green fields and far less multicultural.

Little did I know that I would be the only black girl in a school of 800 young people. As my dad was the local doctor, there was no hiding place for me. Everything I did appeared amplified as I took full responsibility for my actions and conduct. At the time I didn't think anything of it as I was just so excited to start a new school which was co-ed where I could make lots of new friends. I became conscious of this difference, however it was not something that weighed on my mind, as I felt we were all teenagers, loving life, experimenting and going through similar issues. My take away from this favourable time at school and being the only black girl was that it prepared me for my working life where I initially was the only black person in the team.

My new school ignited my love of English, Plays and the Arts as well as contributing to my interest in Shakespeare and love for Stratford upon Avon. Whenever I reflect on my time at school I have many positive memories and still keep in touch with my school friends. My experience at that school taught me something significant; a few lessons which would come back to me later in my life. The one thing that stood out for me was that I had become so used to this situation that I never thought about questioning, "Where are the other black people?"

After school, like many other middle-class teenagers, I went on to university to study Hospitality as I had a passion for food and service. This adventure was a great time in my life as I met many people from diverse backgrounds from Guernsey to Guatemala and everywhere in between. Travelling opened my eyes and mind to life experiences being different from my own because of culture, race and perspectives. During this time I realised that I could seemingly relate and make friendships easily with anyone no matter their background. This skill serves me well today.

After my degree, I found a job in Hospitality, and I soon realised that this was not the career for me as I worked very long hours and it affected my work-life balance. I lasted eighteen months as Restaurant

Manager for a well-known restaurant chain. To escape this monotonous lifestyle I decided to go travelling (another love of mine) to Australia for three months. This travel experience was powerful and impacted my life in a way that I never thought possible. I gained more clarity around what I didn't want to do in life which can be a good starting point for discovering what it is that I do want to do with my life.

Moreover, I discovered more about me and who I was. I have a gift of connecting with anyone from anywhere at any time. I also found that I have something that everyone tells me that I take for granted. That is my smile. I never considered it to be relevant as I had heard it many times from people I knew. Here I was on the other side of the world, connecting with strangers and yet they said the same thing, that I had a beautiful smile. The realisation my smile is powerful, and it must be true is a beautiful part of me. My smile is my superpower enabling me to connect, interact and make a difference in people's lives. I now know I am a woman of influence.

When I returned from Australia I resumed my role as a sales and marketing coordinator at a local restaurant, ironically an Australian themed restaurant! It was a new concept to the UK, so we had to advertise it extensively to the local community. When the lady from the local paper came in to speak with my colleague and me, I was fascinated because

I found it hard to believe someone could get paid for just chatting and having lots of meetings all day and I thought I could do it, so I asked "What do they call what you do?"

"Media sales," the lady replied.

I asked how I could work in media sales, and she pointed me to a website. Within a couple of months I landed my first role as a classified sales executive for a national newspaper! I didn't even know what that meant, but in practice it meant making lots of calls to small business owners and getting them to advertise. It was okay that I didn't know anything because they gave us the best training.

Still feeling unfulfilled, I moved to another company for a cosmetics magazine selling online and print advertising eventually progressing to Sales Manager at several global publishing and events companies serving the financial and Technology industries for six years.

During this time, I met my husband. It was when I was on jury service I kept hearing his name being called out as a juror. On repeatedly hearing his name I wondered who this guy was. He always seemed to be called upon, while I was still waiting for my chance to be a juror. We started talking, and I believe it was my smile that captured his heart. His name is Emmanuel which means 'God is with us.'

Here was another sign of serendipity and that God and the universe were looking out for me. Boom! Eighteen months later we were married.

In 2007 I began to wake up from what I would describe as a 'corporate slumber.' The Lehman Brothers, an investment bank, had crashed and at the time I was pregnant with my first child. Not long after the financial crash happened the company I was working at had an organisational restructure and I was at risk of redundancy. Just imagine, it's your first child, and it's nearly Christmas, and you've made plans for maternity, and now everything was up in the air!

This disappointment birthed the lioness in me. It was time to take control of my life and this untenable situation. Somehow, I found the courage to challenge the leaders in the position and step into my power and voice my point of view. In the end I went through the redundancy process and thankfully I was able to secure another role in a different area of the business.

The lesson I learnt from this situation was never to accept what others say at face value. You have a voice and a right to express it. When challenged you have to dig deep and use your courage to find in what your voice believes. Courage and conviction will give you the power to stand up for what is right for you. Sometimes our choices present us with further challenges.

In 2011 when I was on maternity leave for the second time, I had another 'aha' moment. As I was reading bedtime stories to my daughter I realised that none of the characters looked like her. I thought, someone needs to write a story with black characters. Responsibility did not fall to me and it was not my problem because I believed I was not a writer.

In 2013 I was working on an Awards Programme which recognised trailblazing women from different industry sectors. While I was in this role, I was headhunted by a recruitment company for the position of a key account manager for a Gender Diversity company. This job role opened a new door for me. For the first time I was at events that were created by women for women. I felt aligned with this work because it was purposeful; it increased gender diversity and made me question once again where are all the women in the corporate world that looked like me?

This role led me to understand the insights that impact a women's career. The one area that stood out for me was the importance of role modelling. "You cannot be what you cannot see."

When I considered the issue of lack of senior female role models in the business world coupled with the lack of black characters in children's storybooks, it ignited a spark within me that drove me to explore diversity and inclusion further.

While I was exploring Diversity and Inclusion, within my role at work I was complimented on my writing skills by one of the co-founders. Like the Australian light-bulb moment of realising that my superpower was my smile, here I was again being told I was good at writing, and now I could see that skill as being right for me.

Part of my responsibility was attending events that included panels of women who were sharing their work journey stories about how they took ownership of their careers. Attending these events was a sign of hope for many other women and me. More importantly, it further opened my heart, mind and soul to the desire that I wanted to work for myself. It was time to be proactive, so I decided to quit my job.

Working freelance freed up space in my mind for a more creative approach to life. Now I had the time and opportunity to begin writing children's stories based on Diversity and Inclusion. I have found myself an illustrator, publisher and mentor to make my dream a reality.

Throughout this journey, I now know that my purpose to serve others by becoming a woman who influences change around Diversity and Inclusion.

My vision is to write seven stories where the two main characters travel around the world exploring different cultures.

Highlighting these diverse concepts will give rise to a shared understanding that while we are all human we have exciting differences that expand our minds and embrace the joy and positive aspects of different cultures. The food, sport and music are just some examples of how we can be united.

Awakening awareness of greater diversity and inclusion in children's stories will open countless doors and opportunities to work in schools, give talks and create a range of products that will connect the younger generation to their identity and understanding that we should focus on the similarities and not differences of each other.

My hope is for women to find the courage to step into their power, find their purpose and feel fulfilled by making a difference in the world.

Dedication:

I dedicate this chapter to my husband, children, mum, grandma and extended family who have shown me what is possible and have supported me thus far in everything I've done.

HOPE

Be the Light

Joyce's story is strewn with determination and vision. She is passionate about influencing change in all things to do with Inclusion and Diversity, especially relating to young children and how they are portrayed in books.

When you find a strong 'WHY' you can easily pick up the gauntlet and run. It is for all of us to find such a purpose and create our own missions whereby we can take action to make a difference in the world.

Brenda Dempsey
Creator & Editor

HOPE

BE THE LIGHT

The Art of Feminine Beauty

I AM

Tethered to the Earth with my Dragon
Held up to the sky with my Unicorn,
Healthy Happy Harmonious Awareness
Connected to me.
Full of desires with destination
Abundant Fluent Talented
Capable Well Equipped Real
Likeable Magical Firm yet Nurturing
Joyous Patient Able to Focus
Inwardly Calm
Relaxed & Connected to Nature.

Steady ready poised prepped,
Acceptance of my
Stance my Prance, my Dance
Surrender surfaced splendour
Whole fulfilling days of wonder.
I am span out
I am grounded asunder
absurdly arriving along many a blunder.

Elements decide me;
Earth Air Fire Water
Rain Snow Lighting Thunder

I just smile, kick back, smile some more & ask
myself,

"Is it any Wonder to be so full of awe that all the sky's a Lama & the Stars are like Diamonds of Dew held in light that freeze to ice in the dead of the night?"

"Is it any Wonder" as there is a whole mass of stuff rolling down the Robe, the Sceptre, the Crown.

Wear it well, hold it high
never frown, for your wondrous uniqueness is amidst unbound among the prowess, the silence that ends the sound.

I spend time
knowing me
loving me
Being
Exploring my awareness
Being the Observer
In Joy In Grace In a good place

I think I AM I may I might

Be rising

I am the Empress, The Goddess the one who is watching me, is guiding me home with a new found awareness on a Golden Throne.

Willow Sterrick

VOICES OF HOPE

Juvee Perez - from the Philippines, living in London

Miss Website Ninja

Juvee's story is one wrapped in love, vision and determination.

From the Philippines, Juvee soon learned the Art of Competition from a young age. Living in a densely populated area had created that intense sense of it.

Like all fairy tales, she fell in love and found herself moving to the UK. Full of hope she settled down into British life and was encouraged to find her one thing. Not knowing what that was and being encouraged to work in computers, Juvee soon discovered a passion and a skill in creating websites.

Juvee brings a new edge to Website building as she develops these from the inside out, creating beautiful websites for her clients. I know - I am one of them.

Juvee now dreams big and desires to make an impact on the world through her creative genius.

Brenda Dempsey
Creator & Editor

Transformation #25

Miss Website Ninja

Juvee Perez

Website Designer

"Hope is always there. You have to look in the right places... and sometimes that place is looking within yourself."

Juvee Perez

I was born in the Philippines, a third world country, and I grew up with lots of competition as the population is over one hundred million people. With such a vast number of people, it's about finding the opportunity for you to stand out at the same time as trying to find out what you want to do with your life.

This perspective started for me when I was a teenager. It is a time when you begin to question what you want to do with your life? What will my future hold? What do I see myself doing? You tend to look towards the next five to ten years. At that time I honestly didn't know what I wanted to do. I was lost because I wasn't sure about my skills, my capabilities and my passion. I was still a teenager.

All I knew around this time was that I wanted to travel. Travelling is difficult for people from the Philippines due to poverty and lack of opportunities. People resign themselves not being able to go. My thoughts drifted to finding a career that allowed me to travel, and get paid at the same time; that choice of career path was my challenge at that time.

When I went to college, I enrolled in an International Studies Course because I wanted to be familiar with how international community politics work. I thought that this would give me a path to follow what I want to do, which was to travel. Due to my financial situation at that time, I had to stop going to school and college, and was back at square one.

A few months later, I met my husband. He was from the UK and travelled to the Philippines to meet me. We instantly hit it off, fell in love and got married. He was the person who introduced me to website design. His business mind inspired me to create my own business around website design. From that point I started to read articles, watch webinars and YouTube videos. Everything I learned was self-taught. Throughout this whole process I discovered that I am creative and like website design and enjoy immersing myself in this field. My next move was to live in the UK with my husband.

One of the issues with working for myself and by myself, is that I am easily distracted. However, because I enjoy it so much, I can lose myself in my work. I am in my little world; it's just me. Time flies and I forget the outside world. During this time nobody exists, it's just me and my work. When I am in my particular world it gives me a great feeling especially when I was starting out. I continued to learn about trends, Google analytics and what makes a good website design.

From all of this research, learning and starting a business, my cool business name was born – Miss Website Ninja.

Now that I had discovered that I was good at website design, and I enjoy the creative aspect of my work, I stumbled across a problem. I did not know how to sell myself; finding clients along with being new and not having much of a portfolio to back up my skills. It was during this phase when I committed to myself and my business that I met Brenda Dempsey, who like me, was starting in business. I manifested Brenda that week along with two other new clients. It was a turning point for me as I was thinking about giving up because I didn't know what to do to attract clients.

It was at this time too that my husband said to me that it might be better if I just got a job. As I was stubborn, this was the jolt I needed to focus more and keep going. I am a creative and love website design as well as being good at it. Someone telling me what to do does not resonate with me, so it's at this time I dug in my heels. I am a free spirit.

I am pursuing my dream, and advice to the contrary only fuels my spirit to find a solution. I want to serve people. I want to find people who need me as a Website Ninja. I want to help people with their business.

The learning for me was that when you commit to yourself and your dream, even though you feel you are struggling, the universe seems to give you what you desire. The reward for determination, persistence and keeping going is the answer to your struggle. In my case, it was three new clients when I was at my lowest point. From that time, my business grew. Being Asian, the choice of Miss Website Ninja was a perfect fit for me and my brand.

The name 'Ninja' sticks with people.

As a creative woman in business, it is essential to be inspired. For me this is a perpetual situation I find myself in. When I am feeling down and don't feel like working, I find that this is a time when you have to be kind to yourself. It's the perfect time to take and break and allow yourself to feel the feelings of sadness, frustration or emptiness to wash over you. Let yourself BE. It's also important not to stay down so allow yourself the downtime then tell yourself that from tomorrow you are going to get back up do business as usual and produce quality results for your clients.

Being a woman in business, Self-Care is vital and it is important to schedule time out, as being creative is very tiring; your brain can often feel drained because of all the inspiration and motivational energy that you spend. The design and technical process, as well as thinking, is very much a part of the draining feeling.

As a freelancer, I have the privilege of taking time out that suits me and my schedule. I like to go for massages, go for a walk in nature and visit places so that I can give my mind a rest from all the creativity. Taking care of myself recharges my batteries.

My values are around Creativity, Commitment and Self-Care as well as being good at Communication. You have to understand your clients because whatever you are doing, it's more like Collaboration instead of you working for them. It's you working with them. Clear communication is a must. It's about putting yourself in your clients' shoes so when you do creative design work, it showcases the client's brand so at the same time it speaks to the right audience.

I have recently moved from a more rural environment to the city. Another struggle I face is feeling lonely, because I work from home, and most of the time it is just me. Solitude can severely impact your level of motivation. The isolation has enabled me to look for alternative ways to keep the de-motivation at bay. The solution I have found is networking so that I can meet like-minded individuals. Being in London is helping me with this aspect of my work and I can now seek out other female entrepreneur meet- ups that I can attend once in a while so I can have a sense of community. By doing this, my confidence at putting myself out there has increased. I seek out others who share the same passion or problems that I face. When you connect you are no longer alone and can often find solutions together.

I want to express an air of caution. Just because I am now in London, it does not always exempt me from feeling lonely and isolated. We all know that you can have these feelings even when people surround you. Being in a large city means that there are many meet-up groups and it's about you finding the right ones for you that will help take you out of that place of feeling lonely. You have to be proactive to create the change. The fact that London has so many different people from different walks of life also triggers you into action. It furthers your understanding of people as they are. Being around a lot of people and observing them enables me to do lots of market research as part of the design process. It also inspires me.

We are all individuals, and each of us has different factors affecting our performance, situations and feelings. In terms of being a creative woman in business, a freelancer, website and graphic designer, I have a message when you find yourself struggling. First of all, you have to look inside you for your solutions, before looking outside for factors which you do not have any control over. The only thing that you can control is yourself. Assess the situation that you are currently in, make a list and change your mindset. If you ignore the outside picture and focus on yourself, things will change. You can ask yourself, "What is it I can do now that I have control over?" What can you do to improve yourself and skill set? For example, if you are struggling to find clients you can ask, "Who is my ideal client?" Who are the successful people or brands that you would love to serve?

If your struggle is isolation or lack of motivation, you hve to look inside too and ask What triggers the loneliness? Is it because you don't go out as much, you're too shy to make friends or connect with entrepreneurs or like-minded individuals? Once you know the answers to questions like these you can then do something about it. Once you start to do something about it, the feeling of hope will emerge.

Sometimes you feel hopeless that there is nothing you can do about it, but you have to listen to yourself and do not focus on any outside influences. It's about having a one-to-one talk with yourself and always ask, "What can I do about it now that's within my control?" Take baby steps. Go on social media, Facebook, LinkedIn and learn new skills. Action is key. Movement is a reflection that there is something big that is going to happen in your life. It's up to you to make sure your future is bright. When you take action the rest will follow. Do one small thing, one action, one small step at a time, so you do not overwhelm yourself. When you do this you can achieve your goals and dreams.

Hope is always there. You have to look in the right places. Sometimes that right place is looking inside yourself and so be it.

For me, walking the path of my purpose with passion is working on a much bigger project. Perhaps a big company that focuses on making people's lives easier. I know I want to be part of something that is making a difference in people's lives.

On reflection, I want to be the CEO and leader. I have honed my skills, have great insight and high emotional intelligence. These are great traits of leaders today. I see myself working with different organisations and business whose values are to create a significant impact on other people's lives. I intend to focus on reaching bigger audiences, making a life-changing impact. One of the visions I have is to create apps that enable people to daily shape their lives for the better.

It's essential to visualise building a team, working with amazing start-ups who have great ideas and inventions to make people's lives easier, that require a creative team to produce their vision. It is my vision to be leading the design process of such innovation.

I have now voiced my future of how I want to serve others, and I will wait patiently for the universe to deliver my vision as I focus my energy, efforts and steps to actualising this dream.

Dedication:

To Andrew - who introduced me to the world of web design, who cheers me up whenever I doubt myself and who's there for me through thick and thin. Thank you for believing in me!

HOPE

Be the Light

Like many women today, including myself, Juvee is no stranger to moving from one place to another, putting down roots and transitioning into new adventures.

A women who places great importance on Values, Juvee has a great vision of creating something for the world that will improve lives and make a life-changing impact.

Being Brave, she created such a vision and now dares to take bold steps to make it happen.

Brenda Dempsey
Creator & Editor

VOICES OF HOPE

Tarusha Mittal - Lucknow - Uttar Pradesh, India

The Courage to be Different

During the journey of writing her chapter for Voices of Hope, Tarusha has shown great resilience, perseverance and determination to ensure she contributed to this powerful book.

Tarusha suffered Dengue, a debilitating disease, which impacted on her meeting deadlines set. To her greatness, she made the entry at the eleventh hour.

This strength of character is threaded throughout her story where she fought to have her voice heard and make her own choices, which were extremely challenging within her culture.

Her boldness saw her dare to enter a man's world in India. Not an easy choice at all. With the same determination shown to have her chapter included in Voices of Hope, Tarusha is now paving the way for other women to follow in her footsteps.

Tarusha is a champion of women in India to have the right to choose how they live their lives.

Brenda Dempsey
Creator & Editor

Transformation #26

The Courage to be Different

Tarusha Mittal

Tech Entrepreneur

"Whatever you want to do, if you want to be great at it, you have to love it and be able to make sacrifices for it."
Maya Angelou

The idea behind penning my story was really simple. I really want to introspect to become clear about my own reasons for feeling passionate about causes related to women. I want to other women to know where am coming from so that they can truly know that my mentorship, private coaching, technology businesses are all rolled into one with the same origins and how one thing brought in the other. I want them to realise that freedom of choice is within reach, right there for everyone.

Freedom of choice is a recurring theme in my story.

Freedom of choice when it came to making an unconventional choice, when it came to choosing my subjects in school, to a professional path riddled with a lot of instability and then sticking to my guns down a path of deep tech where there are few women.

I was born in the very heartland of typical India, Lucknow in Uttar Pradesh, one of the most conservative states in the country. Thankfully my family is not that entrenched in traditional, regressive notions but conditioning takes time to shake off.

Growing up in India as a girl, came with its own sets of stereotypes. I was lanky and dark. Now a great combination, but looking back, that is not how I was made to feel while growing up. When I was a pre-pubescent, I was told that a good career for me was to be a model because there was no where else that I would fit in, even though I was a straight A-grade student. I was actually made to feel weird about my height- I was really tall, and I was told that my parents would have a hard time finding a tall enough groom for me.

The idea that a girl can only become a model and that her ultimate destiny was deemed to be about getting married are notions that are hard to shake off, as one grows up.

The good thing is that my family moved around and I studied in the best of schools from Apeejay in Delhi to La Martiniere Girls' - which is a convent school. I have had my ambition sharpened in these institutes.

Convent school came with its own baggage relating to choice, and Victorian rules to do with behaviour of girls.

I was expected to take up science at the plus 2 level in school and remember being slapped by my parents when I went against their wishes to study humanities.

Humanties was where my talent and interest lay. It was a tough choice as all my friends had taken up science and this choice put me in a different section to them.

This was the first time in my life when I exercised my freedom of choice.

It was lonely. Teenagers need support at that stage when they are doing junior college, and I did not have it. This loneliness pushed me into my first relationship but the good thing that came out of my choice was that my school had to constitute an award for me for Literature - I was the first recipient of this award because I was just that good.

Another good thing is that this was also the place where I realised that women supporting each other creates an environment where anything can happen, miracles brew when women come together to help each other.

I realised the problems going back to my childhood and adolescent only in retrospect, when I was diagnosed with depression and went from one abusive relationship to another which was so much worse.

My first real relationship was mired in abuse, sexual, verbal and physical, coupled with a lot of gaslighting. He made sure to make me feel less of a person bringing me down with him, but the turning point was when he tried to put down my ambition as he was not comfortable with my interactions with business partners of the opposite sex.

The patriarchal notions that a woman is somehow less than, the notion that women are not naturally comfortable in public spaces - these are not just stereotypes, this is conditioning that we are brought up with and it reinforces these ideas cementing them in the very psyche of women.

My interest in tech came from actively trying to simplify problems. Technology is for everyone. Technology should aid and abet in making life simpler in this day and age when people are plagued by choices and too much information.

I have two tech businesses and a coaching and mentorship business. My journey started right out of school; my co-founder and I have known each other since we were in school. We were always discussing and talking about ideas, he asked me to be his co-founder and I found myself saying yes. It was and still is an exciting time as we are building and executing ideas. It is pure creation.

The initial struggles were very different from the present ones, initially I was from a completely non-tech background and was always feeling like I was not doing enough for a deep tech company.

I taught myself, so I used to work and learn new things on the go and research and make my knowledge more solid by burning the candle on both ends.

We started as a data centre company- the initial few ideas failed due to lack of capital to scale, and then there were some policy changes that led us to pivot entirely. Data centres or data farm are very capital intensive. We bootstrapped our own data centre and it broke even within 6 months! What we did was this - we used to purchase slighter old servers from Nehru Place -which is the biggest market of computers, in Asia, by the way- and then we used to upgrade them by opening them up and changing certain aspects of the hardware. This was the time when I learnt things like that were very hands on - like lugging servers through a bustling market to opening them up and sitting in uncomfortable server rooms. It was brilliant.

It was amazing to see the look on the faces of the shopkeepers when they realised that I had come alone to purchase servers, looking to upgrade them. Absolute shock, absolutely priceless.

The discomfort that crowded places - especially in India - bring in a woman's heart are innumerable, you have to feel safe and that sense completely goes away here, you feel gawked at and leered at - but the only way out is through. Obviously, use tact. On some days, I glared back, on the bad days, I kept my head down and kept my feet going.

The idea that women were not even part of this discourse or a part of the public space selling and dealing with computers in a big way, still astounds me. Any kind of movement with half the population not being represented is going to be skewed and we do see that, now. Leadership without empathy is the biggest problem in public discourse. The PM of New Zealand is a grand example of how to balance the two ends of the spectrum and come out looking like an absolute goddess.

As we scaled up, we turned it into a cloud infrastructure and management platform - so as to increase scalability. This platform is called Cloudrino and was my very first successful venture.

The challenges here came in the form of being judged as a woman in this deep tech industry, plus the fact that I do not have any fancy tech degrees. I scaled the business, along with my co-founder, nevertheless. The other challenge which is not spoken about enough is capital - people do not talk about it and how the ups and downs of business can really break your heart and shatter your mental health.

Capital being raised by women founders is tiny in comparison to what is being done by men, the ratio is all skewed.

Post Cloudrino, we wanted to start working in blockchain and that is what we did - we started building a decentralised cloud or network and blockchain apps for users and enterprises. This particular venture is called Ethx.

Ethx is about creating an inclusive fintech platform on a decentralised network which allows users to earn/trade in cryptocurrencies and for enterprises to get themselves on blockchain to increase their efficiency in the least resistive fashion. We are incubated at the best tech institute of India.

As a woman in tech, I think all women in tech tend to face this, I noticed how I was not taken seriously by some men, they were always waiting for someone else to come forward and back my opinion, or some assumed that this business belonged to a male figure in my life and not me. On some days, it infuriates me and on some, it amuses me, but the stereotype has to be broken and this is a work in progress, I let my work speak for itself.

I feel very passionately about women in this space and this led me to start mentoring and coaching women entrepreneurs - teaching them about mindset because one does not need to lose one's mind over scaling a business and the pitfalls, setbacks that one sees as an entrepreneur and how to get past them. Both of these things are issues that I still face everyday - there was a very dark period in my life, when I was terribly depressed because business was not doing so well, so I have been there and I have done that and now I want others to learn from my mistakes and get onto their own mistakes super fast so that they can see exponential growth. Mindset is important; having the right information in a concise form customised for you is important, otherwise everything is too generic.

I have recently also launched a podcast called LivingBlockchain - which throws light on women in blockchain by interviewing them.

I have won several tech awards and also been facilitated by the government for my work in technology. It has been a rewarding journey.

The fact that I can speak about women empowerment and their freedom of choice and in the process inspire people, is a blessing and makes me full of gratitude that I am in a position to do this. My story should inspire women to pick their choice, stand by it and remember that ultimately, it is about joy.

I actively help out entrepreneurs who are starting out, by helping them with 1:1 mentoring and self paced courses.

People have asked me time and again if I would choose a path which is unstable and has its own highs and lows - my answer has always been a resounding yes.

This allows me freedom of choice and for that, I would do it all over again, if I had to.

Dedication:

This is for every single woman who is harbouring a desire, who has been told at some point or the other that she is not enough, in one form or another or just simply asked to think before making a choice.

HOPE

Be the Light

Tarusha Mittal is a woman of courage, hope and vision. She chooses to make her life and the lives of women in her country better using technology. She is a trailblazer.

Brenda Dempsey
Creator & Editor

VOICES OF HOPE

Jaswinder Challi - from India living in London, UK

Turning Point

Domestic Violence is prevalent in many cultures. It seems that this abhorrent act continues to exist amongst many communities around the world.

Jaswinder's story is brutal, yet she has found her hope. It is in our darkest moments in life that we implore from the depth of our souls a sound that ignites the spark within us. A tiny flickering flame sheds lights on a deep connection between soul, universe and God, and a knowing is awakened.

From her desperate situation, Jaswinder awakened the spiritual gifts that were innate and now uses them to support others. With a love of learning, she has developed her knowledge and skills to give structure to her work.

Jaswinder is a beautiful soul and when you meet her, her gentle spirit touches you in ways you cannot even imagine. She is a truly gifted lady.

Brenda Dempsey
Creator & Editor

Transformation #27

Turning Point

Jaswinder Challi

Shamanic Practioner, Healer & Therapist

"When everyone else shuts their doors on you, you will find your own door."

Jaswinder K Challi Sahiba

Whenever I have visited India, relatives tell me that our ancestors were well-to-do and our family had riches and abundance; however it all started to go downhill for them during the British Raj years because of conflicts which radiated out from the provinces. As Punjabis, we are descendants of the Indo-Aryan race.

Politics created further division, where Punjab became split and my parents, then children, became forced into deeper poverty, experiencing immense trauma.

I arrived in the UK from India when I was just eighteen months old. My father had already come to the UK before I was born and made arrangements for our arrival.

Before long, I was attending school in England. The culture I came from did not pay importance to educate girls (cultural conditioning), and I was not encouraged to go to school. If my father had had his way I would have stayed at home doing the household chores. However, because of UK law, I went to school, which I loved. The irony of this situation was that some of the children I went to school with did not want to be there; they truanted and got into trouble, whereas I saw school as escapism from some of the drudgery of home life. It represented freedom for me, and I was interested in learning.

As I was growing up, I felt a great sense of pressure as the oldest daughter. I was conditioned to be very domesticated, and my duties included looking after my younger siblings when my parents were working. I would often hear comments like "You have to get it right; otherwise, your in-laws will moan at us." Again, this belief was not unique to my parents, as many women in the community held similar attitudes, and they would make comments to me.

It was the norm back in the 1970s for girls to leave school aged 15 or 16 and not continue their education, as marriage was their destiny. I saw friends who I went to school with already getting engaged and married. I wanted to go to college but was not allowed. Instead I had to go to work until I married at 17. The marriage was arranged for me even though I did not want to get married. Arranged marriages were happening to all the girls in my community, so why was I expecting to be an exception to the rule? I was not.

The Trauma begins…
In this marriage, I was trapped, enslaved and imprisoned. All I was good for was working all day. It was the life of a servitude slave. I married into a family, not just a man; but one who was seven years older than me. My life was sitting at a sewing machine, sewing all day long, day after day. Not only was I their 'prisoner', but they also kept the money I was earning. I was living a servitude life of cooking, cleaning and sewing.

As a consequence of this life, I lost weight and became very depressed, to the extent I even attempted suicide. I decided to take an overdose as I felt I was dying slowly. I was withering away. I had no voice. I had no control. I had nothing. Once a girl marries into the husband's family, you lose all control. Another part of this nightmare is that parents don't usually take their daughter back if trouble comes their way, especially back in the 1970s/80s. I am now aware that some of the girls I went to school with who also ended up in traumatic marriages now experience severe mental health problems.

It was a turn of fate that rescued me from my situation. I am an empathetic person, and my heart always reaches out and feels pain and suffering.

There was a man who used to bring the clothes to the house for sewing each week. He would bring clothes then the following week would return to pick them up and leave more clothes for sewing. One Sunday on the front page of the newspaper there was a large picture of a fire and a picture of two children who died in it. There were also two pictures of a man and a woman; I recognised him as the man for whom I sewed the clothes. As soon as I saw the images, I was very disturbed inside. I was so upset that I struggled to sew the clothes. I was shaking as my heart was crying for them. I could feel their pain after having read the paper and seen the pictures.

Because there were no more clothes to sew, I was just sitting in my mother-in-law's room with her, which is where I used to sew the clothes. When my ex-husband came home from work, he looked around and asked, "Why are you lot not sewing clothes?" I started to tell him the man's story about the fire. Before I could finish my answer, my mother-in-law turned around and replied, "She doesn't want to sew anymore, so she turned him away." I stood in disbelief at these words. There was a man who had lost his two children for which my heart has been crying with empathy. I was feeling traumatised for them, and I could not believe what I had just heard from this woman.

At that point, it was like my kundalini rose within me, my voice came out, and I said, "If you don't believe me look at that paper." I was angry. I turned to my mother-in-law and told her, "How dare you call me a liar?" At that point, my ex-husband started beating me up. He said, "How dare you talk to my mum like that." I shut down again. He beat me up so badly and I was thrown from one side of the room to the other.

Fortunately, my brother-in-law came home from work and saw what was happening. He was shocked and quickly ran to where my uncle and aunt lived at the top of the road.

I was in such a state of fright that parents had brought me back home. I kept fainting as I hadn't

359

been eating. I had lost so much weight and was anaemic. It took a long time before I recovered. I'm not even sure if I ever improved because as time went by, I started getting on with life. I got divorced, and my parents were lenient with me. As a result, I was allowed to go to college and complete a secretarial course followed by a business course. Had my parents not saved me that night, he might have killed me.

Ten years later, I met my second husband. There seems to be a twist of fate with this one because although my auntie introduced him to us, it was weird how it came together. He appeared to be a caring person, but I soon learned that this was assumed to hide his manipulating behaviour. He knew the right words to say, but they were hollow as he was not caring underneath this persona.

From the day we were married, he became verbally abusive. He knew he could control me as I was living at his house and couldn't do anything about it. He started playing games. He would go out all night with his brothers and his friends. On his return, he wanted sex; I often felt sexually assaulted too.

He would throw verbally abusive words my way, like "If you don't get pregnant, I will divorce you." Another phrase was, "I'll divorce you and marry a virgin, she'll be mine and only mine, as you are second-hand goods." Another one, "I only got married because I needed someone in my bed."

His words were destroying me; they were abusive and very cutting -I would often cry and felt so lonely and desperate. It was the most solitary time of my life.

Eventually, when I did get pregnant, he became extraordinarily elusive and abusive as he was now back with an ex-girlfriend, and as they were spending more and more time together, he did not want me around. The day I found out I was pregnant was also the day I discovered he was having an affair with his ex. The loneliness grew and grew.

I returned to my parents. It was also a painful reminder that my parents had experienced much stigma due to having taken me back home after my first marriage had failed. Now I was here again. Things became so bad that my father turned his back on me; it was the only way he could cope with what was happening. Back in India, the suicide rates are very high for women who suffer domestic violence as they feel they have no future.

I felt all choices escaped me. Once I had the baby, a hopeless feeling arose due to my son's father, not wanting to know him or me anymore.

I was entering a very dark period of my life. Everywhere I turned doors were closing: my parents, my ex-husband, family members and the community. People who I once spoke to freely were walking past me in the street as if I had this considerable stigma; they could not or would not look at me. I had no friends.

It was only my son and me at home. I had no contact with anyone. My son would often put his arms around me at times when I was so desperate, and he would say, "It's okay mummy, I'm here for you."

I felt so hopeless and alone. If it weren't for my son I would not be here. I was in such pain. It was during my deepest, darkest, most painful moment that I had an intense spiritual experience. At home I began meditating. During this time I had conversations with God because I felt immersed in pain. One particular day I was sobbing and felt suicidal. I implored to God, "If my life is so crap and full of pain why did you give me a baby to look after?" The agony I felt was so sharp that I was banging on the floor. It felt like my body was being ripped apart in different ways, there was no physical blood, but I saw and felt my veins breaking and blood pouring. I was screaming and crying and shouting at God; I just wanted the pain to go away. I begged for forgiveness. At this point, I surrendered to God. Then, something magical and unusual began to happen. I experienced and saw a white light; it began to fill the room; everything was white. The pain started to go, and I had a sense of calm.

Next, I felt something on my shoulder. It felt like a hand. All I could hear was whispering in my ear.

It left me feeling comforted. At the time, I did not know that what I heard was a Christian poem called 'Footsteps'. Jesus was there with me reciting the Footsteps poem. He said to me, "Now that you have experienced this intense pain you are going to help and heal other people with their pain." I had no idea what this meant. He began to disappear slowly and so too did the white light. I fell asleep. When I woke up everything felt still.

Road to empowerment...
My 'Turning Point', my awakening of reality, my self-realisation of my purpose! It was not the end of problems, but rather it was my learning how to handle them and grow in alignment with my soul.
Near where I lived was a second-hand shop and something made me go inside. I walked around and then to my amazement; I saw a glass plaque on which was the Footsteps poem. As I started to read it, I burst out crying. The lady in the shop came over to me, and when she saw me looking at it, she picked it up and gave it to me. She said, "I know it means something to you, take it as a gift." I was so overwhelmed because I was not used to anyone giving me a present!

Developments...several years later
They say that wisdom comes from experience through challenge; I feel that I have such a wealth of knowledge and have turned it into wisdom. I am a therapist, healing and helping so many people, as well as a teacher of counselling and hypnotherapy,

enabling students to pursue a career in helping others. At the same time, the teaching (much gratitude to Chrysalis Courses), has allowed me to use my voice and express myself.

The journey of unleashing my voice started with my hypnotherapy training with LCCH in London, where working with the inner child helped me enormously. My inner child had no voice, and I had to repair that by building a relationship with her and continue to develop that relationship.

It has taken me a long time to pluck up the courage and share my story with you. However, I have decided to do it with a view that it may help in some way, perhaps give inspiration so that you too can connect with your power. I am now ready to rise and roar, unleashing my inner warrior by taking it to the next level of becoming a motivational speaker and author of my book, sharing my journey with a broader audience. And hopefully do a lot more writing too!

They say that freedom comes from liberation. I spent many years, working on this pattern of 'victim of abuse', something I experienced time and time again, from other sources like bosses, friends, colleagues; however, due to my spiritual experience and awakening, I am growing and recognising it more and more. The more I educate myself, the more powerful I become. I had to learn to develop stronger boundaries with people and stand in my warrior power. My message to you is to armour and shield yourself with knowledge; knowledge is power. Your power is what the kundalini is all about; it is our place of power, so let it awaken, let it rise!

Dedication:

To my parents, who did the best they possibly could under all their hardships and their conditionings. I chose you because you were the right parents for the learnings I needed for my soul's growth.

To my son: You held the light for me in my darkest moments. You enabled me to keep going even when I wanted to give up. I want you to remember; no matter where you are, I will always be there.

Love you all.....

∞

You cannot describe Jaswinder as a victim, her road towards the light of hope has created a victor.

When you are enslaved, Freedom becomes your greatest Value and Jaswinder fuels her desire for freedom with education as she considers it her power.

During her journey she found her voice and talks about her kundalini rising, giving her the courage to speak her truth even though she knew she would be punished.

What strikes you about Jaswinder's story is her tenacity, faith and knowing that her life will get better. What makes her a remarkable woman is finding that strength to continue, especially when faced with extreme challenges.

As she rises and roars, Jaswinder is a gentle force to be reckoned with for the greater good of women and the world.

Brenda Dempsey
Creator & Editor

The Art of Feminine Beauty

Speak Volumes

Photograph by Paula Jarek

The Art of Feminine Beauty

Bravehearts Making a Difference

In the darkness, imprisoned by her taunting thoughts
She rocks her body while tying the knots.
Chained by her beliefs, she's frozen with fright
As her spurious words resound in the starlight

She's forgotten the laughter and love she once felt
If only she realised her power can melt
the gravest of circumstances holding her back
from the life she desires where there is no lack

Dig deep to reveal limitless courage inside
It's time to stand tall there's nowhere to hide
From the Braveheart you are emblazoned and wise
Unshackle yourself, be bold and arise

That flicker of hope's now your beacon of light
As you speak your truth from morning to night
With a new found conviction infused with passion
You're focused and driven as a woman on a mission

To spread love and joy in the service you've found
Making a difference each day you are free and abound
Finding the right path you can finally see
Your Divine Brilliance now living as the best you can be.

Brenda Dempsey

Photography by Michael Bacon

VOICES OF HOPE

Menaca Pothalingam, Sri Lanka - now livng in London, UK.

Resilience Through Courage, Forgiveness and Hope

Menaca Pothalingam is a formidable woman. Once you read her story you will understand why.

Her energy is infectious and you sense an undeniable focus on making an impact on the world. Her life experiences are miraculous. Nothwithstanding her survival of travelling through the jungle during civil war in Sri Lanka, Menaca has one of the warmest smiles I have ever seen and felt.

She is driven to use her intelligence, tenacity and intention of making a difference to raise her profile within her field of expertise so others can experience the ripple effect of her work.

A true Powerhouse, Menaca's story will leave you feeling inspired to take action and make a better choice.

Brenda Dempsey
Creator & Editor

Transformation #28

Resilience Through Courage, Forgiveness and Hope!

Menaca Pothalingam

Entrepreneur - Author - Speaker

"Create the highest, grandest vision possible for your life, because you become what you believe."

Oprah Winfrey

This story begins 25 years ago. I am from Sri Lanka.

The time I want to share with you is during the civil war in Sri Lanka. When you think of a war zone you most likely think that the people's lives are full of trauma. It wasn't for me. I grew up until around eight/nine years of age without knowing what was happening in my country. It is like the movie called "Life is Beautiful". The 1980s was exactly like that. In my world it was perfect.

One time, when I was nine, I was travelling on a coach. At one point some people got onto the coach to kill all the Tamils. I belonged to that ethnicity. I was one of the Tamils. The driver of the bus told us to pretend we were of another religion to escape death. My mum turned to me and said, "Regardless of what happens, pretend to be sleeping."

This was my first experience of war.

What is surprising about this situation were the bus driver and the people who boarded the bus were from the same ethnicity. I believe everything comes down to personalities. You see, the driver who put his life on the line, wanted to protect us despite us being of different ethnicity, while the people who boarded the bus wanted to kill us.

After this incident, life went on. I went to school. I slowly started to see the impact of the war on other children and people around me. I witnessed grief and suffering that war brings. As time went on at school I began to see people missing. During this time my father's medical practice was vandalised. Life began to change.

Every three or four years we would move from place to place as my father was in government service. During this time I was very close to my maternal grandmother who had a major influence on my life. She endured lots of suffering in her life yet she remained optimistic. She is the reason I wrote my book "Resilience Learned". I have learned so much about resilience from her. They say that children pick up from others what they do not what they say.

At one point my father decided to stop working for the government services because he didn't think all the movement was good or helpful for the safety of the family. Gradually I learned that the environment I was living in had a great impact on the lives of those around me.

When I was in my early twenties. I was in university. Life was filled with peaks and troughs. One of the difficulties caused by the war was that the transport links were often broken. Eventually they would be reinstated. It was during one of these occasions that I decided I wanted to go home.

I was only nineteen miles into the journey when the coach driver said that we could not go any further. It was not safe for him or any of the passengers. He had to stop the vehicle and it could not go forward or back. He parked the bus just off the road for safety. Myself and nine other passengers decided we would walk through the jungle. The road ahead was just less than two hundred miles. As a young woman you do not always think it through, so it was an easy decision as I just wanted to go home.

We embarked on this journey. It was really strange because not once did it come to my mind about the wild animals, serpents or any danger we might encounter along the way. I only had a pack of sandwiches and a water bottle! I did not work it through in my mind how long this trek was going to take. It was blind faith, blind hope. We would walk through the night and rest through the day so we would not be spotted by any aircraft that would shoot shells.

Our luck ran out because we were spotted. We knew they could not target a particular person with their weaponry so they blindly dropped shells. The lady right next to me dropped down. She was severely injured. The irony of the situation was that despite my father being a doctor, I was a child who hated the sight of blood. Here I was giving this wounded woman first aid. I tried to help her but it was in vain; she died. The most heart-breaking thing about this was we had to leave her body behind. It would have been impossible to carry her body for another seven days.

Eventually we survived the jungle and came through the other side. This experience gave me my biggest realisation. That team work helped build resilience, being hopeful and being there for each other. Everyone was so generous. They never thought twice about sharing what food and water they had. They were happy to share, to give anything they had to help each other. As a young woman this had a huge impact on my life. It also made me realise how our lives are interlinked. When one person does something, it affects the whole population.

My experience of the jungle sparked a curiosity in me. It made me wonder why some people do certain things. Why are some people really kind, helpful and do generous things, whilst others want to destroy and kill others? This planted a curiosity that is always in my mind. Why do people hurt others? What makes them do what they do?

After this experience I told my father that I'd had enough. I was not going back. I made the decision to go to India. During this time in my group I was the oldest person, I was doing well in school, often being number one in my subjects. But at this time I was not using English and soon my confidence dropped because of this. I sat with a dictionary all the time learning English so I could make sure I was able to catch up with everyone else.

Somewhere along the line of all this hard work I had my eureka moment.

There are so many people dead and gone who were never given these opportunities. I realised I was given this gift and what right did I have to complain? In that moment I decided to change. I thought, 'that's it, I'm going to have a ball. I am going to enjoy my ride in life.' From this point onwards life changed for me. I made many good friends whom I still keep in touch with today. I finished my dentistry course and had the best of my life in India. I relished each day and enjoyed every moment. The wonderful happening of my time in India was that when I arrived I only knew one girl, yet by the time I left I had many friends. This is success for me. I really did something and achieved well.

As a dentist in India I would go into camps and help the poor people. This seemed a small thing to me. It's funny that as you go about your business you don't consciously think you are learning but when you look back you realise that you are learning all the time. India taught me that the rich are really rich and the poor are very poor. My time in India came to an end when I got married and came to the UK because my husband was already living in England

When I arrived it was a struggle in the beginning. I had an exam to pass and get to grips with the

English accent if I were to be understood and if I were to understand them. Communication is key. During this time I watch much TV, BBC News, BBC programmes and Neighbours. I was thinking 'Oh my God; I have to get this English accent.' Although I was thriving on reading and writing, it was the speaking where I felt the biggest competition.

I managed to get work training others but I would do everything in my power not to do presentations. I became that shut-down person as I was very conscious of my voice. It is a self-limiting belief that prevents you from taking risks. The self-talk can destroy your dreams in an instant. Who needs enemies when you can listen to your mind chatter? The most profound words I heard were that I was not good enough. This had a significant impact on me and with a five year old daughter, I found myself divorced. Within my culture and community being divorced is a serious thing, it's taboo. My husband is a lovely person but we are both different people. We were both miserable and we all deserve to be happy. If you stay in a marriage that is not happy what are you teaching your children? My mother told me once that I was the first person in my family and generation to be divorced. I suppose I was leading the way for change. Paradoxically, I got on with my life yet I did not get on with my life.

Again another life changing event took place. On reflecting about my divorce I realised I was courageous. I followed my heart. Despite divorce being something that is not common place in my culture and family, I could not live a lie. Considering everything I have been through I can say I have always been courageous. I had courage to walk through the jungle; courage to try and save the lady's life and courage to go to India on my own. Courage enables you to take the first step to change, to something better.

I take all of this learning into my business as a coach. The first exercise I do with clients is always around Values. My Values are Freedom, Connection and Success. I have learned that when I do not have freedom in my life I have to do something about it. The bottom line for me on this wonderful journey of life is that you have to be true to yourself, not your culture, others or even your limiting beliefs. Living your truth is the best role model you can give to children, others and the world.

Turning to my career and my purpose, whilst I was successful as a dentist, it did not fulfil me. I knew I had something more to do. There is a bigger purpose for me in this world. I embarked on further training – NLP and Hypnosis and the area I worked within as a woman in business is Health Care.

To the outside world I was living this Instagram lifestyle. I was successful, going on holidays, living in a big house, driving a fabulous car. In 2014 I remarried. This marriage did not stand a chance as it was a long distance relationship. I lived in London while my husband lived in Birmingham. I found that I was living a hamster-wheel lifestyle, and something had to give. I was this multi-tasker. I asked myself, "How many more balls can I juggle?" Eventually the pressure was so intense that I began to drop each thing one by one. Everything was compounded by health care issues including a breast cancer scare. In 2016 I was soon diagnosed with 'burnout'. This was my awakening.

It was one day after I had a terrible day at work. When I got into my car at the end of the day I asked myself, "What's happened to my life?" Troubles continued at work until I was first signed off for one month then eventually six months. My world was crashing all around me. Part of my recovery involved going to a public speaking course. I thought to myself I would never become a public speaker because I have a strong accent. It wasn't until a woman from Facebook told me that my accent was a gift. She said that when she listens to my podcasts she instantly recognises that it is me. This conversation enabled me to shift my mindset. It was time to rid myself of the limiting beliefs that my accent was not good enough, my vocabulary was not good enough.

I want to back track to my jungle story. It took twenty-three years, two marriages and a teenage daughter before I decided to tell anyone about that story. It was time to document it in my own book and of course in this chapter of Voices of Hope because my life and what I have experienced and achieved can bring hope to others. Telling your story is so powerful.

I am driven now to help others acknowledge and use their experiences to sharpen their resilience. That is why I have written the book, 'Resilience Learned'. It will form insight so that others can recognise it within themselves and follow making a difference to their lives.

It is with love that I share this chapter with you and hope that there is something in it that speaks loudly to you. When you begin to listen to your voice, it's time to be true to yourself and take action for you have only this life to enjoy every moment.

Dedication:

This chapter of hope is dedicated to my maternal grandmother 'Mummy' for the unconditional love she showered on me, for the encouragement and support she conferred on me and for being my greatest inspiration. Mummy was a symbol of love, an idol of courage and hope, and it is only apt that I dedicate this chapter to her. I would also like to mention my parents, who have been part of my roller-coaster ride, never ceasing to love and support. A huge thank you for my daughter Asha for being my support system, encouraging me to follow my heart and share my trials and tribulations with me.

∞

It is easy to see that the one thing that Menaca Pothalingam has in bucket loads is Resilience.

From her many experiences of surviving war, moving to a new country to study and finally finding courage to live her life on her terms and leave her marriages is nothing short of inspirational.

It is her ongoing fortitude of self improvement that radiates the greatest inspiration. When you find that hunger to serve, change lives and make the world a better place there is no greater mission that fosters impact in other people's lives.

Menaca's message of finding the courage so they can listen to their inner voice is one that is resounded with other like minded women who are also on a mission to make a difference. As we join forces the power of transformation is felt in the tsunami wave of change that is disrupting our world today.

There are 31 such women in Voices of Hope.

Brenda Dempsey
Creator & Editor

VOICES OF HOPE

Kia Bing-Davies - from Philadelphia USA, living in London, UK

Uniquely Me

Our life experiences are not what defines us - it is the actions we take from the lessons we learn.

Kia Bing-Davies uses many of her life lessons, especially growing up and living in a blended family, to gain understanding of others and herself.

Despite knowing what is good for us, we often need to experience some kind of trauma or pivotal moment to sit up and realise what is going on in our lives. In her story, Kia talks candidly of such an experience when it dawned on her that she was not living in her fullness.

Be inspired as you read her story and know that it is only you who can only change your life. Embracing her roller coaster ride she knows the true value of honouring yourself so you can serve others in the highest version of who you truly are.

Brenda Dempsey
Creator & Editor

Transformation #29

Uniquely Me

Kia Bing-Davies
Uniqueness Coach

"You are unique, and if that is not fulfilled, then something has been lost."

Martha Graham

This is the story about my story. I don't typically like to refer to "story" because that denotes attachment to the past. Yet, I know it is our past that defines who we are and I have discovered three things for sure:

- It's hard to tell your story when you are standing in the middle of someone else's;
- Your story is based on your own sometimes faulty child-like perceptions; and
- The centre of your story contains the lessons that you are here to learn from, release and then embody.

So, here is my story. This is not a story of abuse or a hugely traumatic experience. This is one of the subtle pinpricks of growing up with two parents who were weathering the storm of their own unhappiness, how that affected me in life and how I found the way back to me.

I was a sensitive child and my parents used to forbid me from watching nature programs because I would cry inconsolably if any of the animals died. This sensitivity extended beyond the television screen and I quickly developed a deep understanding of my mother and her anger and pain as well as my Dad and his frustration. I say none of this to demean them. They loved me and continue to do so with everything that they have and are. But parents are people who are also acting from their story and, left unchecked, this has an effect on everything.

When I was younger, my parents argued a lot. From what I remember it was mostly about money. I can remember hearing shouting coming from downstairs and me venturing down but getting scared and hiding under the table. My mother found me and shouted at my father for making me cry. Then, they argued about that. I think that was when I decided to stop crying.

From the time I was young, my mother shared a lot with me about what was making her unhappy in their relationship. I started to get angry for her wanting to protect and defend her and that feeling carried on for much of my life. At nine years old, I can remember giving her relationship advice that actually took me out of the equation. I wanted her to do the best for herself and I would be ok with whatever the outcome, as long as she was happy. My role was to make her happy.

So what, you say. Your role became making your mother happy? Big deal! Well, it became a big deal because I had no real sense of what would make me happy. Looking back I can see now that I stopped exploring my own interests and pursued hers and usually this was met with approval. If I ventured too far away from that path, it was met with am almost ire-like force. I learned what she liked and I did that.

Some of my proudest moments were bringing school reports home, believing I had done very well; pretty much all As. My mother would say that it was good but when she was my age, her grades were better. No matter how well I did, I started to dread that time of year knowing that she would one-up me. I came to accept something crucial in that time as well - that I would never be the best.

So, how did those two understandings affect me? I shied away from competition of any sort. As soon as I felt it, I would turn tail and run the other way. When in high school, it was my dream to become a broadcast journalist. I would tell anyone who would listen that I wanted to be the "Black Connie Chung." I researched and applied to one of the most prestigious programs in the US for broadcast journalism, the S.I. Newhouse School of Public Communications at Syracuse University. I was accepted directly into the program and was excited to be finally starting to walk my own path. My mother kept telling me what a competitive profession it was but I continued undaunted. I can remember arriving on campus and attending those first lectures. Looking around at the sea of faces, everyone appeared more capable, intelligent and ready. I changed my major the next year to a safer one and promptly checked out of my dreams.

This kind of checking out continued for much of my life. As soon as it felt too hot, too competitive, I would run a mile. This was hard because I was and continue to be a pretty driven person. I graduated from university, secured exciting jobs in PR and advertising. Wanting more, I returned to law school and upon graduation, worked in family law. Continuing to want more and following a divorce, I moved to the UK where I still reside. However, the thread that runs through all of that is stopping when just reaching the pinnacle. As soon as I became really successful at anything, I would literally start having panic attacks and then I would just run.

I found that my inability to really know myself led me to becoming what I would call a 'shapeshifter.' I could easily mould my personality, likes and dislikes to whomever I was with; family, friends, boyfriends, colleagues. I still had no real sense of who I was but I was liked and accepted so that was fine with me. It was only when I moved to the UK that I started to begin to ask myself what I wanted, what I needed, what I desired. My mother strenuously disapproved and our relationship suffered greatly. Yet, I held onto the feeling. I felt like I was being reborn and I began to explore with childlike wonder, having fun, making mistakes, learning and growing. But, then I wanted more.

Life in the UK was going pretty well. I was married to a wonderful man, had a growing career and a lovely group of friends. Yet, something was pulling at me. I felt discontented and started looking into spiritual practices like meditation and yoga. I caught the bug and eventually found a spiritual counselling and coaching diploma course and as a lifelong learner, I threw myself in. As I looked around at the faces on my first module, I found that I no longer wanted to run. I had found the space where I just wanted to sit, to learn, to discover and connect and that is what I did.

As I was nearing the completion of my course, I was promoted at my job into the Sales Director position. The additional pressure initially felt fine. This was something I had been working toward for a long time. I dived into the role and thought I would enjoy it. Then came the panic attacks. It was like my body was rejecting the promotion and I felt a failure. It was during this time of stillness that I went within. I started to ask what my heart wanted, what my soul needed. I heard the answer. "To be of service. To help those who are ready to heal to heal themselves." Six months later, I left my job and shortly thereafter started my own Spiritual Counselling and Coaching practice. Think this is the end of the story? Think again.

The first year of my practice felt like a disaster. The only clients I had were ones I worked with for free. I felt alone and terrified to make a decision, any decision. I made myself busy without accomplishing much and I invested heavily in marketing programs when I needed something more basic - a deeper understanding of my own UNIQUENESS.

In order to understand what made me unique, I had to understand my story. Not only understand it and embrace it, but forgive any perceived wrongs and make them my rights. I perceived my mother's competitiveness as not being good enough to achieve but, she was trying to shield me from hurt and disappointment. From what I perceived as failing at the final hurdle became a cosmic pivot to learning something new and growing. My journey to finding myself has led me to living around the world, having adventures and meeting incredible people.

I can now see that any perceived slights were never intended to hurt but were actions born out of humanness coated in love. My experiences have made me a UNIQUE expression of God and there could never be any mistake in that.

So now, I currently help clients to release the pain of the past and integrate into the fullness of who they are. I encourage clients to reach for the stars and push themselves further than they could ever imagine. My clients fall in love, some with partners but most importantly themselves. In finding out that they are UNIQUE, they no longer have to remain silent or hide or pretend they are anyone other than themselves. They can be as UNIQUE as their fingerprints and isn't that what living, true living, is all about?

(Launching my signature U.N.I.Q.U.E. program January 2020 and currently writing the Energy of Yes due out Summer 2020)

Dedication:

It is refreshing to hear a woman in business tell her story as it is. The dream of having a business is filled with many spaghetti routes to the numerous successes you enjoy on the journey. It is these twists and turns and ups and downs that attract many people into such a world, as well as having the freedom to make choices that suit you and your lifestyle.

From Kia's story you can see that once you have a calling to live your life on purpose, nothing will get in the way of that goal. The WHY is so strong that you cannot rest until you finally find yourself in that space and place. This is exactly what happened to Kia before she finally left her job to honour her calling and purpose to serve others in finding their Uniqueness.

Story was an instrumental aspect of Kia's journey that helped her understand who she was and make the necessary changes in her mind, causing her to reframe her perspectives of situations and the people who influenced her life.

Your story is power and once you embrace all of it, the good and the bad, you are ready to create something wonderful for you and the world.

Brenda Dempsey
Creator & Editor

The Art of Feminine Beauty

Love to Dance

Holly Campbell

VOICES OF HOPE

Regina Windsor - London, UK

You Can Be Anything You Want to Be

Regina Windsor speaks with assured confidence.

It was not always that way for her, but ready to learn life lessons, she soon realised that making better choices by putting herself at the heart of them would allow her to follow her passion and dreams.

Many of us grow up people-pleasing and Regina is no different. She has exercised diligence and is carving a new life in readiness for a time when she is financially free to make choices without boundaries that limit her soul's calling.

Many of you will resonate with Regina's story and you will be left asking, "What else can I do to make sure I am putting me at the heart of my life?"

Brenda Dempsey
Creator & Editor

Transformation #30

You Can Be Anything
You Want to Be

Regina Windsor
Business Consultant, Legal Officer, Healer.

*"We can't always choose
the music life plays for
us, but we can choose
how we dance to it."*

Unknown

As a child, I grew up on a council estate in London. You could describe my upbringing as troubled. Life for me was living with a father who was an alcoholic and abusive to my mum. Even though it was chaotic at home, my dad still insisted that when I grew up I had to become a lawyer and earn lots of money. I must have heard this one hundred times because it is what I remember most from my childhood. It felt like I didn't have a choice and I didn't know anything better, other than I was led to believe.

From a young age I felt as if I was the adult. I took responsibility for my dad as an alcoholic, as he had many health issues. I also was there to console my mum. Not only was I a daughter to my mum, I was also her friend. Inevitably in this situation I felt like I lost my childhood. I would often think, 'When is this going to end? Why me?' I felt different. I felt less than everyone else.

There was a part of me that believed that if I worked hard and looked after my parents I would make them happy and that things would get better. This deep sense of duty stayed with me and at the time I didn't know any better. This sense of pleasing others carried on at this time in my life as I always wanted to please authoritative figures such as teachers and my parents.

It was a bit of juxtaposition because whilst I wanted to please others, I also was able to stand up for myself. In the back of my mind, because of what was going on at home, I thought 'I am never going to let that happen to me'. As a result I became defensive. It felt like I was responsible for everyone else's happiness at the sacrifice of my own.

Fortunately, I was excellent at school despite everything that was going on at home. I worked hard and achieved great results.

It was when I turned sixteen that things began to change. I'd had enough of everything at home, always being told what to do and the stress associated with exams. It was about this time that I met my husband. Before long, at the age of eighteen, I discovered I was pregnant with my daughter. At that point I thought 'Oh my God, my life is over.' Needless to say, my family thought the same and wondered whether I was going to amount to anything.

My husband too was very young, yet I decided to move out of my mum's house. I didn't really know what I was doing. "What am I going to do with my life now?" were the words that echoed in my head. I had no job. My husband was working and we were having issues. Despite everything that was going on in my life, it was as if something came over me, I thought, I have to do something with my life. I can't sit here waiting for someone to provide for me. I decided to go back to my studies. I had to return to education and I needed to prove that I could make something of myself. Although I felt strongly about this action, I didn't know what I was going to do. I didn't know what law is but it's the only thing I was told to do.

While all of this turmoil was going on in my life, my dad passed away. I remembered feeling the guilt of not fulfilling his wishes. I also felt guilty because he would not see me graduate and become a lawyer. I went on to study law and it was during the third year of my degree that I gave birth to my son. After his birth I decided to do my post graduate studies so I could become the lawyer my father had wanted me to be. Throughout my studies I was still experiencing difficulties within my marriage and bringing up two children. Life was not easy. I had this drive that I had to continue what I was doing as I could not stop, that was not an option for me.

After I graduated I started working full time. I continued to work hard, gaining promotions until I reached the point where I am now. Here I am having reached a goal yet there was something that didn't feel right. I was continuously told as a child that when you become a lawyer everything would be fantastic, things will work out. With all of these achievements something was missing. I didn't feel fulfilled, I didn't feel happy. I didn't feel like I had accomplished anything.

As I endured challenges and difficulties in my life I had always turned to traditional and holistic therapies such as meditation. I was interested in anything natural that I could find to help me deal with all of life's challenges; all of the things I was going through at different parts of my life. It was something I really enjoyed as well. I decided to go on a course with my mum as she had surgery for a breast cancer scare.

This situation was my pivotal moment. I decided something had to change. It was from this point that I began working with the coach who was teaching the course on Theta Healing. I started to work on the issue of feeling that something was missing. I could not understand, I had a good job, I was married, I had kids yet I didn't feel happy. These feelings of misery were compounded as I was going through some issues at work too with my manager which caused me a lot of stress.

I realised I was at burnout. I was on this hamster wheel. I was going to work, coming home, cooking tea for the kids and then straight to bed. There has got to be more to life than this. Surely this monotonous routine was not what life was meant to be like.

I knew that I could not sustain living like this for the next God knows how many years. There was something I was not achieving that I knew I was meant to be achieving. It was time to find out why I am here and what is it that I am supposed to do. There was something telling me that I have bigger things to achieve in this world, it is not simply about being in a job where I am working nine-to-five and being miserable.

I understood I was creating the same patterns over and over again. It was important when doing the programme that I discovered what is it I was passionate about and what is it that sparks me and I am ready to fight for. From this experience I realised it is about working with healers and for healers. It's about the wellness profession and helping other people to change their stories. Essentially, I wanted to bring more healing into the world.

There are many people going through traumas literally every single day. It's about recognising how we deal with it and how we overcome it that determines where we end up in life. I discovered that my purpose is to empower other healers to reach their potential. I support them in the transition stage of leaving their nine-to-five jobs to live their purpose of the life of a healer. It's about helping them find the courage to step into their healing business. I know that my soul clients are women who are transitioning from a routine nine-to-five job into their own business.

As I continue my journey, I have recently decided that something has got to change. One of the first things I have had to deal with is breaking out of the pattern of people-pleasing and that I had to become a lawyer in order to be happy or successful. I now have realised that up until now I was not being me as well as not fulfilling my soul purpose. I now know that it is not up to me to make other people happy. I am here to make me happy.

While I am creating my business I have also experienced a spiritual awakening. As I have been delving into my past and healing, knowing it is about making myself happy and letting go of the fear of judgement, is when I feel alive. I am emerging onto a new beautiful spiritual path.

My vision is to support and empower women, who are experiencing what I have experienced in relation to knowing that there is more to life than doing a nine-to-five job and who want to feel more satisfied and pursue their passion. I can support them into stepping into that passion and create something that makes them happy and proud. They can decide to live a life rather than live for the nine-to-five.

When continuing to learn different healing modalities, I plan to incorporate them into my business. I believe my openness to alternative therapies will only make me a better healer and coach. I dream of a lifestyle that allows me to be with my kids. More than that, as I learn and become more spiritual, I can provide them with tools such as meditation, yoga and healing that they can use for the rest of their lives.

Being a parent today, we are not always around. I dream of a lavish life where I can earn a full time income from a job I do flexibly, a job that I love and where I help many women. Most of all, my experience has shown me that you can be anything you want to be once you release trying to please others and make them happy. We are responsible for our own happiness.

Dedication:

I dedicate this chapter to my children because they have taught me so much and have inspired me to become who I am today.

Regina's story is one of discovering the power of healing. Inspired by its power she went on to train in Advance Theta Healing so she can help others find their passion and live life in happiness.

As a woman who knows and understands the full impact of not living your purpose, Regina is determined alongside her law work, to support women who want to transition from corporate to starting their own healing practice.

It takes great courage to answer your call especially when others around you do not understand the spiritual side of life in the way that you do.

Regina's path is to shed light to other women giving them hope that they too can fulfil their dreams and live life with great happiness and love.

Brenda Dempsey
Creator & Editor

VOICES OF HOPE

Brenda Dempsey - Clydebank, Scotland, living in London UK

Trust the Process

Everybody has a story. We have all experienced the highs and lows of life during our journey. We have all endured crisis and challenges which at the time, seemed like the end of the world. But we survived. And we are still here.

As Jim Rohn says, "It is never the problem that's the problem, but what we think about the problem, that's the problem." So the interesting thing is not what happened, but what we thought about it and did about it. That is why the stories in this book are so valuable. They help us to realise that there is always a solution, even though it might not be obvious at the time.

In bringing together this inspirational group of women from all continents and cultures, Brenda has tapped into the world's wisdom and presented it to us in an accessible and very readible way. The perfect book to dip into for instant inspiration.

Chris Day
Founder and Managing Director
Filament Publishing

Transformation #31

Trust the Process

Brenda Dempsey

Coach, Mentor, Author, Speaker

"Write your Own story and Trust the Universe to deliver."

Esther Hicks

It is easy to break Trust, one of life's beliefs. As you journey through life, you learn to trust some people and not others. Your challenged trust, through experiences, shapes your understanding around who you can rely on. Have they lied, let you down or not kept to their word? When trust breaks, you feel broken. You often project this belief onto others for fear of rejection and heartbreak once again. Allowing distrust into your life creates shadows that keep you in the dark and only seldom do you enjoy the light of life. Relationships are affected, none more so than the relationship with yourself.

I learned not to trust others from an early age. I could not understand why other children could be so cruel to me. I would be ignored, have my face slapped and be the one left out. As a child, this treatment is hard to understand. All my mother would say to me was 'Don't trust them. They are not your friends. People can be horrible.' It's no wonder I had deep-rooted issues and limiting beliefs.

Despite these life lessons, I was a happy child. I loved adventure, climbing and running free. I indeed was allowed to be a free spirit; well, outdoors anyway. There was something special about me, but I did not have the knowledge or understanding to figure it out. All I knew was I loved life and people despite their flaws, and making others feel good. I learned this by doing beautiful things for people, singing, dancing.

Seeing smiles upon people's faces brought joy to my heart and soul.

Childhood passed by in a blink of an eye and before I could say 'white chapel', I was married. My next encounter with Trust or should I say Distrust was discovering that my husband could lie with ease. At first, they were small lies, and I loved him, so I naturally forgave him. I never believed his behaviour was seriously a problem. I felt sorry for him. Again I was left wondering why? Why lie?

My mother hated lies. It was the one thing I never got into the habit of doing for fear of being reprimanded. I was such a loving child, and I always wanted to please others. I loved to see them smile. I always wanted my parents' approval, and this was my experience growing up. I was well behaved but lively. I had a strong moral compass. Naively, I thought everyone was like me.

My husband's lies were more of an annoyance than a problem at first. As time went on and I had a young family – two children at the time – my husband's ease of lying grew darker. He would hide letters, bank statements and began to change in his behaviour. Still, I questioned why? Why could he not directly talk to me? I did not judge him as being a terrible person. Perhaps I had been too lenient, choosing only to see the good in people. I also thought 'this is the father of my two beautiful daughters.'

Before I knew it, I now had four children. The stress of everything was beginning to take its toll. He changed his job from an accountant to a salesperson for an IT company. All the time he was climbing his career ladder, our standard of living was rising. The alluring material world was like honey, and I spuriously believed that we were happy. But facing the truth today, were all the signs of a more significant sinister behaviour. Being married to a man who could not meet his truth was incredibly exhausting. He had this persona that revealed to the outside world he was Mr Wonderful, and I believed deep down he was. However, his dark side became my companion for more than ten years.

Where was Trust? It was eroding bit by bit. It was not a sudden thing for me because I was one of those women who believed I could change her man. This perception was a very shallow view before my spiritual awakening. I was perplexed. Here I was a good wife, mother, and daughter. I was Catholic and went to Mass every Sunday. I went to Mass most days for strength to keep going and top up my spiritual love cup, although I did not realise this at the time. I prayed hard that things would change and my husband's real personality would shine through.

Everything worsened. The tables turned. It was no longer about my trust of my husband but his trust of me. I was accused of all sorts of things usually around being out of the house, what I was wearing and who was I talking with, especially if it was a man. With a strong sense of loyalty and being faithful to my marriage vows, I was aghast and in disbelief at his continued accusations.

Now I begin a dark journey of my trust. I began to believe that I was capable of doing some of the things my husband accused me. I always felt uncomfortable if my friends' husbands talked to me or I spoke to men outside; I began wondering did I fancy them like he said I did. This version of me was scary. It was alien. The more I tried to avoid these situations, the more I found myself in them. Now did I only not trust my husband, but I also did not trust me!

Darkness descended. I was in a living hell. Whom could I trust? What could I do? Nothing, I was a woman with four children and no money.

In my favour, I was young, determined and had stamina. There raged a battle within me between Trust and Distrust. I trusted myself to do the right thing in most situations. I believed that I was a good mum so making a decision affecting my kids would always be true to who I was, as a nurturing and protective mother. I distrusted the woman who was trying to escape from her hell hole because would she do something that my beautiful trusting self would not approve? My inner and outer worlds were at war.

Some days I would scream, cry or do nothing. I drowned in despair. I became battle-weary, but I had children and sick parents who relied on me. They were the ones who I could trust. I always believed my parents. They had never let me down once! What role models; what a feat. They kept me sane.

During this time, my voice was silenced in some ways but not in others. No one would accuse me of having a quiet voice. Deep within me was a fear of speaking out; fear of speaking total truth and a fear of speaking in case others would judge me to be stupid, inarticulate, unimportant. Now the results of my limiting beliefs created from my dark experiences were surfacing.

When was this unbearable situation going to end? How could I trust that something better was waiting for my children and me? I stayed in my marriage until a point when I had to get out or else I may become a statistic. This soul-destroying situation was my first experience of surrender. It was not a tremendous earth-quaking surrender but surrendered I did. All the reasons that had prevented me from leaving previously no longer existed. My WHY changed! It was survival that replaced my previous why of my children having a roof over their head as well as living with two parents.

This life-changing experience was a great lesson in the importance of having a WHY bigger than you. Now I did not have to trust my husband any more.

Now I had to trust myself more than ever. I knew I could do that with ease.

The euphoria of being free diminished as I was in the final year of my teaching degree, without a home, and I still had full responsibility for four young lives. There is no such thing as the grass is greener. It is just a change of challenges, difficulties and problems. Now I had to face them alone. My saviours were my family and friends whom I could also trust to help me when I needed another pair of hands or a shoulder to cry on, although, I am a strong woman and at that time in my life crying was for my alone time.

I was building trust once more. I always tried not to let things get me down for long. Something inside never failed to uplift me. I accepted this as usual but was not consciously aware in an awakened way.

Along the path, this beautiful journey of life as I stepped from the darkness into the light has taught me a series of ideal tools to use in times of trouble. Surrendering to dark and painful situations you don't understand, accepting that there is a lesson even when you cannot see it; letting go of the negativity so you can reframe and allow for something bigger and better to fill the void space and trusting that this process brings joy, happiness and love.

You may experience this time and time again, but there are lessons to be learned. Unfortunately, as humans, we don't always learn the lesson. We are not usually ready to learn it. That is why many people appear to make the same mistake time and time again.

My trust journey had a strong start in life, although an accusation of being too trusting echoed in my ears. Still, I say I would rather be in the energy of trust than distrust because I have learned what that is like, and it is not for me. Negativity, fear, judgement, bitterness and guilt have no place in the life I choose — the life I desire to create.

Having my trust go through testing times shaped me into knowing that Trust is your control and not the power of other peoples. When you abandon faith from your life you are only letting yourself down. Trust begins within you, like love. The more you trust yourself, the more what other people say will not have the same level of impact. Remember, you cannot control their behaviour, only your own and how you respond to situations and people.

My awakened journey began not long after my parents died, and I moved to England. I found a man whom I could trust implicitly. Why? Because I trusted myself. It was a massive leap of faith leaving my home for the last 46 years to move away from everything I knew.

You see, I was beginning to trust that new doors would open, that would create a better life, a different experience.

I was beginning to build my Trust muscle. I gave up my beloved teaching after 25 years to take on the challenge of becoming an entrepreneur. I surrendered to giving that up and trusting that something more incredible was waiting for me. Today I practice regularly surrendering, trusting that everything will work out perfectly for me and my highest good. In these moments, I am a Braveheart. I am a woman of strength. I am a woman of influence, love and compassion. I am making a difference. Start building your Trust muscle today, begin within.

Dedication:

I dedicate this chapter to the voiceless women who have still to find their voice. Through coming together in community we can spark HOPE to light a path that will lead them to their victory.

The Art of Feminine Beauty

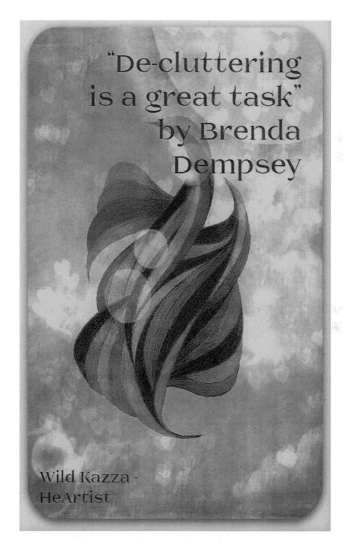

"De-cluttering is a great task" by Brenda Dempsey

Wild Kazza - HeArtist

Art by Karen Hodgson

The Art of Feminine Beauty

You Will Never Know Me

Come and dance with me
Come and hide with me
You know this veil will be
Our secret for ever baby
Oh, oh,oh,oh

You think you know
The kind of girl I am
Just by looking at me
And the way I move on the dance floor baby
But I'm much more
And you'll never guess
Which woman is hidden behind these veils
You'll never know baby

One veil I'm fire
Two veils baby I'm desire
Three veils I'm much stronger
Four veils baby I move slowly
Ah, ah
Five veils and you will never know me

You think you know me better
But it depends on what I allow you to see
Too many veils
But I don't really care
You can take them all away
And you won't find
What you expect
I become what I want to be

And you don't have a say
'Cause is all up to me

One veil I'm fire
Two veils baby I'm desire
Three veils I'm much stronger
Four veils baby I move slowly
Ah, ah
Five veils and you will never know me

Jamy Arafah (Columbian)

Jamy was born in Italy to a Colombian mother and a Jordanian
father, growing up in Colombia until she was 14. She sang and
danced as well as studying the violin, singing technique and
folk dances at the Music Conservatory in Cali. Throughout her
musical career, Jamy has won over the hearts of music lovers
from all walks of life, developing her unique and refined style
that has allowed her to sing across different genres and languages.
Jamy now lives in London and has been collaborating with great
musicians in different live bands projects.
"Cuentos de la Luna"(Moon Tales), her latest project, is the
expression of a romantic, sensual and yet modern Bachata.
The main inspiration is the moon, a passive witness of human
emotions and lives, to whom humanity has revealed its deep
love secrets. This is how you can find songs that speak about
impossible, toxic or unforgettable love, as well as songs that
approach the sentiment with power and pride.

Epilogue

One of the criteria for being a co-author in Voices of Hope was that each woman had to be in business.

Compiling an Anthology is like running a Marathon. It takes stamina, motivation and grit to work with a large group of women who are on a mission to make a difference. More importantly, it takes understanding, patience and a sense of humour to help you provide support to the wide ranging needs of the co-authors for they have a broad range of abilities, skills and self expression.

Like all good stories, Voices of Hope has its own story in its compilation journey. Fear, indecisiveness and self-judgement at times raised their head in the process of the co-authors writing their chapters. Being a coach enabled me to guide them through their challenges, doubts and overwhelms, fuelling their confidence, belief and commitment to writing their chapters.

It is with great admiration for the co-authors that I express my gratitude and appreciation, for they had to dig deep to find their courage and listen carefully to rediscover their voice within. For some, their intuition had been buried for a long time. Once they heard it, they next had to face their truth. Now that takes guts, because it is not always easy to admit to yourself. Finally, they released their fear and expressed their truth through their stories.

Without exception, each co-author agreed that writing their stories healed parts of them. They felt proud of the journey they travelled and who it revealed as a consequence. They acknowledged both the good and bad experiences as part of their learning and chose to use these lessons in shaping the businesses that they now run.

The intention for Voices of Hope was to highlight that each of us, when faced with adversity, will always turn to hope to enable us to ascend once again like the phoenix rising from the ashes. The universal symbol of Hope is a lighted candle, for in the darkness it only takes a spark to ignite hope and travel towards the light. This is true for the thirty women in this book. As they become a beacon of light for others, they know that in lighting the way for others their flame and light will not be diminished.

A common thread for each co-author is that they are driven with love and gratitude for the adversity they experienced and are ready to rise and roar for the next chapter in their lives and businesses. Together they know they can conquer the world, transforming others one by one.

Acknowledgements

I would like to thank all of the wonderful women who said 'yes' and agreed to walk this healing and courageous journey with me. Know you are making a significant difference in the world with the work you are doing.

I would like to thank David Lakey, my partner, who is ever at my side supporting everything I do and believing I can achieve my dreams.

It is always uplifting when others see your vision and agree to be part of the journey and for that I'd like to thank Penny Power OBE and all the other inspiring women who provided the Foreword and Words of Love for Voices of Hope.

I woud like to extend gratitude to Chris Day and his team at Filament Publishing for believing in my work and the difference I am making in the world.

MEET THE CO-AUTHORS

Transformation #1
Selina Boshorin

Selina Boshorin is a Business Systems Strategist, who helps busy overwhelmed entrepreneurs and leaders create order from chaos so they can focus on the important things in their business. With over ten years' experience in careers guidance, hospitality & welfare, Selina has trained, coached and mentored senior leaders & CEOs in Leadership & Personal Development. Selina helps her clients to work more productively and achieve success more effectively without sacrificing their well-being or the need for perfection and overworking.

Connect with Selina:
sboshorin@me.com
Facebook: http://bit.ly/SelinaBoshorin

Transformation #2
Hannah Ingram

Hannah is a Warrior Queen. She is energetic, vibrant, passionate and free. Triggered by the arrival of her son, she learnt to see the world through the wondrous eyes of a child and her zest for growth and life saw her travel the world for a year with him. Hannah is powered by love which fuels a mission to contribute to her son's future. She believes leading a vegan lifestyle is one of the best ways to reverse climate damage, whilst also being good for our health and the welfare of animals. Fitness, travel and people are her passion, and these are nurtured in her event business, which motivates performance and creates memories for employees and customers of her clients. Hannah strives to live each day through joy, and dreams of this for all of us.

Connect: Instagram: @haliwarriorqueen
LinkedIn:Hannah Ingram

Transformation #3
Johanna Burkhardt

Johanna Burkhardt is an Empowerment Coach, Healer, Spiritual Mentor and Speaker who has been seen in numerous transformational summits, podcasts, and several magazines. Johanna has seen darkness and has come out the other side awakened and empowered. She guides women through the steps she took to step into their truth by transcending their limiting beliefs, healing through radical forgiveness and awakening their soul by tuning into a power greater than themselves. She is a mother of three amazing children, a wife to a supportive husband and a divinely connected being. She lives in a one stop sign town on the coast of North Carolina and can be found at:

www.Johannaburkhardt.com
https://www.facebook.com
SpirituallyEmpoweringWomen/

Transformation #4
Phyllis Marlene Benstein

Phyllis Marlene Benstein is an International Speaker, Best Selling Author, a Legacy Founding Leader, Cadillac Earner, and Independent Market Partner with Monat Global, as well as a beauty influencer. Her background is electrical engineering and she is a role model for others to transition from corporate to entrepreneurship and have a successful second career after 50. She is a powerhouse of knowledge and energy combining her background in engineering with her background in many areas of beauty and image. She leads, trains and inspires a team of over 3,400 in North America, the UK and soon to be Poland and all of Ireland . Connect at:

https://www.phyllis.mymonat.com
https://www.facebook.com/Beauty-and-Pampering-by-Phyllis-108828740515204/

Transformation #5
Cathlene Miner

Cathlene is an entrepreneur, home-school mom, wife, mother of four and grandmother (Sea) to two amazing granddaughters and a love of anything that brings a smile and joy, as a self-professed, glass half-full kinda girl. Founder of Manifesting Magic in your everyday life ™, Author of The 30 Day Self Perception Makeover™, The 30 Day Self Perception Makeover Teen Edition™, Manifesting Your Life on Purpose Basics, #1 Best selling Author in Mumpreneur on Fire 3, Public Speaker, On-Air Personality, TV Show Host, Lifestyle Coach, and Non-Profit founder of Hopeful Handbags, Inc. 501c3. Cathlene believes from her own experience that with a healthy Self Perception it is possible to truly manifest a life on purpose and allow your dreams to unfold.

https://www.cathleneminer.com

Transformation #6
Willow Sterrick

Willow has been able to navigate Mental Health and Addictions. She no longer fear these parts of herself and now sees it all as just another available and useful tool for deep inner personal growth & confidence. She is creating a community network in Buckinghamshire that she envisions will ripple out across the Home Counties.

Willow lives with two dogs in her beautiful home in a tiny village and loves to walk & cook and works with adults with mental health issues as a Lived Experience Tutor, with older adults with dementia, and more recently, on an outdoor nature project.

Contact Willow : willowherbpark396@gmail.com
Facebook Page Willow's Wisdom 333
www.willowswisdom.com page live from January 2020

Transformation #7
Louise Matson

Louise Matson is an Intuitive Energy Healer, Channel, Spiritual Guide and Catalyst for Transformation. As an Energy Healer and Spiritual Guide she enables people to understand themselves as they truly are and assists them to reconnect to their inner guidance and universal support system to understand and fulfil their life purpose and be ALL that they are! Louise has trained in various healing modalities throughout her own spiritual journey to heal herself and others. Louise has also worked for over 15 years as a therapist and senior manager within the NHS to enable people to achieve their full potential. She is a mother and lives in Sheffield, UK with her beloved partner.

Connect with Louise at: www.loumatson.com
https://www.facebook.com/
LouMatsonIntuitiveHealer

Transformation #8
Paula Jarek

Paula Jarek is an adventurer, a psychology graduate, and an owner of Speak Volumes. She is extremely passionate about helping women regain their confidence by giving them hair they've always wanted. She is bubbly, creative, sociable, loves a good chat and is passionate about problem solving and all things fiddly, which traits have led her to becoming a hair loss solutions' specialist. Often accompanied by her beloved cat, Spice, keeping an eye on quality control side of things, in her spare time you will usually find her knotting her hair loss systems, painting ceramics or lately, learning to sew.

Connect with Paula at:
http://speakvolumes.co.uk/
https://www.facebook.com/paula.jarek
email: speakvolumeshair

Transformation #9
Caroline Emile

Caroline Emile is a happiness & fulfilment coach, author and cancer thriver, passionate about inspiring and empowering soulful individuals to create lives they absolutely love, full of vibrancy, optimism and abundance. She professionally trained as a Co-Active Coach at the Coaches Training Institute (CTI) after working for almost a decade in marketing communications across various industries, yet continued to feel dissatisfied at her core and that there was more to her than a traditional corporate career. Egyptian-born Caroline is a global citizen who has lived on three continents. She currently lives in London, UK and can be reached at:

www.facebook.com/caroline.emile
www.facebook.com/butterfly.me.caroline.emile/
www.butterflyme.co.uk

Transformation #10
Charlotte Fitzgerald

Charlotte Fitzgerald is a single mum of two children who battled through a toxic relationship over the last four years. She showed great determination to start her life over again. Throughout this time Charlotte qualified as a Pilates instructor and started a health and wellness business alongside a global company. Her journey through pain and personal development has made Charlotte the woman she is today, striving for better things for herself and her children. Charlotte believes that change is possible if you believe it and work towards it. Connect with Charlotte:

charlottefitzgerald@hotmail.co.uk
https://www.facebook.com/charlottefitzgerald.forabetteryou/
Instagram: charlotte_forabetteryou

Transformation #11
Sue Ritchie

Sue Ritchie is a Coach, Mentor, Teacher, Speaker and Author, having already published her book 'Love your Gut: The Practical Guide to Sustainable Weight Loss from the Inside Out', as well as being a co-author of global collaborative book 'The Book of Inspiration for Women by Women' and a co-author in soon to be published book 'Dance in the Fire of Life'. As a result of her own personal "mess to success", where she recovered from Hashimoto's disease, (an autoimmune disorder that makes the thyroid under-active) despite being told that it was impossible, she helps others to successfully transform their health from poor to amazing from the inside out, adopting a totally holistic approach to health and wellbeing. She can be reached via:
www.sue-ritchie.com
https://www.facebook.com/YourEcstaticHealth/
https://www.linkedin.com/in/yourecstatichealth/

Transformation #12
Judy Feldhausen

Judy Feldhausen has had a heart for people all her life. Her corporate employment ranges from electronics to cosmetics. She believes that donating her time is an important part of her life and is chair of the Natural Resource Conservancy Commission and Lieutenant Governor of Kiwanis. Her highest honours are being named Illinois Woman of Achievement, listed in the Cambridge Who's Who and named her community's Business Person of the Year. Because of her own family history of CardioVascular disease, she founded the Cardio Wellness group, whose mission is to eliminate heart disease using screenings and nitric oxide therapy protocol. Connect at:

www.CardioWellnessGroup.com
judy@cardiowellnessgroup.com

Transformation #13
Jane Scanlan

Jane Scanlan boasts more than 15 years of experience within the health and wellness industry, and over a decade in the London Ambulance Service. Jane is on a mission to empower women and help them get super confident so they are able to achieve their life's desires. As founder of Cherish, Transform and Upgrade Your Life Coaching, and Cherish7Sanctuary, she has been helping her local and global community since 2010. Being a healer and women of influence, Jane oozes confidence and power. Jane is no stranger to the spotlight and is a fantastic motivational speaker, having featured on Brooklands Radio, Darren Cockburn's Mindfulness Podcasts and many other online interviews. She has now stepped into the publishing arena and is a co-author of Voices Of Hope where she shares her story from uncertainty to confidence and success. Connect:

https://cherishtransformupgrade.com
https://www.facebook.com/janescanlan78

Transformation #14
Carol Wachniak

Carol Wachniak is an Entrepreneur, International Consultant, Inspirational Speaker, Author, Radio Show Host, Philanthropist, Healer, Super Connector and Mentor to the next generation of birth and postpartum Doulas. She hosted the Positive Impact Radio Show in the Greater Chicago Area, along with being CEO of Genesis 1 Management & Consulting. Her legacy impact continues to this day along with her transformative power to affect communities both local and afar through her holistic health approaches. Carol is the original designer of the UAL Bag Tag for airline baggage, which has resulted in savings for travellers and airlines around the world. Connect at:

https://www.facebook.com/carol.wachniak
https://www.linkedin.com/in/carolwachniak
https://www.seedmilk.com/vsl

Transformation #15
Tiffany Hinton

Tiffany Hinton is a Super Mom, Business Owner, Best Selling Author, Speaker, Functional Medicine Certified Health Coach and Gluten-free lifestyle expert! Tiffany started writing several years ago, while going through treatments for infertility. She was a featured expert on Fox News, The Morning Jam and in HuffPost. She has written 15 cookbooks. She was also a speaker at North Carolina State University during the Gluten and Allergen Free Wellness Event. She is a regular speaker throughout the US, including the award-winning Gluten Free and Allergen Friendly Expo, where she signs books in the Author Area. Tiffany has a compelling story that led to her gluten free lifestyle.

Connect with Tiffany

www.gfmomcertified.com

https://www.facebook.com/tiffhint

Twitter: @gfmomcertified

Transformation #16
Mira Warszawski

Mira Warszawski is a Nurse, Entrepreneur, Storyteller who was born in Poland to keen gardeners and Earth lovers. That love for nature, embedded in her heart by parents, she turned into passion for writing and helping others.

At the age of 33, she was listed in the Lexicon of Polish Journalism (2000), having had written hundreds of articles for local and regional newspapers. Despite a bumpy road of ups and downs in her life, she is a loving and empowered woman, who takes inspired actions every single day, compassionately serving others. She is a mother of a beautiful daughter Klaudia and a grandmother to a smart Gaia. Husband Kris is the love of her life. Mira lives in London and can be found at:

https://www.facebook.com/mirawarszawski

Transformation #17
Trina Kavanagh-Thomas

Trina Kavanagh-Thomas is a Intuitive Personal Trainer, Health Coach, International Author and Co-Author. Over the last nine years, Trina has gained the knowledge to successfully aid people, l go from stuck in self sabotage to flowing in self love with tailor-made life long, transferable tools. Her videos, podcasts and work takes you on a self transformational journey, aiding you through a unique mind body approach to fitness. Her questions to you, right now are: Are you truly happy where you are now with your health? What is stopping you from moving forward? What if you knew you could succeed? Connect with Trina:

https://www.youtube.com/channel/UC_ kgXVHgNhMoBtRv5zunQ6w
https://www.facebook.com/trinakavanagh-thomas
https://www.instagram.com/trinakavanagh1

Transformation #18
Emma Greenslade

Emma is a Mentor to smart women entrepreneurs. She has coached and transformed women all over the world to gain momentum in their business by helping and healing them to create a winning mindset and clear the blocks that prevent them from earning their desired income, gain confidence and have the freedom to do as they choose. Emma specialises in helping women overcome money blocks, limiting beliefs, self-doubt, procrastination, fear of judgement, failure and success. Emma's mission is for her clients to make the money they desire and live the life they deserve so they can impact and empower the next generation and the community around them.
Connect with Emma:
info@emmagreenslade.com
https://www.facebook.com/emma.greenslade1

Transformation #19
Aviv Ortal

Avivit Oz is an inspiring women, author and mum who believes she has a second chance to live life to the full. She is an awakened woman with a beautiful purpose. She is a keen writer and has written The Little Red Dress which has over 16,000 readers. Avivit has also written poetry called 'What's a Thought' and has over 7,000 readers so far.

Avivit's vision is to awaken more women to realise that their thoughts and feelings matter. She is using her writing to inspire other women to take action and make change in their lives.

"One word can change the whole life of someone else."

Transformation # 20
Janet Groom

Janet Groom is an Author and Book Coach. She has published two books; one fiction 'The Naked Knitting Club: Book 1 – Casting On', and one non-fiction 'Write to Heal'. Janet has found power in words and enjoys writing her own stories, as well as helping other incredible people to share their personal uplifting stories into the world. She hosts 'The WRITE Word Show', sharing interviews and insights on writing. Her vision is to share inspirational books with the world. Janet is married to Mark, and they live in a typical chalet in the heart of the Swiss Alps. You can connect with Janet at:

http://www.janetgroom.com/
http://facebook.com/janetgroom.writer
http://www.linkedin.com/in/janet-groom-17926413/

Transformation #21
Fiona Clark

Fiona Clark ('The Zenergizer') is a Transformational Energy Coach, Speaker and Co-author in 'Voices of Courage'. She has a compassionate, down-to-earth and holistic approach to healing her clients on a mind, body and spirit level. Her passion is to inspire and empower them to emerge totally reconnected to their inner happiness, feel energised and recover the courage to be themselves again. As a Life Coach, Solution Focused & Energy Freedom Technique (EFT) Practitioner, who never stops being curious as to how we can 'be the best we can be', Fiona will leave you with your own 'zenergy' chest of skills and techniques. Her passion is her 'Moving Meditation' and can often be seen meandering the country lanes in Surrey raising money for many charities. Connect with Fiona:

https://www.facebook.com/fiona.clark.731

Transformation #22
Indira Kennedy

Indira is Founding Director of Conscious Leadership Australia, an executive development and coaching company based in London, UK. She is also Founder of 'Gorgeous All Over', a spiritual development business for women, and Author of the book 'Gorgeous All Over ~ a daily guide for women with spirit'. Both businesses focus on positive social impact through transcendent leadership, developing multiple intelligences (physical, emotional, mental and spiritual) in ways that elevate the work place, enhance self-leadership and expand people performance. She speaks internationally on women in business, and how to develop conscious leadership. Connect with Indira: https://www.linkedin.com/in/ indirakennedy75332514/
https://www.facebook.com/selfhealingforwomen/

Transformation #23
Leah Adhiambo Ochieng

Leah is a Partner Mentor at Polycom Organization of Kibera slum, working voluntarily for three years. She mentors adolescent girls aged 10-18 years, teaching them Sexual Reproductive Health topics and Life Skills. Leah is also a Counsellor for children with trauma and difficult situations that made them hopeless. She is active with UNFPA (United Nations for Population Funds), Amani Women Network, Female Wave of Change and Chaddy Mission School. Leah has participated in the Young Women Incubator Training by UN Programme Development on Peace Building and Conflict Management.

Leah is an advocate for equality in education. She has featured in the local newspaper as well as a local news telecast. (https://www.youtube.com/watch?v=gQmUMvKHEvw).

Connect with Leah:

adhiambo.leah@yahoo.com

Transformation #24
Joyce Osei

Joyce Osei is an Author, Business Analyst, Agent of change and a Woman of influence. She is a mother of two children, a wife and a lover of travel. From an early age, Joyce has been fascinated with storytelling and loved to create and tell her own stories. Writing is in her blood and she often journaled as a teenager. She also taught English as a second Language. Today, Joyce writes about diversity and inclusion through storytelling for children's books. She is currently writing her first book, "The Adventures of Amma and Kwessi" launching early in 2020. Joyce is a passionate advocate of education for young children and herself.

Connect with Joyce:
www.facebook.com/Joyce-Osei-103567934378463/
joyce-osei@outlook.com

Transformation #25
Juvee Perez

Based in London, Juvee is the Ninja behind 'Miss Website Ninja'. With over five years of experience, she helps service based entrepreneurs from all over the world by designing websites that are stylish, effective and aligned with their brand. Growing up in the Philippines, Juvee had to rely on the internet to teach herself in becoming website and graphic designer. Constantly improving herself, she spends her free time learning about user experience and design trends. An avid fan of travelling, Juvee's goal is to explore the world and inspire others that there's no such thing as impossible and only 'I'm possible!' Connect with Juvee:

www.misswebsiteninja.com
hello@misswebsiteninja.com

Transformation #26
Tarusha Mittal

Tarusha is an award-winning Tech Entrepreneur, who started her journey right out of school. She is a self taught techie and the co-founder of two tech businesses that deal with deep tech, namely blockchain and cloud. She is also a podcast host and is very passionate about furthering and helping women achieve their dreams by mentoring early stage entrepreneurs.

https://twitter.com/tarusham
https://www.facebook.com/tarusha.mittal
https://www.linkedin.com/in/tarushamittal/

Transformation #27
Jaswinder Challi

Jaswinder K Challi Sahiba, is a much sought after therapist. She is a Counsellor, Psychotherapist, Hypnotherapist, Yoga Therapist, Shamanic Practitioner, Aurora Practitioner and Reiki healer. Also a teacher of Counselling/Hypnotherapy and Yoga. Jaswinder enjoys organising group workshops in various areas, and loves working with women's issues. A well travelled person herself, she has been to many countries in search of her healing and has had many psychic experiences. Jaswinder is a very warm, empathic and caring person who has already helped so many people. She is now spreading messages to the wider world through her writings and being an author. Connect with Jaswinder:

jazjourneys@gmail.com
https://www.facebook.com/jaswinder.challi